P9-APH-645

The Rise and Decline
of
The Great Atlantic & Pacific
Tea Company

THE RISE AND DECLINE
OF

The Great
Atlantic & Pacific
Tea Company

by William I. Walsh

LYLE STUART INC.   SECAUCUS, NEW JERSEY

Library of Congress Cataloging-in-Publication Data

Walsh, William I.
  The rise and decline of the Great Atlantic & Pacific
Tea Company.

  Includes index.
  1. Great Atlantic & Pacific Tea Company—History.
2. Grocery trade—United States—History.   3. Food
industry and trade—United States—History.   4. Supermarkets—United States—History.   I. Title.
HD9321.9.G7W35   1986   381'.456412'006073   85-24987
ISBN 0-8184-0382-9

Copyright © 1986 by William I. Walsh

All rights reserved. No part of this book
may be reproduced in any form, except by
a newspaper or magazine reviewer who wishes
to quote brief passages in connection
with a review.

Published by Lyle Stuart Inc.
120 Enterprise Ave., Secaucus, N.J. 07094
In Canada: Musson Book Company
A division of General Publishing Co. Limited.
Don Mills, Ontario

Queries regarding rights and permissions should be
addressed to: Lyle Stuart, 120 Enterprise Avenue,
Secaucus, N.J. 07094

Manufactured in the United States of America

*To my Charlotte, gentle fair lady and wife, who
brings love, honor, courage, and meaning to life*

and,
*with special thanks to our daughter Mary, whose
love and assistance helped in completing this work*

Acknowledgments

This book is a print-out of a lifetime's experience in the retail food business. The author is indebted in countless subconscious and unacknowledgable ways to the great many associates with whom he has worked over the years. These good people have influenced the character and the spirit of this book in more ways than can be acknowledged here, and in that context I now apologize for not mentioning each of them, and express my heartfelt appreciation to all of them.

Specifically, we acknowledge a vast personal library of A&P memorabilia zealously collected over the past forty years. This file includes annual reports to shareholders and a huge assortment of booklets, notices, announcements, notes and reports to which I had routine access as a concerned participant. Worthy of special mention are three books distributed to the organization by John A. Hartford: the original *Manager's Manual, Guard Our Good Will,* and *You and Your Company.* Also special, is the rare, large hardcover titled *Seventy Five Years* published by A&P in 1934 in celebration of the company's 75th anniversary. This treasure contains a priceless photo album showing the parallel progress of the United States and A&P during those exciting years from 1859 to 1934. Finally we cannot forget a genuine antique published in hardcover in the 1890's and titled *The A&P Everyday Cook & Recipe Book.* Written by Miss E. Neil, it was published by A&P, and in addition to over two thousand recipes, this delightful book contains many homey hints to ease household chores and to cure minor health problems common at that time. A special section also provided the ladies with cosmetic beauty secrets of the 1890's.

The author also acknowledges many outside publications, including: Professor Roy Bullock's early history of A&P published in the *Harvard Business Review* in 1933. Edwin P. Hoyt's, *That Wonderful A&P,* published in 1969 by Hawthorn Books, contains an absorbing earlier history of A&P and devotes special attention to the personal lives of the Hartford family. Another hardcover, *A&P—Past, Present and Future,* published by *Progressive Grocer* magazine in 1971, also covers the early history of A&P and later deals substantially with the perceived problems and options facing A&P in the late 1960's.

Vital too was the vast personal collection of articles on A&P gathered over many years from various public print media. Included are newspaper articles from *The New York Times, The Wall Street Journal* and many other papers across the United States. Included also are articles dated from the 1930's to 1984 in *Fortune, Time, Forbes, Business Week, Pension & Investment Age* and other prominent national magazines. Excerpts from outside print media are referenced as they appear in the text.

Also of historical importance are copies of *Hearings and Reports of the United States Senate and House of Representatives* on matters involving A&P, and finally the transcripts of Federal District Court records on matters dealing with A&P.

This book is the sum product of a working lifetime's experience with A&P. As a product of that total environment, it is impossible for me to acknowledge every single source of information and therefore I shall not try. Instead let me again express my gratitude to all both inside and outside the company who added to my store of historical knowledge.

Contents

Introduction

This book had to be written because America's history would be incomplete without it. This story, beginning in 1859, tells of a tiny company whose astounding growth directly touched the lives of millions, and indirectly affected the lives of all Americans.

It is a story of good times and bad, of monumental success and dismal failures. Briefly, it traces the first century of grandeur when a father or his two sons privately controlled the A&P Tea Company. Never in that time did they deviate from the deep-seated principle that the company and employees shared equal responsibility toward each other, and shared a joint responsibility toward providing consumers more good food for less money than their competition. Dedicated to such principles, the company grew to become the largest retailer and largest privately owned company in the entire world.

In this work we shall pry open many previously secret files and examine in detail those unrevealed circumstances and causes surrounding the company's slide into mediocrity and close brush with extinction. The malaise set in when the company went public and that beacon light of principle dimmed following the death of the founder's sons. The infection worsened over a score of years until some 3,000 stores and more than one hundred manufacturing and distribution facilities had been abandoned as incurable.

Finally, a West German entrepreneur gained majority control of the stock, and the company is once more under the effective control of a single individual. Today, having eliminated most unprofitable operations, and buoyed by a massive inflow of cash diverted from an employee pension trust fund, management once more looks to a brighter tomorrow with a company on the threshold of renewed growth. What is likely to happen next?

If indeed the past is prologue, future success will depend upon restoring respect between the company and its employees, and their mutual acceptance of responsibility to provide honest value to consumers in return for patronage. However, such an obviously essential relationship is rarely achieved. It is more often found artfully engraved, elegantly mounted, ceremoniously hung on boardroom walls than thriving in everyday business activity. Its sustenance requires mutual loyalty, integrity and unswerving dedication to a shared business principle.

The scope of our story is such that attempts to recount the names of all who contributed importantly would only serve to blur the story of their deeds. Thus, many who deserve mention shall remain anonymous, supporting this modest paper stage which can only accommodate those chosen to lead that explosive rise to greatness and that pervasive slide toward oblivion.

History has a way of dealing harshly with unsuccessful undertakings. Here, while we harshly criticize failed events and their causes, we press no charge of personal failure, because neither history nor its writers have such right. Personal failure is a private curse that dwells deep within one's soul as the self-inflicted aftermath of despair, resignation of spirit and desire spent. Effort, which far excels success or failure as a measure of human worth, is unfortunately also measurable only from within and thus cannot be properly assessed either by history or this book. Therefore, consider this not a story of personal success or failure but of human strength and frailty, and of business judgments upon which success both smiled and frowned.

If nothing else of value results, let this work assure one truth unchallenged. The loyal employees whose dedication helped build this company were not responsible for its decline—that is an honor to which management is singularly entitled. Yet, as so often happens, we see that those who did the least wrong suffered most by this unwarranted retreat from greatness.

This book is offered in tribute to those thousands of loyal employees whose jobs became fatalities in the crossfires of A&P's recent past, employees who were fired late in life for no cause other than that the company saw fit to abandon their workplace. These, who have suffered financial pains, must bear as well the empty memories of a lifetime spent in efforts now abandoned. Let this book, if nothing else, lift all shrouds of blame from their aging shoulders.

One

An Idea Born Atop a Little Red Wagon

It was a common sight of a summer evening in 1859. Two well-dressed young men strolling along the docks of New York harbor, deeply engrossed, no doubt discussing a contemplated business venture. But these two were not just idle dreamers; they knew that many more businesses were born than lived long enough to turn a profit. Both heads appeared to nod knowingly in accord, as each perceived difficulty was resolved. Enthusiasm grew and each seemed to know instinctively when the "moment" arrived. They stopped, looked each other in the eye, and the deal was struck. The firm handclasp confirmed mutual confidence in the venture, and in each other.

For whatever reason, they never recorded the terms of the arrangement or even the exact date that their business commenced. In all likelihood they never imagined their little enterprise, a century later, would have grown into a collossus, a national institution, the largest retail company on the planet Earth, the one, the only Great Atlantic & Pacific Tea Company.

Almost as many tall tales have been spun about the rise and decline of the A&P as have been told about the rise and fall of Rome. They are part of our business legend, but much of the real story has never been told.

15

As prologue, let us recall a simple fact often overlooked. The standard of living America enjoys today is enhanced by the quality and efficiency of our consumer supply distribution system. Here, as nowhere else in the world, mind boggling assortments of quality foodstuffs gathered from around the globe are presented at their peak of freshness to consumers of every walk of life. Every week of the year, the play is restaged: an unmatched selection of quality products freshly presented in America's supermarkets at costs representing less than 16 percent of disposable income of the average American family, while the balance of the civilized world spends almost twice that percentage for a much less bountiful variety of fresh foods and household products.

For over a century A&P was the driving force molding and improving this distribution system. Before the turn of the century, A&P was that little red-front shop on Main Street operated by a friendly gentleman in a white apron with a pencil over his ear. Some fifty years ago, those little shops began the conversion to modern large supermarkets to better serve the changing needs of a growing America.

A&P has served our nation well. Not only was it singularly responsible for establishing the early standards of the food distribution system we now take for granted, but also, in the process, the Tea Company improved the fortunes of the farmers, food manufacturers, wholesalers, other retailers, and the American consumer.

To get back to our story, we learn that on some unknown date in 1859, one George F. Gilman, a prosperous New York entrepreneur dealing in leather goods, agreed to meet George H. Hartford, a 26-year-old acquaintance from their mutual home town, Augusta, Maine.

Young Hartford had also decided to depart New England to seek his fortune in New York City. He looked forward anxiously to meeting the already successful Mr. Gilman and enlisting his financial support in establishing a business venture employing a new concept for selling tea.

After first leaving Augusta, Hartford had been unhappily selling dry goods in a Boston fabric store. After several years, his older brother John urged him to leave the dreary dry goods business and take over the exciting business which John, for serious health reasons, could no longer maintain. John's business, it turned out, consisted of a wagon and a route selling tea, house-to-house, through the rural countryside presently known as midtown Manhattan.

Young George dutifully took over the business but quickly found it to be even more humdrum and unfulfilling than selling dry goods to the ladies of Boston. He did, however, learn a great deal about tea, and a great deal about selling—the hard way. And during those lonely days atop his little red wagon his idea took shape.

When finally the two former Augustans met in New York, young Hartford, trying not to appear too eager, outlined his approach to selling tea; Gilman, trying not to appear too enthusiastic, hesitatingly agreed to finance the enterprise. Thus, in 1859, along the wharves of New York harbor, on the corner of Vesey and Church Streets, the exact site of the present World Trade Center, two young men founded a small tea company that one day was to change the shape of American retailing.

George F. Gilman, an incurable showman, early in 1861 finally settled on a fitting name for this humble enterprise. He established it as "The Great American Tea Company." Obviously, Gilman already had dreams of sales volumes and territories young Hartford wouldn't dare dream existed.

When young Hartford first rode his little red wagon into the business, tea was retailing for over a dollar and up to two dollars per pound, a staggeringly high price in terms of the pre-Civil War economy. He quickly learned that the high prices resulted from a succession of long profit margins taken by the numerous middlemen between the Asian producer and the American consumer. Included in the group were exporters, foreign exchange bankers, shippers, importers, brokers, wholesalers, and finally retailers. In addition to huge profits being taken at the exchange and wholesale level, it was then the practice in the retail trade to place high margins on tea to subsidize the low prices of other basic commodities such as sugar, salt, and flour, which were intensely competitive at the time. In that era, tea was considered a necessary luxury, and coffee was, by comparision, a scarcely used commodity.

Hartford sensed the opportunity to make the luxury of tea more accessible to the masses through direct buying, eliminating all middlemen, and taking only one small profit per pound for the company. Based upon careful calculations, the two Georges decided they could retail quality teas for well under a dollar per pound. This would surely revolutionize the tea industry, and, at the same time, might prove to be a highly profitable business. And so it began, Hartford working long days and nights minding the store, buying, blending, selling, shipping, keeping books, and planning, while Gilman, from time to time, would stop in and inquire about progress and suggest new ideas for expansion.

George Francis Gilman was born into one of the most well-to-do families in Augusta in the year 1826. Accustomed from birth to the nicer things in life, this flambouyant, incurable high-flyer would grow to consider modest success in life as worse than failure, and hard work the most demeaning curse of all. Well schooled, he fully understood the power of money, and as principal investor he retained full control of the enterprise while young Hartford built the business. In addition to controlling the Great American Tea Company, he continued as a principal in the leather goods and steamship businesses. Hartford was so happily absorbed in the growing success of the Tea Company that he was perfectly content with the arrangement, wherein Gilman approved all important decisions but let Hartford run the store. In later years, with the Tea Company's success assured, Gilman abandoned the workaday world to devote full time to the enjoyment of his wealth as a socialite, a breeder of fine horses, and a sponsor of the arts.

By contrast, George Huntington Hartford was born in 1833 into a modest family with a small farm in Augusta, Maine. He was third-generation American of English ancestry, raised as a hard-working, God-fearing farm boy, who when approaching manhood realized there was little opportunity for a successful career in Augusta. As did so many others of his generation, young George Hartford left the family farm to seek his fortune in the bustling big cities of America.

The early years on that rugged farm left their indelible mark. George Hartford lived with a deep respect for all God's creations and a belief that hard work would provide its own reward. The accumulation of great power and wealth in later life never altered his basic values or changed his simple outlook on life. Devoted to his wife Josephine and their family of three sons and two daughters, happy and fulfilled in his work, he was truly a man at peace with himself with no need for public envy or acclaim to satisfy those yearnings of an empty inner self. In his middle years, as a civic responsibility, he served several terms as mayor of Orange, New Jersey, the town in which Josephine and he had built their home and raised their children. He disdained any further political ambitions but gave of his time and fortune generously, but quietly, to a number of charitable causes.

Two of the young Hartford boys, George and John, upon finishing high school, went to work for their father. They eventually succeeded him in running A&P. The third son, Edward, and daughters, Marie Louise and Maria Josephine, never participated actively in the business but, in accordance with their father's wishes, shared equally with George and John in the profits of the Company.

While it is true that George H. Hartford's private life was exemplary in the finest American storybook tradition, it must also be recognized that his concept of "selling quality goods at the lowest possible prices" was not in any way based upon altruism but rather a Yankee conviction that it made damn good sense to base a retail business upon a consumer-oriented policy. It was just plain good business to treat people right, and earning consumers' trust and confidence provided the maximum potential for growth and profitability. Young George and John were taught and accepted this philosophy at their father's knee, and remained faithful to it throughout their long lives.

While George Francis Gilman and George Huntington Hartford were totally different personalities and seemed unlikely partners for a business arrangement, they worked very well together. Hartford had the intensity and persistence to conceive, develop and operate the business, and Gilman had the vision and flair to promote it in a grand fashion.

Initially, the conservative, hardworking Hartford was embarrassed by the gaudiness and boastfulness of Gilman's early advertising copy, such as the now treasured first ad in the New York *Tribune*, in 1863, which described the fledgling company as: "An Organization of Capitalists for the Purpose of Importing Teas Direct from Place of Growth, and Distributing Them throughout the United States for One Profit Only." Initially, Hartford intended to develop a comfortably profitable business, but Gilman, from the beginning, set out to claim the entire nation (much of which was still largely uninhabited) as the franchise territory of the Tea Company. Hartford taught Gilman how to operate a successful business, and Gilman taught Hartford how to dream bigger dreams. Both learned well.

New York *Tribune* advertisements dated 1865 confirmed the rapid growth of the company: "The Great American Tea Company now Operates Five Branches in New York City Including the Largest Tea Store in the World Located at 640 Broadway on the Corner of Bleecker Street."

To further speed establishment of an enlarged national sales base, a novel idea was developed which had more positive impact on early growth of the company than could have been achieved by the addition of new retail outlets. The company introduced the "Club Plan," a nationwide mail-order device which offered the incentive that, by banding into "clubs," groups of merchants or individuals could purchase quality teas well below prevailing prices. And, as an added inducement, the organizer of each new club was given complimentary quantities of tea. Finally, as a special innovation at a time when shoddy retail practices were commonplace, the Great American Tea Company offered an unconditional money-back guarantee to any customer not completely satisfied with any purchase.

The "Club Plan" was an immediate, resounding success, as in chain fashion members of one club became organizers of other clubs. In the space of a few short years, the Great American Tea Company with both retail stores and mail-order business had captured a noticeable share of the tea market, and had become the envy and the enemy of the Tea Merchants' Establishment.

As early as 1869, articles appearing in periodicals such as *American Grocer* began viciously attacking the Great American Tea Company, charging the alleged "low prices" advertised were for sub-quality teas, or tea which had been damaged in shipment. They charged further that Great American's teas were adulterated to change their appearance, and that "used tea leaves" were obtained from restaurants and other institutions and reconstituted for sale by Great American. Also, as early as 1869, independent grocers around the nation were invited to join in the growing chorus of accusations that chain store monopolies, using devious tactics or dispensing inferior products, were threatening to put local merchants out of business and, thereafter, profiteer on the consumers in the community.

Thus began what was to become a one hundred year war against A&P by politicians on behalf of unhappy competitors. In simplest terms, it was a war against the "high quality—low price" formula offered by A&P. In order to survive, competitors were faced with two choices: (a) to improve efficiency and quality, and to moderate profit margins; or (b) attempt to destroy A&P through political action.

History tells us that the issue was decided, in the long run, by those competitors who decided to compete and, by improving their operating efficiency, soon developed their own successful chain stores. Indeed, A&P had no exclusive patent on this idea. Many, however, chose the second alternative and vigorously supported organized political attack upon A&P. In short order, charges were hurled accusing A&P of "predatory pricing," "destroying local independent businesses," "taking money out of the local communities," and, the most loathesome indictment of America's industrial age— "creating a monopoly."

Then, as now, politicians were very adept at proclaiming lofty motives for waging dirty wars. A "noble cause," such as defending the common man and the American way of life against the scourge of an A&P monopoly, was even more exciting to an aspiring politician than giving him a flag, a cannon, and a military band!

But Gilman and Hartford stood their ground, refusing to let the growing opposition change their mode of operation. Instead, as sales growth continued to increase their buying leverage, they redoubled their efforts to expand further.

It was also in 1869 that President Ulysses S. Grant drove the Golden Spike which joined America's East and West coasts by rail. To commemorate this inspiring event, and to more accurately describe territorial boundaries of the A&P franchise, Gilman renamed the company, to be known henceforth as "The Great Atlantic & Pacific Tea Company."

By now, Gilman's flair for showmanship was shared by Hartford and was evidenced in the copious use of gift premiums as sales incentives. As another idea to encourage sales loyalty, A&P introduced the practice of issuing "trading stamps" which customers could accumulate and later exchange for a wide variety of attractive household items. Before too long, A&P became known as the "Gift Tea Store." So well known was the A&P gift program, that it was memorialized in the punch line of a popular song of the time—"Today's the Day—They Give Babies Away at Your Neighborhood A&P."

In 1871, with the glow still flickering in the embers of the fire started by Mrs. O'Leary's infamous cow, A&P volunteered to aid relief efforts and rushed emergency supplies of tea to the stricken city of Chicago. And, making the most of a new opportunity, the Tea Company promptly opened its first branch store west of New York City's metropolitan area.

To generate still greater volume, A&P began, early in the 1870's, to wholesale tea to independent peddlers who sold their wares from wagons in the rural areas outside the major cities. However, it soon became evident, from numerous verified complaints, that many peddlers were misrepresenting the product or substituting inferior goods. A&P had no choice but to cut off sales to wagon peddlers; but rather than abandon this potentially profitable market, the company established its own wagon routes across rural America, adding an extensive line of condiments and household items, and, of course, exploiting the premium idea. This rural home delivery service subsidiary retained the original name, The Great American Tea Company. It eventually became motorized and remained operative until the mid 1960's.

Throughout the 1870's, A&P quickened its pace of opening retail stores, concentrating in those states which had been least damaged or disrupted by the Civil War. The company expanded throughout New England and as far West as the Mississippi River. By now, a line of coffees had been added to the teas, and the corporate strategy was to sell these products to more and more people each year, using quality, price, and premiums to promote sales volumes. The concept of selling these same customers a greater proportion of their total food needs had not yet evolved. Since tea and coffee were purchased in moderate volume, and purchases were usually made only once or twice a month, a single small A&P could serve the tea and coffee needs of a moderate-sized town. A significant expansion of the product line was becoming an increasingly attactive idea, but would require more selling space and more stores.

By 1878, the company had opened over 100 retail stores and Gilman, now confident that the business was well established and in good hands, decided to retire completely and enjoy the wealth he had accumulated from this and other businesses. Hartford was made a full and equal partner and assumed total control of operations. True to his word, Gilman's only involvement with A&P thereafter was by periodic report and regular receipt of dividend checks.

During the 1880's, under Hartford's direction, the company continued its rapid growth, opening more stores and systematically expanding the product line to include sugar, spices, canned milk, and butter, and enlarging the private label line to include A&P Baking Powder and Eight O'Clock Coffee. In retrospect, however, the most important event of the 1880's was the entry into the business of Hartford's two sons, George L. and John A., who side by side would devote the next seventy years to the development of the organization which their father had founded with George Gilman.

In March 1901, George Francis Gilman died suddenly. In his social circles, he was known not only for his lavish life style but also for his unusual eccentricities, which included the refusal to permit a single mirror in his otherwise elaborately furnished homes, a refusal to come into close proximity to a sick person, or to even discuss illness of any type. He also had an absolute abhorrence of death and refused to attend any funeral service, including that of his wife who had died several years earlier.

Gilman left no close relatives or heirs, and, not surprisingly, he also left no will. A lady friend, who had comforted him in his later years after the death of his wife, did file claim and was awarded substantial benefits from his estate.

As another eccentricity throughout his life, Gilman avoided all written contracts, preferring to rely upon the other man's word and handshake. His equity in A&P, at his death in 1901, constituted the major portion of his estate but there had never been a written partnership agreement with George H. Hartford.

It was only after long and complicated litigation, which lasted four exhausting years until 1905, that Hartford was able to establish satisfactorily his equity in the company based primarily upon records retained since 1878 showing equal division of profits with

Gilman over the intervening period. The court eventually approved a settlement creating a new corporation with capital stock of $2,100,000, of which preferred stock in the amount of $1,250,000 was issued to the administrators of Gilman's estate, and the balance in common stock was issued to Hartford. Thus, at last, Hartford emerged with full control of the business so long as dividends continued to be paid on the preferred shares of stock. And, within a reasonable period of time, Hartford was able to purchase back all of those preferred shares.

By 1906, A&P annual sales were approaching $8 million. The senior Hartford was in his seventy-third year, young George was forty-two, and John A. Hartford was thirty-four years of age. Increasingly, the father delegated more of the day-to-day management and operating decisions to these sons who had learned their lessons well and were making important contributions to the firm.

It was a remarkable coincidence that these two brothers, who respected each other so deeply, and would continue to work together so closely throughout life, had temperaments and personalities every bit as contrasting as had Gilman and their father. George Ludlum Hartford, the elder by eight years, was studious, introspective, and thoroughly conservative. His genius proved to be finance, and until his death he held the only key to the corporate money box. He worked long hours and disdained taking vacations, but his only non-financial responsibility was a lifelong daily ritual taste-sampling of teas and coffees to assure quality standards were being maintained.

John Augustine Hartford, the younger son, was by nature more outgoing. Born with an entrepreneurial flair, ambitious, with broad vision, and dreams without limits, he became the natural leader and the driving force that was to insure A&P's unquestioned position as the originator of American mass retailing. John, however, would always disclaim such personal power and never admit to more than an equal partnership with his brother George. This respect for George never wavered, and John never concluded a major business decision without first obtaining George's agreement on the move.

Mutual agreement on course of action did not always come easy to two such conflicting personalities. It was often preceded by long and heated discussions which associates feared might never be resolved. Nevertheless, the aggressive, often-frustrated John never implemented a major corporate decision without somehow getting George to agree, or at least not disagree so strongly.

By 1912, the company had grown to over 400 stores with an extensive product line which made A&P, in fact, a chain of food stores rather than tea and coffee specialty shops. Volume continued to grow but not at the earlier explosive pace. Inflation during the last decade had seriously impacted the cost of living in general and food prices in particular. The ever-increasing cost of premiums was having a negative effect on profits and the ability to maintain the lowest price structure in the market.

George H. Hartford, the father, was still titular head of the company but now approaching his eighties. John A. Hartford was concerned with the trendlines and sensed the need was at hand for a new direction and a merchandising program more attuned to the times. He warned that the mounting costs of stamps and premiums was undermining the fundamental policy of low price upon which the business had been founded. John then outlined his plan for a new direction which he insisted must be at least explored by the company. His father and brother, however, saw the slackening of 1912 as only a temporary condition which would pass as quickly as it came into being. At that point in time they saw no reason for deviating from the mode of operation which had proven so successful over so many years.

But John persisted, refusing to let the issue rest. Finally, after long and heated argument, perhaps more out of exasperation than agreement, John was given six months to prove the merit of his ideas, on the condition he did not use the A&P name and limited the capital investment to $3,000. He gladly accepted the challenge.

Two

The Merchant Prince Emerges

John Hartford's plan was simplicity itself. He would eliminate every unnecessary selling expense, including such accepted merchandising devices as credit selling, home deliveries, telephone orders, stamps, and premiums, and, indeed, he would dispense with all advertising. He would open for business in a small, unadorned, unnamed store in a secondary sidestreet location. The store would be furnished only with the most rudimentary shelving, a counter, a cash register, and $1,000 worth of inventory. The store would be operated by one person, the manager. The store would be open from nine A.M. to six P.M. but would be closed during the manager's lunch period. Only when volume exceeded pre-set goals would it be permissable to hire a part-time clerk to assist with the stocking and market maintenance. Retail prices were designed to produce an overall gross margin of 12 percent. The total expense rate was projected at 10 percent.

The projected 12 percent gross margin compared to 20/22 percent gross margins then being realized in A&P stores and still higher margins prevailing in the trade generally.

John chose his site, around the corner from a large and successful A&P store in Jersey City. Within six months John's little red front store put the big A&P store out of business. A&P had found itself again and was on its way to true greatness.

What had also happened here without fanfare, or even conscious realization by the principals, was a natural transference of initiative and power from father to son, and the emergence of John A. Hartford as the dynamic force and leader of the company. John created the original mold for "the merchant prince," he was a dreamer of dreams with limitless goals who, had he ever succeeded in capturing 100 percent share of the food business, would probably have been driven by some inner force to take up selling houses, cars, or other commodities.

Still, throughout his lifetime, John refused to admit to being anything other than an equal partner of his older brother George whose major goal was to secure the assets and protect the business which their father had built. Perhaps John was right, perhaps without George's quiet, stubborn, stabilizing influence John might well have driven the entire A&P red wagon over the edge of some ambitious cliff, long before its place in history was assured.

John was assisted in the management of the experimental store by a young store supervisor named Oliver C. Adams. Young Mr. Adams had started his career, when 12 years of age, at an A&P store in Springfield, Massachusetts, in the year 1892. While it was not then extraordinary for a young man of 33 to have over 20 years experience with his company, this young man proved to be most extraordinary. He went on to serve the company for almost 80 years before retiring as Director Emeritus of the corporation in 1972.

It was O.C. Adams who painted and hung the hand-made sign which dubbed the new venture "The Economy Store," and the name stuck. That little red Economy Store, opened in 1912, rang up a sales volume of $400 during its first week. Within two months, and without fanfare, the weekly volume had risen to over $800, which was a most substantial business for a one-man store in those days. More importantly, profit projections were right on target.

A 2 percent net on such sales does not seem impressive in today's economic atmosphere of a billion here, a billion there, but the more than 30 percent annual return on investment was exciting then and would be now. The 2 percent net on sales required no real estate investment, a minimal investment in fixtures, and much of the inventory was converted to cash sales before payment to the suppliers was due.

Mr. George H. Hartford and older son George had grown comfortable with the operating formula which had been successful over the prior 50 years. They had stubbornly resisted this new concept, and had reluctantly agreed to an experiment only after being thoroughly worn down by John's persistence. Now, however, they were happy to join the parade and enthusiastically support John in the expansion of the Economy Store concept.

It had been 53 years since George H. Hartford started in that vacant store in Vesey Street and built this chain of 480 stores and innumerable wagon routes which generated an annual sales volume of over $24 million, a considerable sum in the era of 5-cent bread. The company was securely established and financially sound. Papa Hartford had a right to be proud of the success he and his two sons had achieved.

By now, A&P employees, as people invariably do, had solved the name confusion surrounding the two Georges and the three Hartfords. George H. senior was dutifully tabbed Mr. Hartford, while the two sons became known as Mr. George and Mr. John.

As soon as the Hartfords agreed upon the success and future of the pilot operation, Mr. John contacted O.C. Adams and placed him in charge of carrying out the Economy Store development program. Adams would now report directly to Mr. John.

It should be noted here that the Economy Store was not a totally new concept. Rather it was developed over years of experience and study of numerous retail experiments, the best of which were combined into the precise formula which John believed best suited the needs of the time. The idea was not patentable and was soon being copied with numerous variations by different competitors.

If indeed there were a merchants Hall of Fame, Mr. John's place of prominence should be assured, not so much because he invented this concept but because of the remarkable speed and skill with which he transformed this little idea into a massive reality.

From an established, successful, 53-year-old chain with 480 stores and annual volume of $24 million, The Great Atlantic & Pacific Tea Company was literally to explode over the next 15 years into a retailing Goliath with more than 15,000 stores and annual volume exceeding a billion dollars. Nothing in the recorded history of retailing had come close to that achievement. A&P would become the nonpareil of the retail world. As it happened, the rest of the food industry and the Wall Street community would stand in envy and amazement at this privately owned, closed-mouth company's astonishing success. But closer study of the facts reveals this colossus had not just grown as "fortune's child" but had been carved from stone-hard obstacles by men of extraordinary dedication and skill.

The Economy Store was the perfect embodiment of an idea whose time had come. General inflation and high food costs had become major issues in the 1912 presidential campaign. Customers happily flocked to these new A&P stores which solved their budget problems and proved that the cost of food could indeed be lowered substantially. Excited by the immediate and enthusiastic customer response, and aware that the idea was there for the taking by other merchants, Mr. John resolved to outrace all competitors spreading this low price retailing concept across America under the banner, "A&P Where Economy Rules." Standardization would be the key ingredient to successful rapid expansion.

The simplest possible set of standards was established to apply without deviation to each and every new store regardless of location.

First, $3000 capital was allocated for each store—$1000 for fixtures and equipment, $1000 for inventory, and $1000 for supplies and operating capital. One cash register, a scale, and a small ice-box were installed along with shelving pre-determined to be needed to display the 300 standard grocery items delivered on the standard opening order for each store. For each geographic area, a trained maintenance crew was organized which could prepare a location for opening within one week after signing of the lease.

Second, with an enormous number of openings planned for so short a time, it was anticipated there would be some real estate "location" errors. Thus a standard lease and real estate policy evolved. Leases would only be signed for existing store properties with a minimum size of 20' × 30'. Lowest possible rental was the goal. Lower-rent, sidestreet locations were chosen over higher-rent, Main Street locations. All leases were for the term of one year with nine renewal options of one year each. Under this policy, those few new stores that did not meet projections could be closed unceremoniously and the stock and fixtures transfered to the next location with minimum loss.

The most critical problem of all, however, was how does one mass produce store managers on demand? Success of the enterprise required thousands of store managers trained to operate Economy Stores scattered over 29 states of the Union. So, third, the simplest of store manuals was prepared. In working men's language it explained in most economical terms every single detail an average hardworking man had to know to run an A&P store successfully. The little booklet was designed to fit the shirt pocket always available for reference. With this manual, the area supervisor who hired managers preferred to employ young men with no retail experience, and no built-in bad retail habits.

The manual, which is still a classic, began by emphasizing cleanliness as a matter of first importance. It described the specific maintenance procedures which must be followed to attain acceptable sanitation standards. It then explained the ordering, receiving, and inventory control procedures. Next the strict rules for correctly pricing each commodity display; then followed the simple cash control procedure.

The booklet included rules for control of supplies, utilities, and maintenance expenses as well as rules for personal appearance and conduct. Managers were taught the positive aspects of salesmanship, the importance of courtesy and strict adherence to company policies of correct price, honest measure, and the unconditional guarantee of every product, which A&P stated was included in the purchase price. Next, necessary information to comply with pure food and weights and measures regulations was explained. Finally, the manual forbade sales on credit, home deliveries, or unauthorized local purchases of items for resale.

Along with a "job," A&P offered a man an opportunity for secure career employment. A&P provided such opportunity to many thousands of immigrant and first-generation American parents to raise and educate their families. As a young man, Mr. John realized that the final measure of A&P's success would be limited only by the ability to build and hold the loyalty of an effective organization. He often remarked that "the company's responsibility to a dedicated employee is equal to that employee's responsibility to the company." And, Mr. John did more than preach the subject.

Under his direction A&P generally paid wages above the prevailing scale in the food industry. Before the advent of retail unions, A&P provided its employees with health and life insurance benefits. Starting in 1916, A&P provided pension benefits to retired long-term employees to insure they would be maintained in dignity in their retirement years.

Mr. John introduced the five-day work week into the grocery business, and at his insistence, A&P was the last chain to provide selling hours after six P.M., and during his lifetime he adamantly refused to open the stores on Sunday. He believed these extended hours were not in the best interest of the employees and added an unnecessary cost to store operations which had to be passed along as higher food costs for the consumer.

Because of sporadic but verified complaints of employees not being paid for all minutes and hours worked, Mr. John ordered time clocks into every A&P place of business long before the law required such installation. He insisted that each employee personally initial any alteration to his time card. He was saddened to learn later that many employees believed the clocks were installed to prevent cheating the company out of time.

Mr. John often reminded employees: "You don't have to be brilliant; we teach ordinary people to do extraordinary things." And, he backed this promise with a policy of promotion entirely from within the company. Thus, he provided management opportunities earned by work achievement for thousands of employees who might not have been considered qualified for such positions on the basis of formal schooling alone.

From the beginning, John displayed a genius for building employee trust and loyalty in an industry where hard work, long hours, and little pay was the rule. Even in the most disadvantaged neighborhoods, a career in the grocery business was looked upon not as an acceptable ambition but as a last resort. John tried all his life to change that. As a man he lived by the same golden rule he was taught as a boy. He wanted ambitious young men to be able to regard the grocery counter as a platform from which management careers could be launched. He believed the opportunity for honest employment provides people their needed vineyard in which they can both toil and share in the fruits of the harvest. He wanted A&P to be a good vineyard, and he wanted its harvest to provide the means for its toilers to live in dignity.

By 1915, A&P's increasing share of market had already begun to cause problems in the industry and the first of a series of confrontations between food manufacturers and the Tea Company took place. Cream of Wheat cereal was the nation's largest-selling breakfast food at the time, and that company had a strict policy of selling only to those wholesalers who, in turn, sold only to those retailers who agreed to maintain the retail pricing established by the Cream of Wheat Company.

Aware of A&P's enormous growth, aware that A&P was purchasing for several thousand stores, aware of A&P's argument that they were bigger than most wholesalers, Cream of Wheat decided that A&P qualified as a wholesaler under their definition. A&P thereupon began direct purchase of the product from Cream of Wheat. At that time Cream of Wheat sold to wholesalers for 11 cents per box. The manufacturer stipulated that the wholesaler charge the retailer 12½ cents per box, and the retailer sell the product for 14 cents per box.

A&P, purchasing for 11 cents, decided 1 cent per box was adequate profit, and began retailing the product for 12 cents, which was 14 percent below going retail. A&P's customers were delighted, but the industry was in turmoil. Here was A&P selling the nation's favorite cereal at a price below competitor's cost.

Cream of Wheat demanded that A&P increase the retail price to 14 cents per box. A&P refused, saying property rights changed hands with the payment to Cream of Wheat, and A&P would not forfeit the right to price products which it owned. Cream of Wheat immediately cut off further shipments to A&P. A&P brought suit. The court ruled in favor of Cream of Wheat, saying manufacturers had the right to establish pricing levels on their products. This started a trend of other food processors setting pricing levels on their branded products. Mr. John saw this movement as an unwarranted restraint upon free trade that resulted in unnecessary and artificial increases in food costs to consumers.

Convinced that these monopolistic pricing tactics would spread, A&P decided to compete by further expanding the manufacture of A&P brand products to offer more food of national brand quality to the consumer at lower prices than the national brand items. A&P's enormous volume and efficient distribution was able to absorb large quantities of its manufactured products without any selling or advertising costs, which constitute a significant portion of the cost and retail price of popular national brand items. As the A&P share of market grew many "A&P" label products became better known and outsold the national brand competitive items in A&P stores. As customers purchased more lower-priced A&P brands, A&P manufacturing volume increased, and as this volume increased A&P enjoyed the advantage of manufacturing profits to support low operating margins at retail store level.

Despite all the brand-name food companies' claims to the contrary, private label manufacture was not an ego trip for Mr. John or Mr. George or A&P. John and George were much more concerned with sales and profits than ego, fame, or notoriety. They would never permit a tie-up of capital on private label products whose volumes did not favorably affect the bottom line.

Mr. George H. Hartford passed away quietly in 1917 at the age of 84 years, one year after his official retirement from company activities. His will, carefully drawn, provided that the total ownership of A&P be placed in a one-generation trust with equal shares in the name of each of his five children. The will provided that John and George together, or either as survivor, have exclusive power to administer the trust, and that the trust could not be dissolved and distributed until after the death of his last surviving child. This guaranteed A&P's continuance as a privately owned family business for at least one more generation.

Throughout their entire lives, Mr. George, now 53, and Mr. John, 45, had enjoyed unusually close family and working relationships with their father. Saddened by his death, they dutifully and faithfully administered his wishes, sharing every penny of A&P profits equally with each of the other children, and subsequently with the heirs of those three children.

Both John and George had married but neither marriage produced children. Neither John nor George remarried after their wives died. John and George decided that their shares of the trust would remain intact, and go to the establishment of the Hartford Foundation, which would serve as a lasting family memorial and also as a means of assuring the continuance of A&P and its organization. They desired to perpetuate the A&P Tea Company as a living tribute to their father's name, and as an expression of thanks to the organization that brought honor to that name.

With the end of World War I, the company renewed its upward spiral, opening new stores at an accelerated pace. Each year the standards were revised to provide for improvements in design and fixtures, and the product line was modified to satisfy the changing demands of the American housewife. The suffragette movement and job opportunities created by the recent war had begun the emancipation of women, and the increased availability of packaged and prepared foods enabled women to spend less time in the kitchen.

By 1924, the dairy and grocery product lines had doubled to more than 600 items, including the company's own line of baked goods. That year A&P introduced fresh fruits and vegetables in all its stores and experimented with butcher shops in test stores and soon extended the sale of fresh meats across the entire chain.

In that year A&P also pioneered advertising on national radio, sponsoring Harry Horlick and his "A&P Gypsies." This musical program, which later featured Kate Smith, was an American favorite for many years.

America's population was expanding rapidly, consumers were more affluent and merchants were eager to cater to their every whim. The nation was young, strong, and confident; opportunity was everywhere in those Roaring Twenties. Times were good and the company was never more secure, but Mr. John was troubled.

The product line and in-store service costs were expanding at a rate far exceeding the tonnage increases. Consumers seemed willing to absorb the added costs of variety and service in higher retail margins, and A&P had found itself caught up in the trend. Mr. John considered good times, easy sales, and high profits a warning signal. He thought back to 1912.

He recognized that the principle of volume through low price, upon which A&P was founded, was being eroded and surrendered to a success that was now, in 1925, almost forcing itself upon A&P. While things looked spectacular on paper and from an outsider's viewpoint, John knew it was becoming increasingly difficult to maintain proper control over the operation of a chain which now exceeded 14,000 stores scattered over 29 states from a single control unit. Headquarters, since 1908, had been located in a small corner of the huge company warehouse on Bay Street in Jersey City. Mr. John realized the tree had finally outgrown its root system, and the company's enormous size was becoming its greatest weakness. As he remarked, "A&P's size now prevents the heartbeat from reaching the extremities." Something had to be done to get the company back on course, and keep it there.

After soul searching, study, and discussion, George agreed with John's recommendation to decentralize A&P into six operating divisions, and a manufacturing division. While agreeing to the concept, George prevailed in his insistence that headquarters retain tight control over cash, new leases and renewals, all purchasing, and inventory tie-up.

To implement decentralization, organizational line charts were prepared and operating procedures established, and the best men were chosen to fill each of the important new assignments. Each of the six operating divisions contained approximately 2500 stores, subdivided into six geographic operating units. Each operating unit was headed by a vice-president with supporting, sales, warehousing, and administrative staffs. Each division was headed by a president with a divisional board of directors comprising each of the unit vice-presidents and the divisional directors of sales, warehousing, and administrative functions. Each divisional president was also elected a corporate vice-president and a member of A&P's board of directors.

By November 1925, everything was in place and the decentralization of A&P was officially launched.

The newly appointed executives appreciated their new titles and handsome salary increases and were anxious to get to work and make things happen, using the knowledge gained from experience in their particular geographic marketing area.

John and George realized that decentralization was an imperative, but they believed they could not yet delegate responsibility for the company's future; therefore, they decided to exercise caution with respect to the delegation of authority. Mr. John was determined that no unit or division would have authority to tamper with the sales policy of the company, and Mr. George was determined that no such authority would be delegated with respect to financial, real estate, or purchasing policy.

Under the new arrangement, headquarters maintained exclusive control over all company funds. Procedures required that headquarters approve all capital improvements, all real estate transactions, and all inventory tie-up ceilings for manufacturing plants, warehouses, and stores. Unit purchasing departments required headquarters approval before stocking any new items and even before adding a new size or flavor of items already stocked. All deals and allowances offered by manufacturers had to be approved prior to acceptance, and the headquarters approval stipulated the acceptable limit of advanced buying allowable under the deal or allowance.

Viewed from today's perspective, these purchasing strictures seem particularly heavy-handed and certain to limit a unit's ability to compete effectively in a marketing area. However, they made some sense in the 1920's when decentralization itself was untested, when "new items and deals" were not commonplace, and when a headquarters buyer, negotiating with a supplier, was not limited by a Robinson-Patman Act or similar legislative restrictions.

Mr. John believed that corporate sales policy was the soul of A&P. Policy created the character, integrity, and direction of the company. He insisted that the A&P logo, whether seen on a store in New England or New Orleans, must inspire identical consumer perceptions of confidence and trust, and a sense of "knowing what to expect" in any A&P store. John preached that without such unifying force the great chain would come apart, "A&P" would stand for nothing, would drift in different directions, and become just another indistinct image.

To support his strong feelings on this subject, Mr. John ordered that the following simple statement, which outlined the entire A&P sales policy, appear on a large sign to be prominently displayed inside the front of every A&P store in the chain for both the customers and the employees to read time and time again.

The A&P Policy

Always to:
> Do what is honest, fair, sincere, and in the
> best interests of every customer.

> Extend friendly satisfying service to everyone.

> Give every customer the most good food
> for her money.

Assure accurate weight every time—
16 oz. to each pound.

Give accurate count and full measure.

Charge the correct price.

Cheerfully refund customer's money if for
any reason any purchase is not satisfactory.

THE GREAT ATLANTIC & PACIFIC TEA CO.

As part of decentralization, units and divisions were required to
adhere to other sales operating policies. Mr. John believed that in
advertising, understatement was preferable to overstatement;
therefore, headquarters' approval was required for all advertising
formats and claims, and for any new advertising programs or
promotions planned at unit level. Approval was also required prior
to experimenting with any substantive change in store operations,
or the introduction of any new merchandising concepts.

The entire chain was required to adhere to corporate pricing
policy, which included the following stipulations:

(a) Retail prices were to be reduced on the effective date of the
reduction announced by the manufacturer. Retail prices be advanced only when the higher-priced merchandise is available for
shipment to the stores.

(b) When pennies were important, mulitiple prices were prevalent. In many stores 3/25 cents meant 9-9-7, or two for 18 cents.
Under A&P policy it meant 9-8-8, or two for 17 cents, an important
saving on a week's food purchases.

(c) Multiple pricing must be less than the lowest divisible
multiple. A retail of 4/$1.00 was forbidden. It must be 25 cents
each or 4/99 cents.

(d) The retail price per ounce or unit of measure of an item
available in various size packages must *always* be lower on the larger
sizes than on the smaller sizes so that the customer realizes a saving
by the purchase of a larger size. (This ruled out a practice still
prevalent in many supermarkets today; that is, having a reduced price
sale on only a smaller size and selling the larger size at a higher unit
measure retail.)

(e) Retail prices must be set by the unit sales director and all retail prices in all stores in a marketing area must be uniform.

(f) Selling below cost was prohibited. Exception to this rule was permitted only to match specific below-cost pricing initiated by a competing *chain* retailer who persisted in this practice. And, approval of the divisional sales director was required in each instance.

It appears paradoxical that Mr. John, the originator of low-price retailing, had an absolute abhorrence to below-cost selling. He called this practice insane and a despicable ruse by dishonest merchants to deceive consumers by creating a false illusion of low-price selling. This made sense from his viewpoint. He reasoned that maximizing efficiency and productivity can enable a merchant to sell at low margins, but no amount of efficiency can generate profit from below-cost sales. Selling one item below cost invariably requires taking a higher than otherwise necessary margin on other items to compensate. He disdained the old cliché: "We lose money on everything we sell but we make it up on volume."

However, one can make a good case for the strategy still used widely today, which says: "When you can't meet them on everything, you've got to beat them on something, even if it means going below cost to attract customers."

One of the more unfortunate aspects of the A&P story is that the American consumer never fully believed the depth of the sincerity and urgency Mr. John attached to the A&P sales policy. Even much more unfortunate is that this customer misperception too often resulted from the actions of employees "at the extremities" who hadn't been told about it in strong enough terms, who were too busy with less important priorities, or, for whatever personal reason, chose to ignore the policy that was so prominently visible at all times in the front of the store.

Decentralization, however imperfect, was the only conceivable approach to efficient management of so many stores, scattered over so vast an operating area, faced with problems resulting from differing local laws and regulations and with differences due to varying income levels or ethnic purchasing habits which alter product mix in stores. Added to this, each trading area had its different competitive strategies designed to attract the customer away from A&P.

Decentralization has now become an art form in American business, but no matter how well designed or carefully implemented, it has never worked perfectly or solved all problems and permitted the corporation to live happily ever after.

For whatever reasons, this and each of the numerous subsequent decentralizations organized by A&P were followed by a malaise inherent in decentralization. The decentralized executives eagerly reach out to accept the responsibility to manage the business, but the restrictive limits of their authority soon suggest the new framework was designed merely for passing the buck. One suspects decentralization was invented to allow the Main Office to retain authority, and responsibility for success, while at the same time providing an outlet for delegating responsibility for failures.

Three

Changing Form Without Policy Deviation

A&P entered the new year with a spirit of high confidence because 1925 had been a year of great accomplishment. Decentralization had been completed. Headquarters' office was finally moved from the Jersey City warehouse into beautiful facilities in the new Graybar Building built over Grand Central Station in New York City. While this was going on, the company also opened a record-breaking 2,613 new and larger stores and closed 1,000 older and obsolete stores.

Mr. John was freed from his previous day-long participation in an unending parade of routine operating problems that required his personal attention and decision. He had more time to study and analyze A&P from a broader perspective, and to judge its performance and establish its goals in relation to the national economic prospects of the time. And the new perspective revealed potential troubles on the trail ahead that simply could not have been seen while riding in the wagon.

John realized he had permitted A&P to become a willing victim to an age of affluence. Under the guise of satisfying every customer want, the operation had fallen under the spell of easy living and was slowly but surely betraying its birthright of low price. The newer stores were not economy stores at all. They were large and

40

plush, loaded with expensive lines of groceries, meats, produce, dairy and fresh bakery items with all the attendant costs of services including such amenities as home delivery.

Gross margins in these "combination stores" were again approaching the 22 percent level. John recalled this was A&P's vulnerable position back in 1912 when the first economy store opened with a gross margin of 12 percent. He knew decentralization could not address or correct this problem. He determined to set this company back on its proper course quickly.

George and John knew the yeast influencing the rise in gross margins was the "cost of business," which was increasing at a much faster rate than true sales growth. While total company sales had reached new highs, actual tonnage sold was running behind the previous year in a majority of stores.

In the frenzy to expand, expense control had become of secondary importance. A meeting of presidents of all divisions and all other corporate officers was scheduled for February 3, 1926.

After the exchange of pleasantries putting the group at ease, Mr. John opened the meeting. Pointing to the chart which revealed decreases in actual tonnage in continuing stores on a year-to-year basis, John explained:

"This chart shows the truest picture of our business which can be drawn today. This is the actual tonnage we are selling in the stores, compared from year to year. When I say I am greatly disturbed, I am putting it in mild form. I do not believe there is a man at this table who can look at this chart and say that our business is in a healthy condition.

"I think we are steering the boat wrong. I believe that the operation of this business on a *low volume* and a *high expense rate* is driving us out of the economy business, and unless we can operate in the future along economy lines, I do not believe I can put my heart in the business.

"I do not believe this declining tonnage picture is due to lack of effort, but chiefly to mistaken sales and development policies. I am a firm believer in getting this business into a position whereby we can sell goods cheaper than any concern in the country.

"I have always been a volume man and it is hard to divert my mind to any other policy. If anybody feels this is the wrong policy, I want him to be frank and come out and say so. If you are of the opinion the business can be run better on a low volume all well and good, but I am of the opinion that a big volume is the better policy."

Perhaps some at the table did not share Mr. John's sense of imminent danger, perhaps some disagreed. No one spoke out in favor of abandoning the low price, high volume concept upon which the company had been founded. In the course of discussion it was generally agreed that the development program had taken too high a priority and moved too quickly. It was further agreed that the first order of business was to reduce concentration on new store development and increase concentration upon increasing tonnage in existing stores through lower prices made possible by more effective cost control.

To put matters into proper perspective, and to fully understand the dangers and inherent weakness of A&P's position, we must re-examine the results for the year 1925.

A&P's 1925 sales reached a new high of $400 million accompanied by a new high dollar profit of approximately $10 million. However, this was the product of 14,000 stores scattered over 29 states. While some of the larger stores averaged weekly volumes in excess of $3,000, simple arithmetic discloses that the average A&P store had a weekly sales volume of $600 and an average weekly profit of $14. One does not require any advanced degree in economics to realize how frail this profit margin really was, and how any moderate decline in store volume or further increase in costs would quickly change that meager $14 per store profit to a loss. Further, current trend lines were moving in this direction.

Out of this grim meeting in the winter of 1926 came a rebirth of corporate resolve to reverse these downward tonnage trends through lowered prices and more effective cost control. By year's end this time-tested formula had once more proven effective. Sales volume had increased by 32 percent with an increase of only 5 percent in the number of stores.

A&P's fiscal year ended the last Saturday in February. The annual February meeting of presidents was, therefore, an occasion for both review and resolution. At the 1927 meeting an ebullient Mr. John congratulated the organization for the past year's achievements before discussing future goals. In those moments he now had for solitary reflection, John realized that A&P was now exploring new high grounds never dreamed possible by his father, and never reached by any other food retailer.

Still, he knew the company had just begun tapping into the main lode of the food business. A&P's share of market was estimated at 25 percent of available business in the trading area of its stores. Total national market share was in the 7/10 percent range because there were many trading areas in which A&P was not yet represented. The 25 percent market share in existing stores was limited only by floor space, and the new marketing areas would be represented in due time. He wondered what realistic sales limits existed, if any. He wondered where George and he could lead this organization, or, possibly, where this organization was leading George and him. What had been a recurring dream seemed now to be a realistic target to set as the next major goal.

When he believed the proper moment had arrived, John began to discuss the longer-term future and unfold his objective. He expressed confidence that continuing progress in existing stores, together with a carefully designed and implemented new store development program, could generate sales volume in excess of $1 billion during fiscal year 1930. He acknowledged that this goal, never before achieved by any retailer, would require an increase of 75 percent over existing sales levels. He added that the divisions' outstanding performance in the last year had convinced him and George that the organization was again ready to undertake a powerful new development program without sacrificing progress in existing stores, and he predicted the major portion of the required new business would come from this new store program.

Seated around that table with George, John, and the other headquarters officers were the six presidents of the operating divisions. On average, some 30 years before, each had come from some farm or some city street, as a teenage boy, to go to work for A&P. Despite whatever formal education they may have lacked, they knew the grocery business and understood precisely the goal John was outlining. To a man, perhaps moved by faith as well as reason, they agreed the goal was attainable and would be met.

Now, John knew his dream had become their commitment. Inwardly, he was not totally convinced the target would be reached, because any number of obstacles might arise between now and 1930. But, at the same time, he was fully confident that, if his goal were not achieved, failure would not be due to any lack of effort on the part of the organization. He was never more proud of A&P.

George and John were never really sure what motivated the continued loyalty of so many A&P employees. A career in a grocery chain was not a status symbol and the modest incomes were surely not the incentive. The two brothers, in all probability, discounted the impact their personal conduct had upon the employees. For men of such power and wealth, they displayed an extraordinary "common touch" as they communicated, day to day, man to man, eye to eye, with big and little, rich and poor alike. They behaved as though power and position were temporal circumstances that did not necessarily reflect a person's worth or character. They treated every employee with the honesty and fairness they expected that employee to extend to "our customers."

The two-day meeting ended, and each of the divisions embarked on the quest for the $1 billion sales mark. As fiscal year 1927 began, A&P operated 14,789 stores.

Nineteen twenty-seven and 1928 were record years, and in 1929, one full year ahead of schedule, A&P registered sales of $1.05 billion, an increase of 84 percent over the 1926 sales, and this was accomplished in 15,389 stores, an increase of only 4 percent over the base year. Things were looking good indeed.

A&P stood alone atop the entire retail world when suddenly, on that black Friday in October 1929, the bottom fell out of the Wall Street stock market. In one explosive instant the nation's economic euphoria was shattered, and America was suddenly cast into the dark depths of despair and prolonged depression. Massive unemployment created agonizing and epidemic poverty in a nation that had never contemplated a need for social nets such as unemployment insurance or welfare. So serious was the economic and social upheaval that America's capitalistic system of free-enterprise was seriously challenged for the first time.

While perched at the top and therefore facing the biggest fall, no company in the United States was better prepared for this economic dive into depression than the Great Atlantic & Pacific Tea Company. Mr. George had never yielded on his rule of maximum one-year leases on all stores, or on his rule that A&P rent rather than own store real estate. This policy now provided extraordinary liquidity in the event that individual stores were seriously hurt by the effects of unemployment. Further, the equipment investment per store was nominal and the fixtures were portable. Also, merchandise inventories had been kept under strict control.

Store inventories turned almost 30 times per year, and the company did all its business on a cash-and-carry basis. Over 40 percent of total company assets were liquid. Mr. George had dispersed the funds in numerous banks and in Treasury notes with one-year maturities precisely because the explosive financial Wall Street boom of the previous two years had raised suspicion and concern in his ultra-conservative soul.

In 1930, thousands of companies, including most of A&P's retail competitors, were facing serious losses and possible bankruptcy. A&P, never more secure, was in excellent position to face the economic realities of the time. Total retail sales figures across the nation plunged dramatically because of consumers' empty pockets together with depressed wholesale prices. While per capita food spending was down significantly, A&P's lower price structure attracted more customers than ever before, and company sales actually increased in 1930 to $1.07 billion. As the depression deepened in 1931, A&P sales dropped, for the first time in 72 years, to $1.01 billion, which was still a heady performance for that time.

The Depression persisted into 1932 and the agony of despair become more pervasive. Price, which had been increasing in importance compared to service, convenience, and even quality, now became the only criteria by which most families decided where to purchase food. Thus far, A&P had steered its way through the depression successfully, perhaps much too successfully. During those bleak four years from 1929 through 1932 A&P had earned a record total of $110 million after-tax profits. During this worst period of economic "hard times," the families of each of the five Hartford children earned over $5 million per year in A&P dividends and equity.

To avoid bankruptcy, other operators turned, in desperation, to other measures. Some formed cooperatives such as IGA to gain the benefits of mass purchasing. Others tried various innovative forms of retailing.

Necessity has always been the mother of invention. The necessities of the Great Depression gave birth to the American supermarket.

Those early crude experiments in 1932 bore little resemblance to the modern food emporiums serving the nation today, but did introduce the concept of marketing the whole spectrum of food products, most on a self-service basis, under a single roof, at prices lower than any service store operator, including A&P, could match. This same formula, refined over more than half a century, presently accounts for over 90 percent of America's sales of food and related products for home consumption.

Since the ominous decline in A&P sales in 1931, John had again watched with concern as the old familiar danger signals reappeared. The company's expense rate was rising in proportion to the continuing sales declines. The glory days of record sales and profits were over. Bad times were finally catching up with A&P.

At the same time that the desperado, go-for-broke, pioneer merchants of supermarketing were beginning to attract serious consumer response, a dangerous, insidious philosophy was gaining favor throughout the "food industry establishment," and influenced marketing managers of A&P.

Everyone, including John and George, optimistically expected (and quietly prayed) that good times were just around the corner, and that the recovery would remedy the problems now troubling the business. The reasoning went that since sales were limited by the limits of consumer income, the wise merchant accepts this reality and sets prices to insure profit on existing sales levels rather than chase after higher volumes that may not be attainable, and thus risk any chance of profitability and invite disaster.

This philosophy influenced otherwise routine decisions to close unprofitable operations. Knowing that fixed overhead absorbed by these unprofitable stores would subsequently be added to overhead costs of remaining stores, management refused to bite the bullet and close unprofitable stores, electing instead to further increase margins in a vain attempt to attain profitability, or at least ride out the storms of depression. Today, such corporate suicide is practiced by too many distinguished corporate managers who are driven by a secret inner voice: "If we don't report a profit now ... we won't be here next year!"

Before long, Mr. John's inner beliefs and deeper instincts challenged this surface optimism. He knew A&P had again drifted way off course. This time his concern was compounded by two new outside threats upon the horizon which required serious consideration. They were: (a) the rapid spread of these damn supermarkets; and (b) increased threats of anti-chain store legislation.

The earliest supermarkets were an assortment of bare-boned operations. Most were called "public markets," others became known as "supermarkets." They experienced early growth in the Los Angeles area before coming East and invading A&P territory. In 1932, a huge market opened under the name "Big Bear" in the vacated Durant Motor Car plant in Elizabeth, New Jersey. The owner/operator devoted one entire floor of this gigantic warehouse to selling dry grocery items out of opened shipping cartons, off the floor, at his cost. He expected to make his entire profit by renting the balance of the warehouse space to various concessionaires offering customers all types of perishable food products and household items.

Big Bear's advertised low prices, together with a new amenity, plenty of "free parking," attracted consumers in carloads from miles around. The total operation generated sales volume estimated to be at least $100,000 per week. This positively astounding sum was equal to the total weekly volume of the 100 A&P stores in the surrounding Newark/Elizabeth area.

Mr. John was furious and frustrated by these revolutionary tactics that so effectively checkmated the A&P game plan. But he waited.

At about the same time, Michael Cullen, a former A&P employee, sensing the extraordinary opportunity, opened a supermarket in Jamaica, in Queen's County, New York City. He soon followed with several additional supermarkets in the county to become the first "chain supermarket." King Kullen, as the chain was and is still called, controlled all departments, including meats, produce, and dairy, as well as dry groceries stacked in original cases on wooden platforms on the floor of large stores occupying space in vacated garages, factories or similar-sized facilities. Each King Kullen market achieved volume equal to that of at least ten A&P stores in the competing area.

Uncharacteristically, John continued to watch and wait, hoping that this ugly innovation was just a passing fancy the public would surely tire of as soon as better times returned and they could afford the convenience and services of the familiar neighborhood store.

Throughout the country, additional supermarkets continued to open in many forms and configurations. Most were successful in attracting large sales volumes, although a goodly number soon faded into obscurity because of inept management. In almost every instance the impact on nearby A&P store volume was devastating. Attempts to lower A&P retails to combat this supermarket competition were futile because the service-oriented physical design of A&P stores simply could not handle the high volumes required to justify the lower margins. When such competitive price tactics were tried, only nominal volume increases resulted and heavy losses were incurred.

In 1933, A&P volume dropped 19 percent to $820 million, and despite higher margins, profits declined by over 25 percent. By now John realized that the culprit was not the Depression but the growing epidemic of all those damn supermarkets.

Nineteen thirty-four offered the first glimmer of hope that perhaps the nation was emerging from the seemingly endless agony of depression. But, as 1935 approached, A&P had endured three devastating years of sales declines, and marginal profitability was sustained only through steadily rising retail margins, which John despised.

George, now 70, and John, 62 years of age, reflected and considered their options. Together they had spent a lifetime building this network of 15,000 stores into a powerful chain operating across 30 states and Canada. They were proud of their accomplishments and wanted desperately to believe that this organization had the strength and resiliency to bounce back from what they had considered temporary challenges of depression and its offspring, the supermarket fad. They tried not to face the prospect of seeing this 15,000-store chain dismantled; and they wondered whether at this time of life they possessed the energy and will to undertake the long and difficult task of converting these 15,000 service stores into perhaps some 3,000 supermarkets to serve existing marketing areas. Indeed, this was a far greater challenge than building the chain had been.

Perhaps age and personal wealth played a part in delaying the decision, but their innate pride and character simply would not permit them to duck the issue and permit the company to expire gradually.

John had known in his heart for some time what had to be done. The supermarket, in whatever modified form, was clearly the wave of the future. A&P had no choice, if it was to survive, but to bite the bullet and convert its operations as quickly as possible. George was not at all so sure of the future of the supermarket, or the need to alter A&P's course so radically. He argued that the larger stores required higher fixture and inventory investment, and longer lease commitments at higher rentals. He believed such diminished liquidity was the primary cause of most bankruptcies in recent years. He argued against abandoning the existing network completely, for less concentration on volume for volume's sake, and for more concentration on more profitable product mix with particular emphasis upon private label.

While the brothers Hartford argued and anguished over the decision, the entire company seemed to grind to a halt and languished in a sea of confusion awaiting new direction. Meanwhile, supermarkets, in increasing numbers, continued gnawing at the vital life lines of the A&P Tea Company.

A deep spirit of doom and gloom had fallen over A&P when, in 1936, Mr. George finally relented and agreed to an experiment with 100 supermarkets. By the spring of 1937, at John's urging, it was agreed to increase the experiment to include 300 supermarkets. At last the giant had awakened.

While A&P had been agonizingly slow in making the decision to enter the supermarket arena, it was the first major chain store to ever attempt a rapid and total conversion of a previously successful formula. Most of the other grocery chains of that time simply expired during their sleep.

The Tea Company never did claim credit for the invention of the supermarket, but the astonishing speed with which it converted to supermarkets once that decision was made created the perception across most of America that A&P in fact invented the idea. However, A&P did open the first supermarket ever seen in most cities of the nation. By 1938, the company was operating over 1,100 supermarkets successfully. Sales growth had been reestablished, and A&P was on the way to greater heights than ever before experienced or dreamed of. Those one-year leases in the older stores being closed once again provided the liquidity that permitted the closing of six to ten smaller stores in the trading area of each new supermarket.

The Harvard Business Review of 1933 contained an article by Professor Roy Johnson Bullock on A&P's early history. His summary findings about the success of A&P to 1933 are worth repeating. Professor Bullock stated that the history of A&P, rather than being the result of exploiting a single idea, was one of successfully developing and then discarding a succession of different and occasionally conflicting ideas.

He continued: "The keynote of A&P's progress has been adaptability. Although the ebb and flow of the tides of economic change have wrecked many enterprises and have left others to stagnate in isolation, this concern has consistently ridden the crest of the wave, appearing, on occasion, even to anticipate the action of the elements. For a business to survive its founder is not an everyday occurence. For it to exist over seven decades, in a country as young as our own is an achievement. For an enterprise to retain its place in the vanguard, to remain a pioneer to follow economic trends without following ruts, is almost without parallel."

By 1938 Professor Bullock's conclusions based upon the history of A&P to 1933 proved to be prophetic. The Hartford brothers once again demonstrated that A&P's true genius was the adaptability to change the outward form swiftly, efficiently, and *en masse*, without deviation in the basic underlying corporate policy upon which the business was founded—namely, providing the most good food for the money.

The aggressive program for opening new supermarkets was proceeding on-target, employing standards updated but as disciplined as those employed back in 1913. Supermarkets were designed and scaled to serve at least a 25 percent market share of the trading area in which they opened. A model store in which layout changes and equipment innovations could be studied was maintained at headquarters. Following George's dictum, all supermarkets were in leased premises with standard leases calling for no more than a five-year initial term, and no less than five options, each of five years duration, often at reduced rentals.

The past seven years had been excruciatingly difficult, and at times the very survival of A&P was in doubt, but now George, 74, and John, 66, seemed to have gotten their second wind. The company was back on track, bigger and better than ever. They were buoyantly looking toward the future. There was, however, a deadly attack being launched from a source outside the business.

Four

The Years of Political Warfare

By 1936, political pressure to "break up chain stores" had become a national issue led by Congressman Wright Patman of Texas as its major advocate. Congressional investigation revealed that large chains, because of high-volume purchasing power, were extended price advantages by the manufacturers which were not made available to smaller operators purchasing lesser quantities. Congress dismissed the argument that large-volume orders created production efficiencies to which the purchaser had rightful claim, and viewed the practice as one in which food manufacturers were helping the big chains put the small independent out of business. Congress passed the Robinson-Patman bill establishing that sellers offer identical prices, allowances, and terms to the entire trade.

In 1938, Congressman Patman took the next step to advance the cause which had brought him national prominence by introducing a federal chain store tax proposal. The bill called for a per store tax that would increase as the number of stores in the chain increased, up to a maximum tax of $1,000 per store per year. Further, the federal tax so established would then be multiplied by the number of states in which the chain operated to determine the total tax amount due the government. Under this formula, the chain store tax on A&P would exceed $300 million per year, or approximately 30 percent of total sales, which had finally returned to the billion dollar level. Surely such punitive legislation, even greatly modified, would destroy A&P.

Over the years, George and John had shunned personal limelight, and had gone out of their way to avoid corporate publicity, preferring to let consumer trust and acceptance of A&P policies create the corporate public image by word of mouth. Extremely sensitive to the often-repeated charge that A&P took money out of the local communities, they believed it made good business sense to play down personal wealth or power. While they sincerely believed that the benefits A&P brought to a community by way of lower food prices outweighed any disadvantages of an "absentee owner" concept, they never chose to debate the subject publicly with an angry local operator.

A special tax on chain stores had first raised its head as a local issue back in 1930. The idea was embraced in a number of states but never constituted a serious threat to A&P. The Hartfords steadfastly refused to engage in any public discussion or political activity against such a tax. Privately, they often commented, in true New England Yankee fashion, that the American public had the right to tax A&P out of business if it chose to do so. If indeed that was the will of the people, A&P would accept it and close up shop because, after more than half a century of hard work, they were not about to hold out a tin cup or beg for favors from anyone.

Up until now, chain store tax measures had been discussed and considered at state levels, and there is little doubt that the Hartfords and A&P would have quietly packed their bag and departed any state where a chain store tax made continuance in business unprofitable.

But this Patman challenge was at the national level and represented a matter of life or death for the entire company. The business which their father had founded and which they had worked all their lives to build and protect was now threatened, not by competition in the market place, but by political actions.

They had always believed the chain store tax idea would fail because of its inherent lack of merit, but now the risk was too great for them to stand idly by and depend upon political good sense to solve the problem. John and George knew the time had come for action on their part and considered the course of action open to them.

They had always acted in the belief that it was somehow improper to seek political support for the purpose of obtaining any kind of leverage or help for the A&P Tea Company. They disdained the normal political approach and decided that the company should be judged by the American people based upon their judgment of the "good or evil" of the enterprise and the service it rendered to the general public and its own employees.

Putting aside their personal negative attitudes toward publicity and corporate public relations, having decided, "We'll be damned if we will let this happen without a fight!" John and George finally came out of the corner swinging.

For the first time in its long history A&P released a public statement on an issue of the day. John and George Hartford brought their case to the American people on behalf of A&P and all other chain stores.

Over 1300 newspapers across the United States carried the two-page advertisement which is historic, because to the food trade this was the first public pronouncement ever issued from the mysterious labyrinth of marble halls high atop New York's Graybar Building whence the Sphinx-like lords of A&P were imagined to look down upon the rest of the food industry. It was historic for the more important reason that it uncovered the spirits, interests, and dedication of two most extraordinary, ordinary citizens who were American pioneers in their own right. It read as follows:

A STATEMENT OF PUBLIC POLICY
by THE GREAT ATLANTIC & PACIFIC TEA COMPANY

The Honorable Wright Patman, representative in Congress of the first district of Texas, has announced that he will introduce in the next Congress a punitive and discriminatory tax bill frankly designed to put chain stores out of business. In the past, Mr. Patman has been very successful in securing enactment of legislation which he has sponsored. He has demonstrated that he is a very able lobbyist and propagandist for his own bills. The management of the Great Atlantic & Pacific Tea Company is therefore faced with the necessity of deciding upon a course of action in relation to this proposed legislation, whether to do nothing and risk the possibility of the passage of the bill and the resulting forced dissolution of this business, or to engage in an active campaign in opposition to the bill.

In arriving at a decision, the interests of several groups of people deserve consideration—the management, the 85,600 employees of the company, the consuming public, the millions of farmers producing the country's food, and labor.

1. *The Interests of the Management:* The interests of management can be dismissed as of very little importance.

The Great Atlantic & Pacific Tea Company is managed by George L. Hartford and John A. Hartford under an arrangement made by their father, George Huntington Hartford, the founder of the business. George L. Hartford has been actively engaged in the grocery business for 58 years, working generally six days a week, 52 weeks a year during that entire period. John A. Hartford has been actively engaged in the grocery business for 50 years, working generally six days a week, 52 weeks a year during that period.

Both of these men could, of course, retire without personal or financial inconvenience and live very comfortably if chain stores were put out of business. The record of the last calendar year shows that out of any money earned annually from the business, in the case of George L. Hartford, 82 percent is paid to government in taxes; in the case of John A. Hartford, 83 percent is paid to government in taxes. As neither of the brothers has any children, any monies left out of their earnings would accrue to their estates, and in the event of their death, inheritance taxes would probably amount to two-thirds of such accrued earnings, leaving approximately 6 cents on the dollar as a motive for continued personal service.

It is therefore apparent that the interests of management need hardly be taken into consideration in arriving at a decision.

2. *The Interests of the Employees:* The interests of the employees of the company are, however, a matter of very grave concern.

It is simply a statement of fact to say that the employees of the Great Atlantic & Pacific Tea Company generally throughout the United States receive the highest wages and have the shortest working hours of any workers in the grocery business, whether chain store or individual grocer. Many of them have devoted all their working lives to the interests of the company.

The management, therefore, has a definite obligation and duty to defend the interests of these 85,600 employees against legislation intended to throw all of them out of work.

3. *The Interests of the Consumer:* Since this business has been built by the voluntary patronage of millions of American families, we believe that we must give consideration to their interests in this matter. Millions of women know how acute is the present problem of providing food, shelter and clothing for themselves, their husbands and their children out of their

present income. When food prices go up it is not a question of paying more for the same food. They do not have the additional money with which to pay. Therefore, they must buy less and eat less. A&P food stores last year distributed at retail $881,700,000 worth of food at a net profit of 1 percent.

This food was sold to the public at prices averaging from eight to ten percent lower than the prices of the average individual grocer.

Literally, millions of sales were made at prices twenty-five percent lower than the average individual grocer. This saving of eight to twenty-five cents on each dollar is of vital importance to these millions of families. If they were denied the opportunity to buy at these lower prices it would simply mean that in millions of homes they would have to leave meat off the table another day a week, eat less fresh fruits and vegetables, give the growing child one bottle of milk less every week or stint on butter, cheese, poultry, eggs and many other of the most nourishing foods.

In the last 10 years during the greatest period of chain store growth, the number of individual dealers has increased rather than decreased. We maintain that there is nothing wrong when these dealers charge more than we charge. They must charge these prices in order to make a fair profit. The average grocer will, upon request, deliver the groceries to the customer's door and in many cases extends credit to some of his customers. Delivery service costs money. The grocer must put this added cost in the prices to his customers. In the same way the extension of credit involves the expense of bookkeeping, the tying up of capital, and credit losses. There is nothing wrong in the higher mark up of the individual grocer, because he is rendering a service that justifies his prices.

If some customers can afford and voluntarily elect to pay a higher price for groceries and meats because they want credit or because they want delivery to their homes it is quite proper that they should pay an additional price for such service. However, the millions of families in this country whose income is limited and who can have more and better food because they are willing to pay cash and carry home their own purchases, should not be denied this opportunity. Millions of families of limited income can only enjoy their present standard of living through these economies and savings. These millions of American families have helped us build a great business because they believe we have rendered them a great service. The company, therefore, has an obligation and a duty to protect the interests of these customers.

4. *The Interests of the Farmer:* Eight million farm families are engaged in producing the food consumed by the American people. All of the farm

homes in America, therefore, comprising one fourth of all of the population of the United States, have a direct interest in the methods of distribution by which the products of their labor and of the soil are marketed.

Approximately 30 percent of their production is marketed through the chain food stores; about 70 percent through individual grocers. Their fruits, vegetables and other food stuffs are sold through the chain stores at prices averaging 8 percent to 10 percent cheaper than the prices at which they are sold by many grocers. If the farmer sells a given product to both at the same price, the individual grocer must charge the public more to take care of his higher costs. Thus 30 percent of the farmer's products reach the public at low prices and 70 percent of his products reach the public at higher prices.

If the public cannot consume a given crop of apples, potatoes, berries or any other product, at the prices at which they are offered, these goods do not move from the grocer's shelves; a surplus accumulates and the farmer finds that he either cannot sell the balance of his crop or must sell it at a substantial loss. Only too often a situation arises when it is literally cheaper for the farmer to let his apples or his peaches rot on the ground than to expand the labor costs necessary to pack and ship them. Every farm economist knows that a 10 percent surplus does not mean 10 percent less return to the farmer but often more than 20 percent less return.

In other words, the farmer's problem is to sell his products at the cost of production plus a fair profit and to get them to the public with as few intermediate costs and profits as possible. It is therefore obviously unfair to the farmer to propose legislation which would, at a single blow, wipe out 30 percent of his distributing machinery—and that 30 percent the part which maintains the price to the farmer yet reaches the public at low cost because of economical distribution. It would be just as unfair to the farmer to propose putting out of business all of the individual grocers of the country who distribute 70 percent of his produce. Both chain food stores and individual grocers perform a distributive function vital to the interests of the farmer. If either failed to function the farmer would be faced with tremendous surpluses and heartbreaking losses.

For years A&P has dealt with the farmers both as producers and consumers. We feel that we have a definite obligation and duty to oppose any legislative attack upon their best interests.

5. *The Interests of Labor:* Every business in this country has a vital interest in the purchasing power of labor. When labor has high wages and great purchasing power, everyone is prosperous. When labor's purchasing power is curtailed, all business suffers and the American standard of

living is impaired. For many years it has been the wise policy of the national government to protect real wages and the purchasing power of the worker's dollar.

Combinations or agreements to raise prices, thus reducing real wages, have been declared illegal. It certainly seems strange that it should now be proposed to destroy a group of businesses for the frankly admitted reason that they furnish the necessities of life to the wage earner and his family at low prices. There are approximately 900,000 workers directly employed in the chain store industry. What course is open to us but to oppose the action of a man who, at a time when more than 1,000,000 wage earners are already out of work and 3,000,000 families on relief, proposes a bill that would add almost another million to the roll of unemployed, wipe out 30 percent of the distributing machinery of all the farmers of the United States, and raise the cost of living of the wage earners of the United States.

We believe that our organization has rendered a great service to the American people and that it is as a result of that service that we have prospered. If we consulted our own interest it would be very easy to stop and enjoy whatever leisure we have earned. No one is dependent upon us except our fellow workers. However, after the fullest consideration of all interests, we have arrived at the decision that we would be doing less than our full duty if we failed to oppose, by every fair means, legislation proposed by the Honorable Wright Patman.

As we have said, Mr. Patman is an able politician, an able lobbyist and an able propagandist. In that field he is an expert. We are experts only in the grocery business. We believe the chain stores have a right to present their case to the American people. We will not go into politics nor will we establish a lobby in Washington for the purpose of attempting to influence the vote of any member of Congress. We expect only a full and fair opportunity to present the case for the chain stores as a great service organization for the American people.

Since the task we have set before us is one involving the widest dissemination of complete information to all of the American people, and since this is a profession in which we are not expert, we have engaged Carl Byoir & Associates, public relations counsel, to do this work. We realize that our views are seldom news. We know, therefore, that we must be prepared to spend a substantial sum of money in telling our story to all of the American people. We declare now that this money will be spent in the dissemination of information through paid advertising and every medium available to us, and in cooperating in the work or formation of study groups among consumers, farmers and workers, which provide open forums for a discussion of all measures affecting the cost of living.

WE BELIEVE THAT WHEN THE AMERICAN PEOPLE HAVE ALL OF THE FACTS THEY WILL MAKE THEIR DECISION KNOWN TO THEIR REPRESENTATIVES IN CONGRESS. AS AMERICANS WE WILL BE CONTENT WITH THAT DECISION.

GEORGE L. HARTFORD   JOHN A. HARTFORD

Congressman Patman struck back, promising his bill would be H.R.#1 when the House convened in January 1939. He aimed 15 charges at inter-state chain enterprises including those such as F.W. Woolworth as well as food chains. He argued that chain stores:

1. Destroy community life by avoiding duties of local citizenship.
2. Reduce local reserves of credit and destroy local banks.
3. Lead toward eventual monopoly in business.
4. Destroy local insurance companies.
5. Destroy local newspapers.
6. Destroy local printing shops.
7. Destroy other local independent businesses.
8. Destroy individual initiative and ambition of the young people.
9. Destroy free competition.
10. Narrow the market for farmers and destroy farm prices.
11. Encourage dishonesty and short weight and cheat the public.
12. Aid large cities to the detriment of other parts of America.
13. Cause business dictators which will bring Fascism to America.
14. Cause concentration of wealth in the hands of a few.
15. Ignore the general welfare and benefit the rich Barbara Huttons and the childless Hartford brothers.

But A&P's media campaign had been successful. With the support of labor, farm, and consumer groups, the voice of the people was heard. The Patman bill died in Congress in 1940 and similar types of pending state legislation also quietly expired.

John and George were thrilled and looked to the future with renewed confidence both because of the performance of their 1,100 new supermarkets, and also with the feeling of hope that all major political obstacles to future success had finally been laid to rest.

However, having once stepped upon the stage of the public and political arena, the Hartfords soon found out that retreat to the pleasures of personal privacy was now impossible.

Neither the public nor the press was aware of a most unusual event that occurred on March 29, 1939, right at the height of the heated debate in Congress about the chain store tax and abolition of chain stores.

The general counsel of A&P, Caruthers Ewing, came to see John and George in the Graybar Building. He told of a meeting he had had with a long time friend, Bill Sirovich, who was then serving as a member of Congress. Sirovich advised that President Roosevelt had contacted him relative to helping his son, Elliott, obtain a $200,000 loan for the purpose of purchasing a radio station in Texas; and the President suggested that, possibly through Mr. Ewing, an approach could be made to obtain that loan from the Hartford brothers. Caruthers Ewing explained that the purpose of his visit was to pass on this message.

All their lives John and George had avoided personal politics like the plague. They had never been introduced to, communicated with, or campaigned for or against Franklin Delano Roosevelt, and of course, they had never met or communicated with the President's son Elliott. They sat flabbergasted and stunned as the story unfolded and Ewing created the unmistakable impression that they had been earmarked, by name, as potential underwriters of this loan. By modern sophisticated standards, the Hartfords were sheltered country boys totally inexperienced in politics and the mores of politicians. Their immediate reaction was the question of propriety. Was there not something sinister about this extraordinary request coming at the very moment Congress was deciding the future of A&P?

It did not take George long to react. He stated bluntly, and with finality: He was not interested, and would neither make, nor contribute to, the making of the loan. That was that!

John always admired George's bluntness almost as much as his financial instincts. Perhaps, inwardly, he wanted to add, "That goes for me too! Tell the President our answer is no." But those words would not come. George, now 75, had spent his years behind the desk guarding the safe while John, now 67, still had to live in the real world as a citizen, dealing with problems of the employees, the customers, and the country. He simply could not force himself to give a fast "no" to the President of the United States.

John did not want to even entertain the possibility that the President of the United States would connect a financial favor to his son with support on the resolution of a current political struggle.

When Ewing explained that proper contract would be drawn to support the loan agreement and that securities of the radio station would be offered as collateral, John agreed to at least take the next step and meet with Elliott Roosevelt.

The next day, March 30, 1939, Elliott visited John Hartford's apartment in the Plaza Hotel in New York City. John's own words record the substance of that meeting:

I inquired of Elliott Roosevelt whether his father knew of his request for the loan and stated that I certainly would not make such a loan without the President's approving it. Elliott Roosevelt stated, "Let's get Dad on the telephone," and that there would be no difficulty about obtaining his father's approval. When the connection was made, Elliott said, "Hello dad," and after some preliminary conversation... said, "Here's Mr. Hartford," and handed the receiver to me.

I said, "Hello, Mr. President," and I heard a familiar voice, a voice I had heard over the radio many times, say, "Hello John." I then told him that Elliott was in my apartment and asked him what did he think about this $200,000 loan Elliott wanted to make in connection with the radio business and the President said that he was entirely familiar with it, that it looked good and gave assurance to me that it was a sound business proposition and a fine thing. He said he would appreciate any assistance and consideration that I would give to Elliott in this matter and extended to me an invitation to call on him at the White House. I then told Elliott, "I am going to make the loan," and the only reason I was making the loan was that his father practically asked me to make the loan, and I further told Elliott that I was not interested in radio and that I was not asking any favors.

In response to later questions as to whether any representations were made as to possible benefits that might accrue if this loan was made, John replied: "No sir, after the President was so enthusiastic about it I felt that I was on the spot and I had to make a decision right then and there and I did not want to do anything to incur enmity of the President." He added that he did not think it was good judgment to turn down the loan after a direct approach in which the President of the United States stated this was a sound business proposition.

The very next day, forty-eight hours after being approached by Caruthers Ewing, John advanced $200,000 to Elliott Roosevelt, completing the loan. George had refused to even discuss the matter further.

As swiftly and privately as they had entered John Hartford's life, as swiftly and quietly did the Roosevelts now depart. The loan was never repaid. John Hartford was infuriated by what he considered a betrayal of trust.

After three years of silence and no repayment, John had occasion to be in Washington on business matters and was called in to see Mr. Jesse Jones, then Secretary of Commerce in President Roosevelt's cabinet. Mr. Jones advised John that Elliott and his wife were without financial means and could not repay the loan, and the collateral was worthless. John asked if any part of the loan would be paid and Mr. Jones suggested a settlement of $4,000 in exchange for the collateral securities. Although very disturbed, John agreed to settle the debt for $4,000. This was in March 1942.

Convinced he had been victim of a bad debt loss, John immediately took a $196,000 deduction on his 1942 personal income tax return. The Internal Revenue Service allowed the deduction, and the matter would have never come to light, had not columnist Westbrook Pegler got wind of the story, and with a loud splatter, the feces hit the fan.

The long investigation of the matter by the Ways and Means Committee of the House is summarized in House report #1033 dated October 1, 1945. The above quotations of John Hartford appear in that document along with other interesting commentaries. The majority opinion of the Committee agreed with the IRS conclusion that Hartford was entitled to the deduction. The Republican minority expressed dissenting views. They concluded that as the result of this transaction someone was escaping payment of tax on $196,000 that was due the United States Treasury, and argued that if Hartford is entitled to the deduction, steps should be taken to collect the tax from Elliott.

The minority report also stated Hartford did not bring suit because he was determined not to do anything to embarrass

Elliott's father. They added, surely a taxpayer has not pursued reasonable efforts to collect a debt when he declines to do anything that would add to the worries of the debtor's father. Summarizing, they said in fairness to Hartford that the record clearly shows that he was a reluctant participant; that the President of the United States, Franklin D. Roosevelt, not only played an important part in effecting the $200,000 payment to his son by Hartford but went further and initiated the settlement by his cabinet appointee, Jesse Jones. The shares of stock returned to Jones by Hartford were later given to Ruth G. Roosevelt by the President.

John had taken the deduction on his 1942 tax return and since forgotten the matter. He was mortified when all this publicity and investigation broke in the public media in 1945, shortly after President Roosevelt's death. How he wished now he had listened and agreed when George said no to any participation in the transaction. How he wished now he had simply taken the loss without the tax deduction which would have saved this embarrassment to the President's memory and had now incurred enormous political and public enmity toward the A&P Tea Company, which was not party to the loan.

John's deepest regret was that by his personal actions he had denigrated the reputation of A&P when all through his life he had tirelessly preached to all employees their need to GUARD OUR GOOD WILL, which he described as the most valuable thing they as an organization possess. His message to the employees said: *The single most important thing about this business is the individual customer who enters our store. This customer places confidence in us, and, this delicate human confidence, GOOD WILL, is the foundation of our business. No customer should have reason to feel we undervalue that confidence. No parent who confidently sends a child to our store must ever be dissappointed in us.*

But enough of politics, scandal, and regret. It was 1945, and George, 81, and John, 73, still had mountains to climb. World War II had ended, the country was in a jubilant mood. A&P had successfully survived the war years marked by food shortages, rationing, and food stamps. At year's end A&P had 1,700 supermarkets and construction was starting again.

But alas, the Hartfords' hope that political activity and government pressure against A&P had ended, was short lived. In 1945, the Antitrust Division brought a new version of an old action against A&P into Federal court in Danville, Illinois. The indictment charged the same criminal violation of antitrust laws which had been dismissed by a Dallas court in 1942. The government's attorneys had started and then, in 1944, dropped the appeal of the Dallas case to the circuit court in New Orleans. With all of its other problems, A&P did not take the new Danville case too seriously. The charges were familiar:

(a) A&P by the size of its manufacturing, wholesaling, and retailing resources constituted a food monopoly.

(b) Because of size, A&P was able to demand and obtain preferential allowances and discounts from suppliers.

(c) A&P used manufacturing profits to subsidize retail operations and operated stores at a loss in certain areas to drive competition out of business.

(d) A&P's produce subsidiary, The Atlantic Commission Company, controlled markets by buying more than A&P's needs and then selling, as a broker, the lesser quality and surplus products to competition.

Literally hundreds of thousands of documents were submitted as evidence, and as the trial dragged on into 1946, A&P realized the matter was serious indeed. After 18 months, in September 1946, Judge Lindley held for the government and fined A&P $175,000.

The case was appealed but in February, 1949, the conviction was upheld by the circuit court in Chicago. A&P concluded that seven years was enough and decided to pay the fine and dissolve the Atlantic Commission Company, which Judge Lindley found to be the only "rotten thread" in the A&P fabric. In his decision, Judge Lindley conceded that many of the charges the government made were without merit and he complimented A&P, saying: "To buy, sell and distribute to a substantial portion of 130 million people one and three-quarters billion dollars worth of food annually, at a profit of 1.5¢ on each dollar, is an achievement one may be proud of."

To add to John Hartford's chagrin, during the period this case was before the courts various politicians and governmental agencies had made allegations of rampant overcharging in A&P's stores, and pointed to "stock gains" as evidence to prove their claim. In

George Huntington Hartford, founder of the Great Atlantic &
Pacific Tea Company.

George Huntington Hartford (seated) and employees photographed in the 1890's on the roof of the company headquarters on Vesey Street in Manhattan. John Hartford is third from left in the rear, and George Ludlum Hartford is at extreme right.

An 8-horse team pulls away from the company headquarters on Vesey Street.

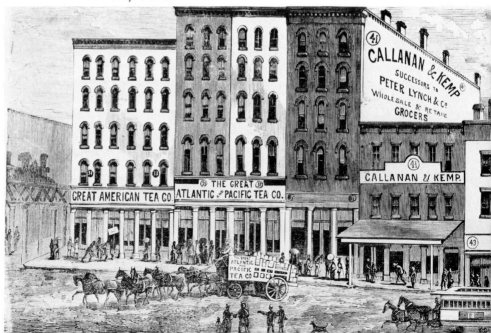

A 1908 photograph taken at a formal dinner celebrating George Huntington Hartford's 75th birthday. Among the company executives on hand were son George L. on the founder's left, and son John A., at the extreme left.

George Ludlum Hartford at his desk in the Graybar Building in Manhattan.

John Hartford, the merchant prince of the retail grocery business.

The two founding generations of the Great Atlantic & Pacific Tea Company: George Huntington Hartford and his sons John and George L.

Another 8-horse team delivering PURE GOODS to an A&P store.

This red and gold A&P wagon was a travelling store, selling tea, coffee, and spices in the early 1900's.

July 7th 1888.

Gentlemen,

I find on Chemical analysis that your "Baking Powder" is composed of pure materials.

When mingled with dough & baked, it produces bread or biscuits which are light and perfectly wholesome.

For economy, as well as health I cordially commend your Baking Powder to the general public.

Yours respectfully

R. Ogden Doremus M.D. LL.D

Professor of Chemistry, Toxicology & Med: Jurisprudence in the Bellevue Hosp: Medical College.

To the
Great Atlantic & Pacific
Tea Co. N.Y.

From its earliest days, A&P was obsessed with purity of product. Here is an 1888 testimonial from an unimpeacheable source. Who could have the slightest doubt that it was unsolicited?

The early stores (circa 1900) were as much premium centers as grocery stores, to judge from the window displays here. How could anyone distrust these gentlemen, who seem to be pleading only to be given a chance to serve you?

the A&P system all grocery products were billed to the store, and inventoried at the store, at the retail price to be charged to the customer. When notices of price changes were issued by the local office, the stores were required to advise the office, by mail, of the numbers of units of each product reduced or advanced. When the monthly inventory was taken, the difference between the actual inventory and the inventory the accounting department estimated to be on hand was the shrinkage or gain.

In those days most items were sold at fractional prices, such as $3/25$. All items were charged to the store on the premise that they would be sold at the fractional price. A small inventory gain was created when, as often happened, such items were sold singly. However, when a store inventory resulted in a stock gain, it was usually considered to indicate some form of "hanky panky" at store level.

The charge of being a "crooked merchant" infuriated John. He ordered that retail prices be marked on every single item for sale in the store. This was considered an unheard of and unnecessary expense at that time, when only shelf tags informed customers of item prices. John also set up an elaborate system of surprise price checks by company auditors in all stores to insure that prices were correctly marked. Finally, he charted the inventory results of every store in the country and demanded a thorough investigation and explanation whenever a stock gain was reported.

Throughout his lifetime, John insisted upon absolute corporate honesty to both employees and customers, and he demanded from all employees absolute honesty to both the customer and the company. Every A&P employee knew that if he were completely honest with the company and the customer, and applied himself reasonably to the job, his employment was secure.

John was also a realist, who understood the nature and practices in the real world of retailing. Competition was fierce and profit margins extremely low. Damage, spoilage, and pilferage could quickly wipe out profits unless rigid control was maintained.

In A&P then, as in retailing now, sometimes the best and most honest of store managers found it most difficult to achieve profit or budget expectations for their store. This was particularly true where a store was poorly located, or surrounded by competition operating in better facilities, offering wider varieties or lower prices. Human nature has not and does not change. Supervision and middle management tend to downplay the impact of these outside influences when setting budget goals and monitoring profit results. Usually, all stores are expected to meet the norm, and must meet the budget. Under such pressures, ambition being what it is, even the most diligent of managers is tempted to bend the rules just a little bit to help attain his profit objectives and remain in the good graces of his superiors.

The trouble is, bending the rules a little bit is like being a little bit pregnant; both lead to bigger things. John was fully aware of such temptations, but despite his repeated admonitions to both the supervisor and managers alike, A&P did have its share of "flip-magilders" as he used to call them. Those caught were promptly dismissed. Some, of course, were never caught, and perhaps a few had long, nominally successful careers cheating both the customers and the Tea Company, because a person who will steal for the company will also steal from the company.

But, back to February, 1949, the appeal in the Danville case was lost and George, now 85, and John, 77, decided not to take the matter to the Supreme Court. They just wanted to get back to going about their business without interference or assistance from the government or the courts.

But it was not to be. In September of 1949, the Attorney General of the United States filed basically the same charges under the civil portion of the Sherman Antitrust Act. This action demanded complete dissolution of the Atlantic & Pacific Tea Company.

John and George were heartsick, but fed up with the lawyers and determined not to passively stand by for another long period, waiting for their fate to be decided by some federal judge. They decided to use the public relations weapons which had worked successfully ten years earlier in the 1939 struggle against chain store taxes.

A series of full-page newspaper advertisements were prepared to state the A&P position to the American public at large. The campaign generated overwhelming public support in favor of A&P. Response came from a wide variety of sources, including farm groups, organized labor, suppliers and even a number of retail competitors. Quoted below is the ad in the *Boston Daily Record* dated September 30, 1949. Typical of the series, it starts out asking the question in bold type:

WHY DO THEY WANT TO PUT A&P OUT OF BUSINESS?

The answer is to be found in the formal complaint "they" have filed with the court. By "they" we mean, of course, the anti-trust lawyers from Washington who are out to destroy A&P.

They say... *and these are the anti-trust lawyers' own words...* that we "have regularly undersold competing retailers."

TO THIS CHARGE WE PLEAD *GUILTY*

We confess that for the past 90 years we have constantly stepped up the efficiency of our operations in order to give our customers more and more good food for their money.

The American people have seen nothing wrong in this. By their ever-increasing patronage for 90 years they have shown us that they like this low-price policy.

Apparently the people still see nothing wrong in this today. All during the past week—since the anti-trust lawyers made their charges—we have been deluged with phone calls and letters from men and women in all walks of life who want us to know they are opposed to this effort to put A&P out of business.

An enormous number of customers are telling our store managers and clerks that they want to continue to enjoy our low prices for quality foods.

Farmers and other suppliers are asking what they can do to preserve this efficient outlet for their products.

Our 110,000 employees are asking us to protect their jobs and pensions.

Labor leaders are wiring us their opposition to this threat to Labor's living standards.

If all these people will be hurt, why then do the anti-trust lawyers want to put A&P out of business?

LOW PRICES DON'T HURT ANYONE

The anti-trust lawyers say because we are able to sell food cheaper than other grocers, we make it impossible for those grocers to compete with us.

If this were true, we should have all the food business in the United States by this time.

Just the opposite is true. In 1933 we had 11.6 per cent of the nation's food business. Now according to the anti-trust lawyers, our share has decreased to 6.4 percent in 1948. Anyone can see we have nothing even approaching a monopoly.

As a matter of fact, there are about 30,000 more individual grocers in business today than there were ten years ago.

There are about 275 more food chains in business today than there were ten years ago.

In other words, we have more competitors in the food field and do a smaller share of the nation's food business than before.

Where is this alleged destruction of other grocers?

Where is there any evidence of their inability to compete with us?

DO YOU WANT HIGHER PRICES?

As anyone can see, the only purpose that would be served by putting A&P out of business would be to raise food prices.

Who would this benefit?

We were the first merchants to set the pattern for low-cost, low-profit distribution. Our example to our competition has led other grocers to keep their prices down.

Remove A&P from the picture and food prices are bound to go up.

Remove A&P from the picture and the way will be cleared for the destruction of every other efficient large-scale distributor.

Is that what the American people want?

Is this in the public interest?

This copy, professionally set on a full page of the daily newspapers across America got the A&P story to the public attention in a hurry.

The response, including editorial response, was so one-sided in A&P's favor that political wisdom influenced the Justice Department to back off. Eventually, the case was settled out of court with A&P signing a "consent decree" in 1954 which required no significant change in A&P's structure.

Five

O Captain, My Captain!

Despite the critical nature of the Antitrust actions which threatened the dissolution of the company during the 1945 to 1950 post-War years, John and George would not allow attention to be diverted from their primary goal of completing A&P's conversion from small service type stores to supermarkets.

By the end of 1950 the conversion to supermarkets was virtually complete. Some profitable service stores were retained in locations which A&P believed could not support supermarkets, or in areas where A&P had not yet found a suitable supermarket location. At year's end the company operated 4514 stores of which approximately 4,000 were supermarkets. Sales had increased to $3.2 billion and after-tax profit was $32 million, or 1 percent of sales.

To put this achievement in its proper time perspective, A&P's sales volume then exceeded the combined volumes of its two largest competitors, Safeway and Kroger. Working six days every week George, now 86, and John, 78, had accomplished this seemingly impossible task. They had rescued an entire chain of 15,000 small, high-operating-cost service stores faced with certain annihilation by the onslaught of supermarket competition. In a remarkably short space of time this entire operation was converted into a chain of over 4,000 of the most efficient supermarkets extant. Once again they had kept A&P's promise "to provide the most good food for the money." The Hartford brothers accomplished all this while engaged in a life-or-death struggle with the Antitrust Division, and while also recognizing they were soon coming face to face with an inevitable fact of life... death.

Both brothers brought a missionary zeal to, and found real joy in, their work at A&P. They never seriously considered retirement or relinquishing the task they felt so driven to complete. They were intent upon building and preserving A&P as a lasting memorial in tribute to their father. Both widowers and both childless, they had earlier agreed that their combined 40 percent share of the company would be donated, in its entirety, to the Hartford Foundation, which they had established in their family's name. The foundation which carried the family name would provide benefits to medical research and also serve the ancillary purpose of perpetuating the A&P organization so that it, in turn, could preserve the Hartford policies of providing more good food for less.

They established that the original board of trustees of the Foundation would be composed of senior A&P executives and representatives of the heirs of their two deceased sisters and brother Edward.

John wanted to build the organization to the position of strength where it could provide its own leaders and renew itself to meet the challenges of the unknown future. He realized that supermarkets were a lot more complex than small service stores; he knew that the next generation of leaders in the food industry, and American business as a whole, must be better educated and prepared to comprehend the complexities of an advancing technology. He organized and elevated personnel and personnel training to a position of high priority in a company where for over a century the only training was apprenticeship, a school where the performance of menial tasks over a period of time gradually resulted in one's attaining the ability to perform the job his boss performed. Apprenticeship continued at every level. It took a damn good man an average of 30 years to rise from store clerk to a position of high responsibility such as president of a division. Unfortunately, most who reached those positions knew only what they had learned from their predecessors and were not exceptionally well equipped to meet the challenges of the post-war world.

While recognizing the advantages of and need for modern training methods, John did not want A&P philosophy and policy, which he believed were the underlying support of the entire enterprise, delegated to any lesser position of importance. He prepared a booklet entitled "You and Your Company," intended for all potential management personnel and store managers in particular.

John opened this 44-page booklet with a personnel message discussing the employee's place in the company's plans. He restated the founder's belief that good capable employees "were the best assurance that A&P would grow and prosper." He pointed out that today, practically every officer and director of A&P was one who started with the company at the bottom. He added: "Promotion from the ranks expresses our policy of advancement. Just how well you and other managers are prepared to take your places on the higher rungs of the A&P ladder will determine how well A&P will serve and prosper in the years ahead." He related his and George's great desire: "to perpetuate A&P as a great public service, to have it stand forever as a monument to the integrity, perseverance and human understanding of the man who founded it, George Huntington Hartford."

The second section of the booklet was devoted to the explanation of company policies. John stated that all the policies of the company could be summarized in fifteen simple words: "Always do what is honest, fair, sincere and in the best interests of our customers." He went on to explain that each neighborhood store "is" the A&P Tea Company, and the treatment consumers receive in each store creates the national reputation of A&P. He followed with detailed discussion of four major components of the policy to customers:

(a) Courteous, prompt, attentive, patient, service to every customer with particular attention to children confidently sent to our store by their mother. "Make sure their purchase is well wrapped and their change put in a safe pocket or purse."

(b) The A&P guarantee, included in the price of every purchase. "If a customer returns merchandise, not satisfactory to her for any reason whatever, refund her money cheerfully, promptly and without question."

(c) The company policy of selling at the lowest possible prices. "We believe it is sounder to take a small profit on many sales than a larger profit on a few sales. We believe that in giving our customers the best possible value, we need not worry about our own success."

(d) Correct prices, correct weight and full measure. "It is the policy of your company to give every customer sixteen ounces to the pound. Honest intentions are not enough. Haste is no excuse. It is the policy of your company to charge every customer the exact same retail price set by the sales department for your territory."

The third and fourth sections of the booklet described the structure of the A&P organization from the individual store to the nationwide chain, including the widespread manufacturing facilities and their products as well as the many products purchased from outside suppliers under the A&P label.

Finally, the fifth section positions A&P in the American way of life at the time. It discusses America's mastery of mass production and the equally important need for mass distribution. It points out the part A&P has played in improving mass distribution systems and the reputation A&P has earned: "A&P is said to be expense conscious. A better description would be that we are waste conscious. A&P has seldom spared expense that would contribute to efficiency."

John very much wanted to personalize his relationship with each store and its personnel. He apologized for not being able to visit every store and explained, that this booklet was an attempt to substitute for that visit.

With each passing year, George and John found themselves wanting to devote more and more time to the organization. In 1946, they decided to share some of their success with the organization by instituting a Christmas bonus at a cost of over $2.5 million, almost 10 percent of the company's after-tax profit. Most corporate managers would distribute such an amount proportionately to where they expected it would do the most good for the company. John and George, in their typically untypical fashion, decided that each and every one of their 110,000 employees should receive identical Christmas presents, a check in the amount of twenty-five dollars along with an expression of appreciation and best wishes for the holidays.

While this distribution didn't sit well with some of the "brass hats," as John used to call the big-shot executives, it brought a great deal of Christmas joy to the families of those 110,000 workers whose weekly wages averaged less than fifty dollars in those days.

In 1916, George H. Hartford had started a pension plan under which long-service employees received monthly checks throughout their retirement years in amounts sufficient to maintain those ex-employees in dignity and which differed according to individual needs. John and George had always continued this plan in effect. In 1947 they decided that the time had come to formalize this practice by the establishment of a retirement plan covering all of the 110,000 A&P employees. Again the Hartfords were way ahead of their time in improving benefits to employees in the food industry.

On August 31, 1948, John Hartford in a letter "To Our Employees" stated: "I am very happy to announce a Retirement Plan covering all full time employees has been approved. The Plan will go into effect on October 1, 1948, and the company intends to bear the entire cost of the Plan." After mentioning that details of the plan will be covered fully in a booklet soon to be released, he concluded:

"In adopting this Plan the company is giving recognition to the loyal service of its employees who have aided in the progress and success of the company. The continuation of a Plan as costly as this requires the continued successful operation of the company. I am confident that, with your continued loyalty and cooperation, we can look forward to such successful operation in the future."

The A&P retirement plan provided benefits equal to half of the average annual wage earned during the last five years' employment, less primary social security benefit, when an employee had accumulated 33 years creditable service upon reaching age 65. To install such a plan in a company that was already 90 years old was extremely costly. Many of the 110,000 covered employees were already at or approaching the mandatory retirement age of 65. Additional thousands were at or approaching the early retirement age of 55 years. Funding costs during the first ten years of the plan's life, as expected, exceeded all the net corporate earnings in the previous ten years.

Kenneth C. Goodell, Treasurer of the Eastern Division, whose office was in the Graybar Building, was chosen to coordinate data and oversee the presentations on pension costs and benefits during the eighteen-month period the pension plan was under study prior to approval. He recalled this experience in a letter written during

1983 when A&P's intention to divert some $300 million surplus in this plan for corporate uses was being contested by a class action of the plan membership. Ken recalled the enthusiasm with which the Hartfords welcomed this plan, and he commented that it was his firm belief that the Hartfords intended this trust for the sole benefit of members, and if in 1983 the Hartfords were still alive and A&P was facing bankruptcy and they were also broke ... they still would never have attempted to touch a penny of that trust fund which they intended for employee retirement benefits only.

In addition to extensive travel visiting A&P stores throughout the country, John also organized a managers' and supervisors' conference which was held each week in Newark, New Jersey, starting in 1947. Small groups of managers or supervisors were selected from representative areas of the country and gathered for a one-week conference in Newark. Ostensibly it was an advanced training program for already successful managers and supervisors who enjoyed the trip to New York and the opportunity to meet with each other and compare ideas and experiences. In a real sense it filled Mr. John's need to get closer to the organization. Without fail he would spend at least one day each week with the group in session so that, after putting the group at ease, in the ensuing bull session and question-and-answer period he could get the pulse of what really concerned middle management out at the extremities, in Dallas, Los Angeles, Toronto, or Milwaukee. At week's end every group departed with a greater sense of security and pride in being part of A&P.

A&P with sales volume of $3.2 billion in 1950 had now become the largest privately owned company and the largest retail organization in the world. Its sales volume exceeded that of U.S. Steel and Standard Oil, and was second only to General Motors in total sales volume for corporations of any kind.

A portrait of George and John adorned the cover of *Time* Magazine on November 13, 1950. The four-page feature story provided a rare insight into A&P and the two brothers responsible for its growth. In describing John and George as perhaps the most unusual business team in U.S. history, the article says:

"Both brothers are widowers; both live only for the A&P. But there the similarity ends. John is thin, George is plump. John is bold and expansive, George cautious and conservative. John is gregarious and full of quips, George shy and sobersided. John stands and talks, George sits and listens. Plain and unpretentious George, in his drab black suit, sedate tie and stiff collar, could easily be taken for a retired motorman dressed up for Sunday. Nobody would make that mistake about John, who looks the merchant prince from the tip of his elegant shoes to the top of his wavy-maned handsome head. He dresses as fastidiously as a latter day Beau Nash. A symphony in greys, he orders as many as a dozen suits at a time from exclusive Manhattan tailor James Bell. He always sports a deep red carnation in his buttonhole, tucks an expensive handspun monogrammed linen handkerchief in the pocket beneath it. His silk and poplin shirts are custom made by Sulka with a special high soft collar. His oversized, flowing bow ties give him a faintly poetic air."

The article goes on to explain how the brothers live as differently as they dress. George dwells in a spacious house in Verona, N.J., where he lives what seems to be a lonely life with television, an electric organ, jig-saw puzzles, and tinkering with radio and television sets as his hobbies and amusements. He maintains a summer suite at the Monmouth Hotel in Spring Lake, N.J., but has never taken a vacation and commutes to work every day.

John, also a widower and childless, lives like the lord of the manor in a rambling Tudor stone mansion in Valhalla, N.Y. He played golf on his private nine-hole course with his wife Polly, but since her death in 1949 he has given up the game. He rides the paths of his 365 rolling, wooded acres on one of his thoroughbred horses or in a fringe-topped surrey. He keeps fit raking leaves or laying stone walks near a cozy cabin overlooking a large pond which has become his favorite retreat on the estate. He enjoys tossing shreds of ground meat to the fat trout in the pond, remarking with a wink, "when you catch one of those meat fed trout it tastes like lamb chops."

The article in *Time* ended by quoting Mr. John saying: "I don't know any grocer or anybody else who wants to stay small. They all dream about building something bigger. The whole country's growing, our cities, schools, labor unions, everything. I don't see how any business man can limit his growth and stay healthy."

Some time earlier, in another of his rare interviews, he said: "The secret of chain store profits lies almost entirely in a rapid turnover of merchandise, and a rapid turnover simply means unceasing attention to the needs and the buying habits of your customers."

John also maintained an apartment at the Plaza Hotel in New York where he usually stayed during the week. On pleasant days he would walk the sixteen blocks to his office in the Graybar Building. He also put off vacations and worked every day, although in later years he had accepted directorships on boards of several major corporations and charitable institutions, which got him away from the office on occasion.

On September 20, 1951, John enjoyed his morning stroll from the Plaza down to his office. The company was prospering, it was autumn in New York, and, all was right with the world. He arrived at the office shortly after nine, reviewed the mail and had the usual routine discussions with George and the executive staff. At 1:30 P.M., advising George he would be back by four P.M., he left the office, crossed Lexington Avenue to attend a board meeting at the Chrysler Corporation. After the meeting, coming down in the elevator of the Chrysler Building, on the way back to his office, John was stricken. The heart which had carried him through seventy-nine exciting years had finally stopped. He never regained consciousness.

Suddenly now, the eagle had fallen. John was gone, leaving George, the eldest child, now 87 years of age, alone to guide the future destiny of A&P.

Across the country newspaper editorials eulogized Mr. John:

The New York Journal-American: "John Hartford perhaps accomplished more than any other man in making the high American standard of living available to families of even the most modest means."

The San Francisco Call-Bulletin: "John A. Hartford belonged to a little group of Americans whose energy and vision made us the most prosperous nation in the world. He pioneered in foodstuffs just as Henry Ford did in transportation. Their philosophy was blunt and simple, just as most works of genius are simple: "Sell more for less.""

The Chicago Daily News: "John Hartford has often been called, "the last of the merchant princes." Such individuals have largely disappeared in the multiple and anonymous management of large corporations. But it will be a sorry day for the American way if their competitive genius should ever prove to have died with them."

The Columbus Georgia Ledger: "What Ford meant to transportation, what Edison meant to electricity, what Burbank meant to horticulture, John Hartford meant to food retailing in America."

The Davenport Daily Times: "In the death of 'Mr. John' there passes a retail Napolean.... He had a grocery empire as Ford had an automobile empire, Rockefeller an oil empire, Carnegie a steel empire. We shall not see their like again."

The funeral service was conducted at the Valhalla estate by a priest from St. Catherine of Sienna Church. John A. Hartford rests in Hillside cemetery in Middletown, New York, alongside his wife Pauline, who had died two years earlier.

The Tide Ebbs Slowly

Although both George and John had been blessed with exceptional health throughout their lives, they knew plans had to be made for the transference of authority to assure the continued prosperity of the Company after their passing.

In 1949, John who had held the title of President became Chairman, George retained the title of Treasurer with which he was most comfortable. Together they decided upon the candidate most qualified to succeed them and appointed David T. Boffinger as President of A&P. Boffinger, at an early age, had gone to work for A&P in the Lake George, New York, area. Rising through the ranks he had served for many years as head of A&P's vast purchasing network. Unfortunately, Mr. Boffinger died suddenly in December, 1949, just nine months after becoming president.

In June, 1950, John and George chose Ralph W. Burger as president and successor to run the company after their passing. Burger had also started with A&P as a youth, had worked in the headquarters office for many years, and had worked closely for both John and George. He had earlier been appointed secretary of the company. While Burger had never held a position of high executive authority, over long years of personal contact he had earned the friendship and complete confidence of the Hartfords. After Pauline Hartford's death in 1949, Burger had become John's closest friend and confidant. Ralph and Mrs. Burger often spent weekends with John at Valhalla; and Ralph was constantly at John's side in travels around the country or in the office. Burger was also chosen to be president and chairman of the Hartford Foundation. The power to vote the Foundation's stock would insure his authority after the brothers' passing.

So long as John lived, Burger's presidency had little or no effect upon the organization or the operation of the business. However, as might be expected, his selection was not a popular choice with the divisional presidents or the other headquarters executives, each of whom undoubtedly considered himself more qualified. Burger had never been active in the nuts and bolts, buying and selling parts of the food business. He was considered no more than an office boy who had matured into an executive's secretary... a highly paid "get me or go for" this and that. Of course, such thoughts were never expressed publicly or at meetings.

After John's death, George, now chairman of the board, retained full and absolute authority over the company. Nothing of importance could be decided without his full consent. However, George had never taken active personal interest in the day-to-day operation of the retail business; that had been John's job. George preferred keeping control of the assets and passing judgment only upon major operating decisions of the company. At 87 years of age he was not inclined to change things and prefered that Ralph Burger handle all day-to-day operating decisions.

Burger was fully aware that he had no proven track record in retail operations and was also aware of the awkward, rather distant relationship that existed between him and the rest of the organization.

His first action after John's death was to visit each of the six divisions and each of the thirty-seven operating units of A&P and meet with the executive staffs and store supervisory personnel. He was remarkably relaxed and candid at these meetings, admitting his lack of field operating experience and relating why Mr. John told him he was chosen: "Because, Ralph, during these last years you have been closer to me than anyone else; more than anyone else you know how I feel about this company, and as new problems arise in the future I believe you more than anyone else would know how I might react to that problem and you are most likely to react in that same way."

He told of his close personal association with John, and how Mr. John had insisted that he take a salary of $25,000 per year as president of the Hartford Foundation. He had refused, but after some additional discussion he agreed to accept one fresh red carnation from the Valhalla greenhouses each day as his added salary for heading up the Foundation. He explained that was the reason for the red carnation in his lapel button hole; and standing, he added: "This is Mr. John's suit I'm wearing." He had adopted Mr. John's stylish look he said, "Because we were both the same size and John would not have wanted those famous grey suits to go to waste." He assured each group of his intention to carry out John's desires to take care of the organization. He left the field organization feeling satisfied that A&P was in good hands.

Back and comfortable in John's old office, not wanting to appear weak or uncertain by asking advice from the field, Burger decided he would run the company through the headquarters staff with whom he felt more comfortable and secure. Perhaps, unwittingly, he had already decided to do precisely what Mr. John would never have done.

The 1950s were growth years for America and the food business. The population was growing, the cities were vibrant and large new housing tracts were springing up in the suburban areas to accommodate new families and the baby boom.

A&P's development program had slowed somewhat, but the supermarket formula was successful and company sales and profits were increasing each year. The company's volume passed the $4 billion mark in 1954 and things looked great . . . on the outside.

The consent decree, signed in January 1954 as final settlement of the antitrust action brought by the Justice Department in 1949, represented a solid victory for A&P, because under it A&P had only to dissolve the Atlantic Commission Company and its produce brokerage dealings. It did not otherwise materially reduce the company's ability to procure fruits and vegetables competitively and in adequate quantities. Other than that, the decree prohibited A&P's selling or wholesaling to the outside trade and accepting or demanding allowances or prices not available to the trade as a whole; and A&P had not, or been able, to do this anyway.

However, the decree gave Mr. Burger and his headquarters staff additional excuse for tightening the already suffocating controls imposed upon the operating divisions in the field. The decree provided the legal department the opportunity to become part of the command staff and issue orders to field purchasing, sales, and accounting staffs. These orders, much more restrictive than the court decree, were intended to guarantee that no misinformed person in the field could conceivably embarrass headquarters by even the most minor or remote violation of the court order. This overkill produced tons of trivia files and resulted in field personnel taking underaggressive positions in relations with suppliers.

In a period of rapid expansion in food manufacturing, with new items, deals, and allowances exploding onto the retail food scene, headquarters tightened its grip on control. Every new item or new size, every deal or allowance offered, had first to be approved by headquarters. Oftentimes a buyer in Kansas City, for example, would have to justify to a New York purchasing director why his stores should stock an item that was heavily advertised and already selling in volume in competitors' stores in Kansas City. Such policies not only stifled initiative but seriously reduced A&P's competitive effectiveness in the marketplace.

This policy had the added effect of discouraging suppliers' salesmen in the field to the point that A&P often became the last rather than the first customer to whom a deal was offered or a new item presented. A&P also closed its doors to close-outs and other special offerings.

Headquarters also imposed rigid inventory ceiling budgets based upon weeks' supply formulas not in keeping with realistic needs based upon volumes, size, number of deliveries, or other circumstances. This often resulted in lost sales due to out-of-stocks in warehouses or stores simply to satisfy headquarters' fanaticism to avoid or minimize financing peak period inventories.

Headquarters' warehousing and transportation department contributed by establishing productivity goals not calibrated to the size, physical characteristics, or schedules of various distribution facilities. As a classic instance of bureaucracy in action, this group decided they would solve the distribution problems troubling the New York area divisions. They planned, designed and built a massive distribution facility in Elmsford, New York, without even consultation with the operating units of the area. Upon its completion, fully equipped, including underfloor tow chains, the responsibility for its operation was turned over to the operating unit along with productivity goals set by the designers. To meet projected tonnage figures, headquarters decided that the facility must service stores of a New Jersey unit as well as the New York unit stores. On opening day, national warehousing experts turned over the responsibility and all related costs to the unit, but continued to have the plant superintendent report directly to them. A long-term disaster resulted because headquarters personnel had not considered or provided for the resultant rebellion by the Teamsters over tonnage and personnel displacements, had not provided for the complete product line required to be stocked for the stores to be serviced, and had not provided for adequate service levels. Costs far exceeded projections, labor problems became a way of life, service to stores was worse than before, and, of course, the unit was held completely responsible for the failure.

Headquarters' administrative committee approved all new leases and renewals. All leases were to be on a standard A&P lease form with any changes separately approved. During the 1950s new store leases were expected to be for a term of five years, with five renewals of five years at rentals not to exceed $2 per square foot per annum.

As property values and building costs increased, developers required longer lease terms and higher rentals to finance new larger shopping centers. Other chains with more aggressive new-store programs began to outbid A&P for prime sites by offering to rent more space at higher rentals for longer terms. From the units' viewpoint, headquarters' policy seemed to be to flatly reject requests for longer-term leases or higher square foot rentals until it became evident the developers were not just bluffing and the Tea Company had lost out on numbers of prime locations. Then, grudgingly, little by little, the standards would be raised, but always, it seemed, to a level six months to a year behind the conditions in the real world.

Labor relations did not escape headquarters' purview. The units of the Metropolitan New York area, comprising New York City, Long Island, Westchester, Rockland and Orange Counties of New York, Fairfield County Connecticut, and northern and central New Jersey, from the earliest days represented the major bulwark of A&P. In the early 1950s this Metro area had volume in excess of $1

billion annually in approximately 750 stores. This represented
about 25 percent of A&P's total volume and an even greater share of
A&P's total profits. The area since late in the 1940s had been
threatened by unionization of its stores. The activity was greatest
in New York City and Long Island, where both the retail clerks'
union and the butchers' union were trying to organize their
portions of the stores. Time after time elections were held. Time
after time the unions failed to gain sufficient votes to represent the
store employees; however, as time went by the vote was getting
closer. In 1952, headquarters decided that efforts to keep unions
out of the stores were futile; they further decided it would be
better to deal with one reasonable union than attempt to deal with
two different unions in each store. Suddenly, the word came out
from headquarters that on the next election the company would
like to see Max Block's butchers' union win the right to represent
the store employees. That is precisely what happened, and for the
next thirty years the Metro units were saddled with the highest
labor contracts in the area.

On a national scale, perhaps the most oppressive long-term
devious weapon was wielded by headquarters statisticians. Retail
food has always been a labor intensive business. Store wages
constitute the largest item of controllable expense by far. Without
effective control of labor costs it is impossible to operate a store
profitably.

For many years the standard criteria of store labor efficiency was
"clerk hire rate," the result of store wages divided by sales. Volatile
food price inflation, and varying increases in hourly labor rates,
made it difficult, if not impossible, to obtain a true measure of
labor productivity by the "clerk hire" standard. Over the years this
problem has been resolved by carefully studying each component
of store labor—stocking, pricing, checkout, meat cutting, wrap-
ping, floor care etc.—to ascertain hourly productivity targets for
each job. Using lower part-time labor rates where possible, the
store staff is assembled and the productivity performance of the
various tasks is monitored. Today's computers tell the store not
only what staffing is required but also how the schedule should be
set by day and by hour.

Early in the 1950s, headquarters statisticians devised an onerous
"pounds per employee hour" gauge for measuring productivity in

stores. It was predicated upon the retail value per ton of food sold in stores, updated each month using a complicated formula which reflected changes in food prices across the United States. Weekly, each store divided total sales by the current "price per pound" formula to determine poundage sold, and divided that number by total store hours to calculate "pounds per employee hour" performance.

This calculation could record trend lines in productivity, if there happened to be a single store anywhere in the United States that was reflective of the whole nation, and there was no change in inventory position. Despite being unnecessarily cumbersome, it might have been an acceptable guide for measuring continuing productivity in any single store. However, when a target, such as 120 pounds per employee hour, was arbitrarily imposed upon *all* stores as a measure of acceptable performance, store managers believed it made no sense at all...and they were right. It made no allowance, for example, for the small, crowded city stores with no back rooms, where freight was dropped on the sidewalk, and where apartment dwellers shopped daily carrying home small purchases. It made no allowance for neighborhood or regional differences in product mix. It was not adjusted for "pay weeks" or slack weeks, or whether chuck meat or ham was featured. If and when a manager got his staffing in line, the index would change suddenly, and he would find himself again overstaffed according to the formula.

The two most important criteria for judging managers' performance became the ability to achieve satisfactory control over "pounds per employee hour" and stock losses. In far too many instances this resulted in managers arbitrarily cutting back store labor hours to meet a formula they did not understand. Further, they had no choice but to cut the lower-cost, part-time hours. Customer service levels, particularly at the checkout stands, deteriorated rapidly, and this soon reflected itself in weekly volume drops which started the deadly cycle all over again.

At a later point, headquarters finally decided to eliminate the calculation of individual store profits. They reasoned that, since certain costs, allowances, and expenses were charged to stores on an arbitrary sales basis, the store profit was truly not accurate. More importantly, if A&P didn't calculate store profits or losses, the government could never prove the company was operating stores at a loss intentionally.

The word "potential" took on more importance than profit. This "potential" additional profit available for each store was calculated based upon that store's deficiency with respect to various "norms." Calculations were made to point out the total potential additional profit available if a store's stock losses, gross margins, credits, pounds per employee hour, supply, maintenance, and other expenses had been in line with the expected norms.

The cost of store labor as rated on sales actually increased, while managers tried everything, including understating store labor hours, to solve their problems. Store conditions deteriorated further. Cleanliness, stocking levels, service, and courtesy were all negatively affected.

The logical question is, how in hell could this have gone on in a company of this size without rebellion in the ranks? The answer to that question is interesting but somewhat complex. From the viewpoint of Mr. George and the family, things were never better. Mr. George never communicated directly with the store organization, never visited stores, and, only occasionally, even peered in the front windows to see what was going on. From 1952 through 1956, Ralph Burger's management had rung up five consecutive sales and profit gains, each a new record high. No one noticed that new stores accounted for more than the average 4 percent annual sales growth, or that this five-year growth was less than half of the industry average. Dividends were higher than ever. Mr. Burger's regime was most successful.

Mr. George never knew, and in all probability Ralph Burger never realized, the deterioration in morale and stagnation that was setting in at store level in many areas of the company.

From the store viewpoint, protocol required that the store manager complain to his supervisor, the supervisor complain to the unit vice-president, the vice-president, if he thought it serious enough, complain to the divisional president, and the divisional president, if he dared, complain to Mr. Burger. Large multi-level corporations tend often to abide by the old military adage that a little dissension in the ranks is a healthy thing. Management tends to expect a certain amount of griping and dismisses it too often as lower-level excuse making.

In this case, the unit vice-presidents were well aware of the managers' feelings and sympathized with those feelings. Most vice-presidents made their feelings known to their divisional president with varying degrees of vigor. One or two divisional presidents even broached the subject gingerly to Mr. Burger at meetings in New York. The response cut the questioner down to size, suggesting that he had best spend his small talents trying to recover the enormous "potential" profits being wasted in his division rather than question formulas which headquarters and the rest of the organization agreed were sound. There is a corporate axiom that says: "Challenging the wisdom and authority of a successful chief executive officer, at the peak of his career and power, is a short route to the back exit." The wiser, older heads fall back upon the old reliable, "This too shall pass."

Mr. George, in his 93rd year in 1957, had every reason to think things were going just fine. He continued to come into the office frequently arriving about 11 A.M. and departing, after his ritualistic testing of all A&P coffees every afternoon, around two P.M. In 1908, George had married the former Mrs. Josephine Burnett Logan. Together, they lived happily in their large stone mansion in Verona until her passing in 1944. Josephine had a daughter by her previous marriage who had now also passed away. After the daughter's death, her husband, Sheldon Stewart, came to stay with George in his later years. Mr. George passed away quietly at his home on September 23, 1957, just one month shy of his 93rd birthday, and after having served A&P for more than 80 years. So little was known of his private life that his many obituaries were really brief historical sketches of A&P.

George wanted no acclaim in his lifetime. In one of his rare public comments, made during those 1940's antitrust struggles, he summed up his life: "We're just a couple of grocery boys trying to do an honest business."

The trust which George H. Hartford, the founder, had established in 1917, providing for equal distribution of A&P's income and stock to each of his five children until the death of the last surviving child, could now be dissolved.

George L. Hartford, the eldest son and the last child to die, left his entire share of the trust to the Hartford Foundation.

Ralph Burger, as president of the Hartford Foundation, could now, therefore, vote the 40 percent of A&P stock willed to the Foundation by John and George. In the period between John's death in 1951 and George's passing in 1957, the non-active heirs of

A&P had voiced few objections to the Burger presidency, and were apparently satisfied that the business was in good hands since sales, profits, and dividends increased each year. With the acquiescence of holders of just 10 percent of the stock, Burger could maintain complete control of A&P's destiny.

The third, and youngest, brother, Edward V. Hartford, had never taken an active interest in the grocery business, but as a young man was much more interested in engineering. Declaring, "at least one of the Hartfords ought to be a gentleman," he went off to college. Later, successful in his own business, and very interested in automotive engineering, he invented the Hartford shock absorber and was responsible for other improvements in automobile design. Edward enjoyed the good life but unfortunately was not blessed with good health; he died at a relatively young age in 1922. He and his wife Etta, who passed away in 1950, had two children. Their son, George H. Hartford II, later became much better known as Huntington Hartford, patron of the arts and playboy of the western world. Their daughter, Josephine, in her third marriage became Mrs. John F.C. Bryce. Huntington Hartford and Josephine Hartford Bryce each inherited 10 percent of the trust.

The founder's daughter, Marie Louise, married A.G. Hoffman, who later became a vice-president of purchasing for A&P. They had two daughters, Marie and Josephine. Daughter Marie by her second marriage became Mrs. Robertson; daughter Josephine married Allen McIntosh. Mrs. Marie Robertson and Mrs. Josephine McIntosh each also inherited 10 percent of the trust willed to them by their mother Marie Louise who passed away in 1928.

The founder's other daughter, Maria Josephine had married John Clews. They had two children. Their son, George Clews who passed away in 1940 left his share of the trust to his daughter who had become Mrs. Rachel Carpenter, and now inherited 10 percent of the trust.

Maria Josephine Clews's other child, daughter Josephine, married Wm. G. Wrightson and they had five children. The mother, Maria, daughter Josephine, and husband Wm. G. Wrightson had all passed away by 1944. The five Wrightson children, therefore, shared the final 10 percent of the trust, with 2 percent going each to son William and daughters Oliva Switz, Martha Ramsing, Cynthia Twitchell, and Marie (Minnie) Besch.

The heirs, Huntington Hartford (10 percent), Josephine Bryce (10 percent), Rachel Carpenter (10 percent), Marie Robertson (10 percent), Josephine McIntosh (10 percent) and the five Wrightsons (total 10 percent), all either attended or were represented at an informal family meeting with Ralph Burger. The meeting was held at A&P headquarters in the Graybar Building in October 1957. Those present expressed agreement that present company management had been highly competent. Preliminary discussions were held regarding possible wider stock ownership at some future time, but no immediate changes of any kind were recommended.

Up until now, these ten family members had no control whatever over their stock, which was locked into the trust established by George H. Hartford in 1917. Some years earlier, seven of this group had entered into a formal agreement to pool their voting power when the trust was finally dissolved. Josephine Bryce, Rachel Carpenter, and Cynthia Twitchell had refrained from joining in this agreement. Individuals in the splinter group of seven, notably Huntington Hartford, had expressed skepticism and concern at what they regarded as Ralph Burger's arrogance, and the dictatorial power he apparently wielded.

Burger was aware that some of the heirs would prefer new management, and he was most anxious to avoid controversy that might split the voting power down the middle and create a management crisis. Expecting this eventuality, in recent years he had campaigned diligently to gain the confidence and support of Josephine Bryce and Rachel Carpenter. They now voiced their support of his continuing in management, and with 60 percent of voting stock, Ralph Burger remained in complete control of A&P's destiny. Josephine Bryce even accepted Burger's invitation to join the Board of Trustees of the Hartford Foundation, which up to that time was comprised of Burger and two A&P executives, John Ehrgott and Harry George.

Aware that other foundations had found it wise to diversify their investments, Burger did not want to release large blocks of stock for fear this would lead to outsiders taking control of A&P contrary to the expressed wish of John and George to keep the organization and its policy intact.

The heirs, on the other hand, would be forced to sell some portion of their A&P holdings in order to pay the estate tax with which they were confronted. As the financial community predicted, A&P went public in 1958 and the stock was listed on the New York Exchange. The heirs sold moderate amounts over varying periods of time, but the Foundation held fast.

The heirs as a group were responsible for the selection of six outstanding outsiders to sit on the board of directors of A&P. This group was not selected to represent the special interest of the heirs but to bring a depth of outside experience and viewpoints to the consideration of future A&P management decisions. This group included:

R. Manning Brown—Vice-President, later Chairman of New York Life Insurance Company.

John L. Burns   —President of R.C.A.

Jay E. Crane   —Vice President, Standard Oil of N.J., retired.

Donald K. David —Former Dean, Harvard Business School, Director of Ford, G.E., Vice-Chairman Ford Foundation.

Gwilym Price   —Chairman of Westinghouse Electric Company.

John E. Slater   —Partner, Coverdale & Colpitts, Consulting Engineers.

After their first board meeting the above group reported they had no hostility to A&P management or the 14 inside board members who comprised the balance of the 20 member board. They indicated instead an attitude of curiosity and anxiousness to learn more about this company and its business.

As 1959 came to a close, Burger, now 70 years of age, was still in control of A&P with 60 percent majority vote of the foundation and heirs, and a 14 to 6 majority of inside directors on the board. He remained genuinely dedicated to carrying out the Hartfords' wish to preserve A&P, its policies, and organization. Unfortunately, he also had the guts and obstinacy to point the company in the direction he thought best to achieve that goal. He decided that increased profits and increased dividends would provide the best prescription for the perpetuation of the company even if it had to be achieved at the expense of sales growth.

Ralph Burger, and the company he loved, were betrayed by his lack of vision and failure to understand that A&P's long-term protection could be assured only by continuing growth sufficient, in the minimum, to maintain present market share in each division. He was done in by a failure to understand that unchecked erosion of market share, whether in a store, unit, or division, leads inevitably to loss of profitability for that entity and the company.

During the four-year period ending with fiscal 1962, after-tax profits continued upward at record levels, averaging $57.2 million. An incredible 92 percent of that amount, or $52.5 million, was distributed each year in dividends. Over those four years the Foundation received $84 million, each of the ten percenters received over $20 million, and each of the two percenters over $4 million. A&P stock, which had opened at $59 on the New York exchange in 1958, was selling at $70 per share in November 1961.

But what had happened to sales volumes in that period? A&P sales had increased an average of 1 percent per year while the total industry was growing at a rate ten times that. Volume for 1962 totalled $5.3 billion, up 4 percent over the $5.1 billion sales of 1959. On a tonnage basis, 1962 results were actually lower than 1959's.

When the sad day finally arrives when A&P is no more, let it not be written that this giant was driven to extinction by a government's oppression nor by fierce competitor aggression. Let the record show it was death by its own hand, and let the epitaph contain one single word "suicide." However long it finally takes, it started the very moment John died.

In a period of explosive national growth, A&P's development was severely curtailed by management policy that siphoned profits into dividends, had an obsessive passion against borrowing, and looked only to depreciation as the source of funds for capital development. Thus, in the four years ending in 1962, A&P development was limited to replacing an average of 205 obsolete stores per year and opening approximately 55 additional new stores per year. In a 4,500 store chain, this amounted to 5 percent annual obsolescence replenishment and 1 percent new store increase.

These grim statistics fail, as most statistics do, to reveal the whole story. The pitifully few stores A&P was opening did not compare favorably in size or furnishings with the typical new supermarkets opened by the industry at that time. And, of more lasting import, A&P was replacing obsolete stores in obsolete inner cities of the country while the competition was leaving those cities, following consumers into the newly built suburbs and the booming sun belt of America.

From the outside, A&P appeared awesome in 1962. With sales of over $5 billion it was more than twice the size of its nearest competitor. With an enviable debt-free balance sheet it was in an extraordinary position to capitalize upon the baby boom and the nation's economic expansion.

On the inside, management looking at the economic boom could see only the shadow of depression certain to come, and postulate how well off A&P would be when the "big bust" came. From the inside, this magnificent Goliath was being tied down securely by the Lilliputian minds of a small army of statisticians who could not see the beach for the sand. They carefully examined each reported number, but only in relation to a norm. They knew not, and cared not, whether the "norms themselves" of the expenses and gross margins they studied were too high. Their limited vision could never look up from the sand and see the whole beach, and grasp the biggest "potential" of all, the effect on profit of lost sales.

When, in mid 1961, it became evident that sales for that year would be behind the previous year, headquarters management dismissed lack of aggressive development, rapidly increasing gross margins, and deteriorating store conditions as causal, and decided the introduction of Plaid Stamps would provide the vehicle to boost sales at least 15 percent without capital expenditure; and, with a 15 percent sales increase, the stamp cost was to be self-liquidating.

Early experiments, starting in mid November 1961, proved what carefully monitored early experiments in carefully chosen test markets always tend to prove... this experiment succeeded in this market at this time. In his annual message to stockholders, dated May 16, 1962, Mr. Burger commented upon the success of the pilot experience and said: "We are now committed to a course of steady and orderly expansion of this program. We have stamps in approximately half of our stores and are in the process of introducing them in other trade areas as the circumstances indicate." As with most high-pressure, high-cost promotions, the early response was favorable, but it wore off quickly because there never has been a gimmick that can offset quality, price, availability, and service.

By late 1962, the Plaid Stamp bloom was off the rose and all six outside directors decided to act at last. They allegedly threatened to resign en masse unless Ralph Burger stepped down. Mr. Burger resigned the presidency on January 24, 1963, resigned as chairman on April 11, 1963, and took retirement on May 1, 1963.

An era had ended, an eleven-year period of deepening stagnation had ended. A&P, still powerful king of the retail hill, would soon reassert itself. By this time the stock had dropped from $70 per share into the $30/40 dollar range. Shareholders and employees looked forward to better days ahead.

Before going on with the story, we should pause and examine the size, condition, and character of the A&P Tea Company Ralph Burger left when he resigned as president and chairman of the board.

No one ever doubted Burger's total devotion to the Hartfords. All agreed he gave one hundred percent of his effort and ability to his job. Most agreed he tried to form his decisions and run the company the way he believed John and George would have done it faced with the same problems. But Burger saw himself faced with a problem which John and George had never encountered. No one had threatened or challenged their absolute control over the affairs of the company because no one ever could make such challenge.

The Foundation's holdings now represented about 34 percent of total A&P shares, and Burger was convinced that dissident shareholders could represent the major threat to continued inside management of A&P. Evidence of such discontent had already been expressed by some of the heirs holding large blocks of company stock. He decided to meet this perceived threat by increasing profits and dividends. History's major criticism of Burger is that his concern for current profits blinded him to the opportunities for growth offered by the post-war economic boom. At the time, his counterargument to more aggressive development was, "This is not the time to rearouse the Federal Trade Commission, or other agencies of government, which is what will surely happen if A&P becomes overtly aggressive now."

Despite the fact that sales stagnated and job opportunities were reduced during his tenure, no one doubted his personal loyalty to the organization. In 1960, he approved an employee stock purchase savings plan under which the company contributed 25 percent of employees' wage savings. Over a period of time this Thrift Plan became second to the Foundation as A&P's largest shareholder. Burger foresaw the day when employees and the Foundation would gain majority control of A&P stock.

In Burger's defense, it must be remembered that John and George had not gained preeminence by being first to spot the need for change. Their success had come from the speed and efficiency with which they moved the company once the need for change was recognized. However, we can be sure that John would have seen that need sometime during the decade of the 1950's, and he would have pressed forward with the development program needed to maintain A&P's position of preeminence over all competition in providing more good food, for less money, to more people, how and wherever they wanted that food.

Certainly, the Tea Company Ralph Burger turned over to his successors in 1963 was still in strong position to assert itself. Current assets were more than twice current liabilities, the company was debt free, with an impeccable credit rating, and, with its strong reputation among consumers, was the most sought-after tenant in any new shopping center.

A&P was still the dominant force among the top ten super-market chains in the country. Besides A&P, this group included Safeway, Kroger, National Tea, Acme, Winn Dixie, Food Fair, First National, Grand Union, and Jewel Tea Company.

In 1962, these chains enjoyed a combined volume of $15.657 billion, of which A&P accounted for $5.311 billion, or 33 percent. A&P operated 4,475, or 36 percent of the total 12,445 super-markets represented by the top ten chains. A&P's average per store weekly volume, however, was already $4,000 lower than the average of the group. This reflected the competitors' much more accelerated rate of growth over the past ten years. Not only were the competitors opening proportionately more new stores than

A&P, but their new stores were usually larger, better equipped and better located than the competing A&P. As store volume stagnated, Tea Company margins were raised to maintain profit levels which played right into competitors' hands, and slowly compounded the problems.

The most pointed comparison of 1962 indicates that A&P, with 33 percent of the volume and 36 percent of the total number of stores, expended only 18 percent of the capital investments in stores made by the top ten chains. More noticeable was the fact that Safeway, the second largest chain with less than half of A&P's volume and numbers of stores, was already investing twice the amount of capital in store development as the A&P Tea Company.

At this time, the company consisted of seven operating divisions directing 38 operating units in the United States and Canada. The Canadian Unit had been opened in 1927 and reported to the New England division located in Boston. A&P stores served consumers from Calgary, Canada, to Key West, Florida, and from Lubec, Maine, to Bremerton, Washington. In addition to distribution warehouses serving each unit, the company operated some 67 manufacturing and processing plants producing A&P products for all stores. A&P also operated over 80 field buying offices in growing areas throughout the United States and coffee buying offices in Brazil and Colombia. The Great American Tea subsidiary still operated home delivery routes from 13 distribution points.

The Hartford family heirs, and outsider members of the board, who finally convinced Ralph Burger to retire, were more pleased with their accomplishment, perhaps, than they had a right to be. For while Burger left active employment with the company, he still continued to rule over the Hartford Foundation and controlled 34 percent of A&P's stock proxies. Also, that group which ousted Burger as chairman had no effective measure by which to choose his successor. They were willing to accept almost any change as an improvement, and, as things worked out, it was Ralph Burger more than anyone else who decided the line of succession.

Three months before his retirement, Burger approved the selection of three potential candidates for the top position in A&P and each was then elected executive vice-president. The trio included Steve Shea, vice-president, Director of Sales, and Board Member since 1953; Frank Bucher, President of the Central Western Division and Director since 1961; and, Mel Alldredge, President of the Central Division and Board Member since 1961.

Shea, an insider with no store experience, was considered the most likely successor by the trade based upon his demonstrated executive talents, toughness, and reputation as a man of his word. Bucher, starting in warehousing, eventually became vice-president of the Detroit unit before being named president of the central western division. He had achieved outstanding results through an ability to earn the respect of and motivate employees at every level. Alldredge started as a clerk in the stores, managed the sales and purchasing departments in Louisville, served as vice-president of Detroit following Bucher, and then was elected president of the central division headquartered in Pittsburgh. He was the Dale Carnegie type of self-made man, bright, well spoken, and by A&P standards a very young 51 years of age. He had been most persuasive in convincing his superiors of his abilities, but some considered his talents more political than retail oriented.

On April 11, 1963, in a surprise move, John D. Ehrgott, the treasurer, was elected Chairman, Alldredge was named President, and Bucher assumed the new position of Vice-Chairman.

Ehrgott had come to work for A&P 40 years earlier fresh out of New York University and had worked directly for George Hartford until 1957, when he was named treasurer after Mr. George's passing. He never went near the stores, was introverted, but was extremely well liked by those few in the company who knew him. He did not seek the chairmanship and accepted purely on an interim basis.

Ralph Burger retired from active A&P employment on May 1, 1963, but immediately signed a consulting contract guaranteeing him payment of $200,000 for the fiscal year 1963, "because his advice and consultation are expected to be of benefit to A&P." On June 18, 1963, Mr. Burger was elected to the board as a non-management director and president of the Hartford Foundation. At the insistence of the family heirs, four additional outside directors of their choosing were nominated and elected to the A&P

board at the June 18, 1963, shareholders' meeting. The board now comprised 10 outside directors, 13 management directors, and Mr. Burger, a total of 24 members.

John D. Ehrgott, newly elected chairman, took little or no active part in the day-to-day operation of the business. His role was to provide the steady experienced hand to whom Alldredge could come for advice, and to hold the loose but secure leash to make certain that Alldredge remembered this was a test run, and that his performance was subject to scrutiny from above. Under these conditions, young Mr. Alldredge found himself placed in charge of the store with the responsibility for reversing the downward sales trend lines of recent years.

Nineteen sixty-three turned out to be a very disappointing year. Sales for the 53-week period were $5.189 billion compared with $5.311 billion during the 52-week period of 1962. On an average weekly basis, sales for 1963 were down 4.1 percent and tonnage was down 6.2 percent. Profits dropped 4.5 percent to $57.5 million, or $2.37 per share. Dividends totalled $1.84 per share, 80 percent of earnings.

The annual message to shareholders included some interesting explanations and comments: "In the face of comparative sales declines from the previous year, we embarked on a program of holding the price line—and, in some cases, actually reducing prices—by not passing on to our customers all of the rising costs that beset the industry. This decision was motivated, in part, by great competitive pressures. The lower net earnings for the year were due in great measure, therefore, to the fact that we actually reduced our profit rate in order to maintain our competitive position and to build for future growth."

In this bowl of pablum, A&P for the first time introduced the "apologia" that competition, not management, was the source of the company's troubles. In the twelve years since Mr. John's passing, price had been sacrificed for profits. The company had little factual knowledge as to where it stood comparatively, pricewise, in the industry, yet embarked on a program of "holding the line."

The message went so far as to suggest that "not passing on all rising costs" constituted "actually reducing prices." Later, in the same annual report, the statement of income and expense reveals that gross margins for the year actually increased by 2.2 percent.

Much more significant was the message to stockholders concerning the company's plans for 1964.

"We plan to continue an aggressive development program during the coming year. This includes attention to the physical plants as well as concentration on improved services in the stores. Much attention will be given to the development of new products that show promise of becoming profitable additions to our already well-established lines of exclusive merchandise."

The same annual report disclosed that capital expenditures of $49 million were the lowest since 1958 and were financed almost completely by depreciation and amortization of $43 million. Worse, during a period when the tonnage sold in stores was in steady decline, more than half of capital investment was being diverted to manufacturing or distribution facilities whose design capabilities required massive tonnage increases to achieve projected efficiency standards. A 1.5 million square foot plant costing $25 million was under construction on a property of 104 acres in Horseheads, New York. A bakery plant, reputed to be one of the largest in the industry, was under construction in Flushing, New York. Final cost of this plant was $16 million. New distribution facilities were approved or under construction in Atlanta, Jacksonville, Charlotte, Detroit, and Salem, Ohio. New store openings were the lowest since 1958. The company closed 154 outmoded units and opened 198 new stores for a net increase of 44 new stores. The annual report concludes by stating: "A face lifting program enabled us to revitalize 495 stores last year and improve our competitive position locally at considerably less expense than would be entailed in new store construction."

This apparent overemphasis on manufacturing investment served to improve manufacturing profits, which were becoming the major, and most reliable, source of corporate earnings. However, failure to make comparably sufficient investment in the retailing arm conflicted with total long-term corporate interests because the inevitable erosion of retail strength would eventually idle those manufacturing facilities now being expanded.

Looking more deeply into what appear to have been misguided judgments, we come upon elements of an enigma which confronted Ralph Burger, and those of his successors who were both executives of A&P and trustees of the Hartford Foundation. Throughout their lives, John and George Hartford believed their personal long-term interests coincided with the long-term interests of A&P, and they consistently subordinated short-term profits and dividends to longer-term goals. However, in establishing the Foundation, the brothers Hartford unwittingly placed their successors in a classic Catch-22 situation, since the best interests of a foundation, and a corporation in which it holds stock, are sometimes in conflict.

A trustee, in the execution of fiduciary responsibility in the best interest of a foundation, must act to nourish and employ its assets so as to provide for continuance of projected charitable grants. A tax-exempt foundation must not expose its financial best interests to the vagaries of declining fortunes of any company, including that company which was the primary source of income to its owners who parented the foundation. The prime responsibility of a trustee so confronted is not the replacement or improvement of corporate management, but the disposal through sale of necessary quantities of that parent company stock to diversify the trust portfolio sufficiently to provide greater assurance of continued satisfactory income.

Similarly, the corporate director, in the execution of fiduciary duties in the best interest of all shareholders, must act to nourish and employ corporate assets to assure continuing satisfactory return on investment. At times these corporate interests are best served by the increased use of surplus for reinvestment rather than dividends. A director should not be unduly influenced by the needs of special interests, including those of the largest stockholder, a foundation, almost totally dependent upon that dividend for income.

In the execution of fiduciary duty neither a director nor a trustee can effectively wear two hats or serve two masters. The Hartfords, while acting on the noblest of intentions, apparently did not foresee the potential conflict that would surface in a foundation established to serve the dual purposes of a charitable trust and a means of perpetuating A&P.

In today's complex environment of overlapping business interests and growing numbers of quasi-professional directors sitting on multiple corporate boards, perhaps it is asking enough to have directors perform in the best interest of all shareholders without subjecting them to make judgments on potentially conflicting interests. In all probability, the well-intentioned efforts of some Hartford Foundation trustees to improve A&P's management, together with the empathetic instincts of some A&P directors to perpetuate Foundation control of large blocks of A&P stock, contributed to the deepening paralysis which immobilized A&P. To both frustrated insiders and analytical outsiders, the symptoms reflected a comatose management awaiting corporate rigor mortis.

Ironically, later in this story, we shall again witness an A&P board presuming to wear two hats. Along with responsibility to shareholders, A&P's board also assumed full authority and fiduciary responsibility to administer its non-union employees' pension plan—"solely in the best interest of plan members"—as required under ERISA (Employment Retirement Insurance Security Act). We shall see A&P's board vote to seize, for corporate purposes, the entire bulging surplus of this plan without sharing a single dime of that surplus with retirees whose modest pension benefits had been ravaged by the very inflationary factors generating surplus in the plan. Few retired plan members can see their best interest represented or enhanced by this board action.

Similar conflicts sweep our nation today. Many corporate boards, eyeing temporary pension surpluses resulting from high interest rates, have chosen to exploit the "termination" loophole in ERISA and wipe out long-standing pension trusts to enhance short-term corporate profit. In the fifteen-month period ending April 1984, the PBGC reported processing 8883 pension plan terminations which is graphic evidence of the rapid demise of the "defined benefit" pension system for non-union employees.

But now we must return to our story.

Seven

Playing It Safe—Means Losing the Game

Wise men have learned that even "experience" has a shelf life, and John often remarked, "You can't run a retail business from memory." Success requires a constant presence in the market place, checking the product line, assessing realistically comparative conditions in the competitors' stores, obtaining first-hand customer reactions to your stores' cleanliness, quality, product availability, service, and price. There is peril in placing reliance upon memories of past experiences, trade report publications, or gossip exchanged at manufacturers' golf outings.

Unfortunately, some of John's successors saw little need for continuing update of a business they thought they had mastered years ago. Isolated and insulated high in the marble halls of the Graybar Building's throne rooms, top management was the first to learn the bad news but often the last to know its cause. Lacking something better to do, the Foundation and the board engaged in games of management musical chairs when confronted by continued unpleasant results whose true cause they did not comprehend.

On June 16, 1964, immediately following the annual shareholders' meeting, the board elected Mel Alldredge Vice-Chairman. John Ehrgott remained as Chairman, and Byron Jay was elected President and Chief Operating officer replacing Alldredge.

This announcement provoked widespread speculation within the company about the position of vice-chairman. It appeared to have been created as a position "in waiting." The question now was, "Waiting to come, or waiting to go?" Alldredge, who had been the unquestioned number-two man, now seemed relegated to the number-three spot.

The other two considered "potential heirs" to the throne, Frank Bucher, Vice-Chairman, and Pat Shea, Executive Vice-President of Merchandising, obviously now by-passed, announced their resignations prior to that shareholders' meeting.

Byron Jay graduated from the University of Michigan during the depths of the Depression and came to A&P in preference to the only available alternative at that time—driving a cab. He had not intended A&P as career employment but soon found himself caught up in the flow of opportunities the Tea Company offered and forgot all else. Most of his A&P career was devoted to merchandising and sales management until being appointed vice-president of the Louisville division.

Tall, slender, unpretentious, soft spoken, but warm and friendly, Jay had created a Lincolnesque image among employees, most of whom he knew by name, in the stores of Louisville and Lexington on down to Hazzard in rugged Harlan County, Kentucky. He had respect and affection for his people and they responded to his leadership.

He believed that the greatest asset A&P possessed was the reputation for quality and low price of its many private label brand products. He often preached that there was nothing A&P could do in merchandising Heinz ketchup or Hellman's mayonnaise that the merchant down the street couldn't do equally well, or better. No matter how low A&P priced national brands, a competitor could meet or beat that price. When A&P sold a national product—it made a sale; but when it sold the A&P brand—it made a sale, and probably a regular customer.

Jay was not overtly anti-national brands as much as he was pro-company products. He was proud of their quality standards and fought hard to preserve or improve those standards. For years A&P brand canned fruits and vegetables carried the U.S. government grade "A" label when a grade "A" could not be found on any similar national brand item in the store. Stories have been told of how Jay, when introducing a new A&P product at a sales meeting, would taste a sample and offer it to all present, even if the item were a new flavor of A&P pet food. Jay, and many who worked in the more impoverished areas, knew A&P sold many more cans of pet food than could possibly have been consumed by pets. In those days, and in most product categories, the A&P brand products far outsold the comparable national brand products throughout the A&P chain.

Jay brought a totally new and different personality to the presidency of A&P. Alldredge was more outgoing and seemed to enjoy public speaking and meeting with the press. The most discussed and remembered event of his brief presidency had been his guest speaker appearance at the Grocery Manufacturers annual get-together at the Waldorf-Astoria Hotel. Alldredge seemed to revel at the opportunity to be the first A&P executive to ever address such a large, distinguished body of food industry leaders. The enthusiastic standing ovation following his speech signalled the long-awaited debut of "Grandma" into the social whirl of the food industry—it was her "Cotillion Ball," but it was short-lived.

Byron Jay would not have been comfortable addressing this group and would have found some reasonable excuse for turning down the invitation. Jay was much more at home with gatherings of A&P people where he could expound his philosophy of attaining retail success through well-stocked, pleasant stores featuring exclusive A&P brand products at prices substantially below national brands.

In 1964, the company, while continuing to drag its feet on new store development programs, began exploring alternative means of expanding sales and profits. Under the name "Golden Key," the Newark unit experimented with two fast-food hamburger operations in Paramus and Teaneck, New Jersey. The Paramus store enjoyed outstanding sales and profit growth until the state took possession of the property for construction of a highway overpass on Route 17. The Teaneck store had achieved moderate growth and marginal profitability. A&P's corporate participation in these ventures had been kept secret to provide maximum flexibility and avoid attracting the attention of the unions. After losing the Paramus store, the company decided to drop the idea in the belief that any rapid expansion of fast-food operations under the A&P

banner would bring inevitable unionization, which would erode the profitability which depends upon staffing flexibility with minimum-wage, part-time employees. Besides, management already had more problems than it could handle in the supermarket business.

In the early 1960's, A&P began attributing its misfortunes to competition, and particularly to the advantages the smaller regional competitors and independent operators had over major chains such as A&P. Divisional executives throughout the company had been complaining about the labor-cost, purchasing, and administrative expense advantages which the smaller operators enjoyed. Now, headquarters wanted to prove or disprove this allegation once and for all.

In spring of 1965, the Newark unit had a proposal in headquarters recommending leasing a defunct independent supermarket in Warrenville, New Jersey, and re-opening it as a new A&P. In a rare abridgement of protocol, this writer, then the Newark unit vice-president, was summoned to the hallowed halls of the Graybar Building for an unusual meeting with top management.

Headquarters asked whether the Newark vice-president could operate this store independently without any identification or logistical support of A&P.

The ground rules were clear cut. A&P's name would not appear anywhere in the operation, and A&P's sponsorship of the store would remain top secret. The store could not employ a trained A&P manager, department heads, or any A&P store union personnel. No merchandise would be supplied from A&P warehouses or manufacturing plants. No A&P brand label products would be stocked for sale. Other than the Newark vice-president, no other supervisory personnel could visit the store or communicate with this store's employees. If any union secured sufficient signatures of store employees, the store manager would negotiate and sign the resultant union contract. The services of A&P's purchasing, sales, advertising, and warehousing personnel must not be employed in any fashion. The store manager, under the supervision of the Newark vice-president, would establish retail prices, prepare the store's advertising programs, and operate as if he owned the store independently, dealing with suppliers and others as believed necessary and appropriate to insure a successful operation.

The Newark vice-president agreed that the experiment could be carried out successfully, and when asked how soon the store could open, replied "three to four weeks." After brief discussion, headquarters gave a verbal approval to proceed. No written approval was ever granted, perhaps because no corporate officer wanted to sign such a document. The "Golden Key" corporate name was affixed to the store, but the Bardy Farms name remained to identify the shopping center.

This proved to be a remarkable experience for A&P. The opening took place on schedule under the direction of a very capable manager hired from a regional competitor. On opening day, the Golden Key supermarket had approximately $20,000 on deposit representing advance income on deals from many of the very same suppliers A&P dealt with, but who would never negotiate similarly with A&P, knowing that A&P would not dare accept such unwritten allowances. For the most part, these were cash payments for exclusive delivery rights, or for rights to fixed amounts of display space on shelves or in refrigerated cases where the paying vendor's product was displayed exclusively.

Where practicable, direct deliveries were arranged from the major suppliers such as Proctor & Gamble and General Foods in accordance with their minimum drop standards for mixed-product truck deliveries. In many instances, this store was able to obtain greater amounts of "cents off" and other deal merchandise than were available to the A&P stores in its marketing area, and at a lower cost than would result from delivery through the A&P warehouse. A wholesale supplier was used for delivery of the balance of the national brand line, and certain of that supplier's private label products were stocked as price items. The manager purchased meats and produce direct from the local markets.

The store manager hired key department head personnel from competing (non-A&P) stores. The balance of the store crew was hired at favorable wage rates without serious problems, and an amicable union contract was signed.

At that time, Warrenville was a thinly populated rural area. This store had been built ahead of its time by a family who had farmed the area and wanted this supermarket to carry on their name as a matter of family pride. *The Plainfield Courier*, which carried approximately twenty full pages of supermarket ads each Sunday and Wednesday, now added a small weekly, home-made type advertisement proclaiming the merits of Bardy Farms. The store was projected at $50,000 weekly and met this average, which was considered moderate but by no means "big volume" at the time. On this volume, the store generated a pre-tax net of between 5 percent and 6 percent, which by A&P standards was astounding.

Headquarters had placed so much importance on itself, on sales and purchasing support, on volumes of reports and layers of paperwork, on supervision, on personnel programs and costly advertising programs; and now this single store comes along and suggests that all of that is just so much unnecessary overhead. After a little more than one year, headquarters, on the pleadings of the legal department and convinced there was little more to learn from the experiment, ordered Golden Key closed and later reopened as a standard A&P. The store carried the A&P logo thereafter, although the shopping center remained Bardy Farms. Interestingly, although in this growing area the A&P eventually did a much higher volume than the experimental Bardy Farms, profits were never again nearly so good.

Meanwhile, other strange things were happening at A&P. The Mafia was allegedly attempting to influence private label detergent purchase.

In 1963, the brothers Gerardo and Eugene Catena were reported to be among the most important Mafia family members in the United States. Included among Eugene Catena's many interests was a brokerage firm he operated in Newark, New Jersey, under the name Best Sales Inc.

One of Catena's clients was the North American Chemical Company, a New Jersey firm controlled by Nathan Sobol, President, and Louis d'Almeida, executive vice-president, who together had built a reasonably successful business selling private label detergent products to regional supermarket chains in the New York metropolitan area but had few accounts in other areas of the country.

Testimony from hearings by the United States Senate in October 1971 on "The Effects of Organized Criminal Activity on Interstate and Foreign Commerce" deals with North American Chemical's attempts to secure A&P's private label detergent business.

The Senate record discloses that since 1961 North American had pursued this account through normal channels, which included soliciting assistance from friendly outside management members of A&P's board of directors. John Schiff, senior partner of Kuhn, Loeb & Co., of Wall Street, was also a director of A&P and uncle of Louis d'Almeida. John T. Cahill, head of Cahill, Gordon, Reindel, A&P's outside law firm, was elected to A&P's board of directors in 1963. Senate hearings exhibits included the following correspondence between Louis d'Almeida and John T. Cahill:

September 5, 1962: "Dear Mr. Cahill: Having just returned from my California trip I hasten to write you regarding our brief phone conversation in which you asked me to send you a memo on my product for A&P.

"In view of the fact that I have been in contact with various people at A&P, it would seem to me more propitious to meet with you, even if only for a few minutes, in lieu of the memo. You would be able to give me the kind of invaluable advice which can only be obtained through a personal visit. Any time, any day, any place.

"Hoping you can spare a few momemts in what I know must be a hectic schedule. Sincerely, Louis d'Almeida"

September 11, 1962: "Dear John: I want to thank you so much for meeting with my partner and myself yesterday. If we ultimately get the A&P account it will certainly be due in part to such seemingly insignificant person-to-person meetings.

"I am confident that at the right time and in the right place you will put in a good word for us.

"Looking forward to seeing you again soon. Sincerely, Louis d'Almeida"

April 9, 1963: "Dear Louis: Thank you for your kind letter on my being named director of A&P. I am delighted to be associated with the company and with your uncle John Schiff. Sincerely, John T. Cahill"

Such formidable acquaintanceships as Cahill and Schiff resulted in friendly meetings with all the right A&P executives, but since A&P had an in-house detergent manufacturing facility with ample capacity, no justification existed for purchasing this product outside.

The Senate hearing discloses that North American Chemical signed an agreement with Best Sales Inc., effective December 1,

1963, designating them as agent and agreeing to pay Best Sales a commission of 3 percent on all of its sales whether or not effected by this agent but reserving North American's right to make such sales as it desires without the aid or assistance of Catena or his firm, Best Sales Inc.

In the fall of 1964, Irving Kaplan, president of the Almalgamated Meat Cutters, Local 464, asked Bob McKee, A&P's labor relations executive, for an introductory meeting with Bill Kane, the recently appointed president of the eastern division of A&P. In the course of the meeting, Kaplan inquired of Kane as to the procedure for introducing a new product into A&P. Kane introduced Kaplan to the divisional purchasing director who would explain the procedures involved.

Several weeks later Kaplan called McKee asking to arrange a meeting with A&P's purchasing department for an acquaintance who was selling soap powder. A short time later, Nathan Sobol visited A&P and made his proposal to A&P's detergent buyer and left sample product for the company's inspection. Several months went by and nothing happened.

In mid-December, 1964, John Mossner, manager of A&P's store on Soundview Avenue, Bronx, New York, advised his supervisor that he was concerned by the repeated insistence of two threatening males that he stock a particular detergent product. He stated that he repeatedly advised these two individuals to contact the buying agent in the Bronx office of A&P.

Upon closing his store on the evening of December 18, 1964, Mossner observed two males attempting to throw what looked like a plastic container onto the rear roof. He ran after them and they ran away. At three A.M. the following morning the neighboring A&P store on Bruckner Boulevard exploded into flames and burned to the ground.

On December 27, 1964, John Mossner tentatively identified a photo in the FBI file as looking like one of the two men he saw in the back of his store on December 18, 1964. The picture he identified was one Joseph A. Maselli, a convicted arsonist.

New York City detective Bateman described for the Senate hearing the events of February 5, 1965, as Mr. Mossner drove to his home in Elmont, Long Island. "This is a residential area, a rather quiet area, which I had visited. I also went over the records of the homicide with the homicide squad, Nassau County, and it appeared that Mr. Mossner drove his car into the driveway, and departed from the auto, turned around facing the garage door. Somebody fired a shot, the first one striking him in the abdomen; the next shot went into the overhead garage door.

"His wife was inside watching television. She heard the car come into the driveway. She thought she heard two firecrackers. She went outside. She did not see anything. A witness in the area said she heard what sounded like firecrackers. One person said she walked to her window. She thought she heard a car starting up. She looked out the window and saw a dark car turning the corner, approximately 200 feet from where Mr. Mossner lived.

"It appears from the investigation we did that Mr. Mossner, when he was shot the first time, charged the person shooting, causing the second shot to go into the overhead garage door. The person firing ran down the driveway, Mr. Mossner after him; the car pulled away from the driveway. Mr. Mossner must have gotten tangled in the fleeing car. As the car turned the corner, at the intersection, Mr. Mossner fell off. At the time his body was found, it was thought he was the victim of a hit-and-run.

"He was taken to the hospital, cleaned off, and they found that he had in addition to one bullet in his stomach, that he had two bullet holes right between his eyes, exactly one half inch apart."

In April, 1965, during the course of an arbitration hearing, Kaplan complained to McKee about the inaction of A&P's part in concluding the detergent contract. After inquiring of headquarters' purchasing department, McKee was told that Sobol's detergent samples did not meet A&P's lab specifications and would not be purchased. McKee so advised Kaplan.

In the wake of the above events and several additional mysterious store fires, A&P sought the assistance of the district attorney and the FBI, and decided that under no circumstances would they take on Sobol's products.

Robert Kennedy as Attorney General of the United States had led a vigorous drive against Jimmy Hoffa, labor racketeering, and their possible connection with organized crime and the Mafia. To aid this campaign, the Justice Department permitted the FBI to establish an elaborate network of bugging devices in the environs of all sorts of suspect individuals including Catena. Based upon investigation of the unusual events occurring at A&P and information obtained by "bugging," Justice Department officials decided they had sufficient evidence of conspiracy and extortion to present to a grand jury. Catena pleaded the privilege of Fifth Amendment rights in response to every question posed before the grand jury concerning A&P or detergents. While he was not indicted, he got the clear message that the FBI was serious. As it happened, the Justice Department was not prepared to go to trial based upon bugged evidence, because such evidence had been refused admittance by federal courts, and disclosure of the "bugs" would destroy their future use as information-gathering sources. Following the grand jury presentation, the Justice Department asked A&P to keep them informed of any future suspicious activities and indicated that A&P would now enjoy at least a temporary period of tranquility.

In May of 1965, prior to the start of major labor contract negotiations, Kaplan again asked McKee to arrange an appointment for Sobol to visit A&P headquarters to "clear the decks" on the detergent business before starting labor negotiations. Shortly thereafter Sobol visited A&P headquarters and was told his detergent would not be purchased by A&P for a number of reasons, including his "association with unsavory characters." Word came back promptly through McKee that Sobol was insulted and would probably sue, and the company had made a mistake and had better retract its statements to Sobol. A&P passed back the word that the "association with unsavory characters" was information supplied by the FBI and no retraction would be forthcoming.

On July 30, 1965, Sobol, by telegram, withdrew his bids and offers to sell detergents to A&P and requested prompt return of samples submitted. When asked by the Senate Committee on whose advice he sent that telegram, Sobol responded that it was on the advice of John T. Cahill, director and outside counsel for A&P. When asked if Cahill, director and attorney for A&P, was also his (Sobol's) attorney, he replied: "Mr. Cahill is a personal friend of John L. Loeb and if I remember correctly, that when we saw Mr. Cahill, I think it was his advice to just withdraw and I think he told Mr. d'Almeida to let things go by four or five months or so, I just don't remember."

Sobol also admitted his anger about the linkage with organized crime inferred by A&P, and admitted he had threatened to sue over that. The Senate Committee then expressed curiosity about the role of Cahill, who was an attorney for A&P and yet was giving Sobol advice also. When asked, "Is the Mr. Cahill who had written letters to the A&P on behalf of your company before you ever signed the agreement with Best Sales, the same Mr. Cahill who is a director of and counsel for A&P?" Sobol replied: "I don't know Mr. Cahill, the director and adviser to A&P," adding that in this instance Cahill's interest was a personal one and he was not paid by North American.

In December, 1965, North American Chemical entered into a new contract with Best Sales releasing both parties from the 1963 agreement designating Best Sales as selling agent for North American. Under the 1965 agreement Best Sales was to receive payments of $25,875 per annum for 13 years and was given options to purchase 3,000 shares of North American stock at ten dollars a share over a period of six years.

On July 8, 1966, Louis d'Almeida, who must be given "A" for effort, wrote the following note to John Cahill: "I have just spent the weekend at my mother's with John and Peter Loeb. In the course of our conversations, John asked me what we were doing with A&P?

"It would be most helpful to me if I could see you for a few minutes at your convenience this week, as I need some advice which only you can give me. Sincerely, Louis d'Almeida."

North American's selling efforts continued for some time, but A&P had long since decided to continue to manufacture its own detergent products.

Getting back to A&P's historical record, 1964 turned out to be another poor year. To display a unity of purpose toward improvement, A&P's management announced its "Target 1965" as follows:

"Management's primary objective is the further development of an in-store personality and appearance that will be more pleasing, more attractive and more magnetic than anything ever offered to the American consumer. A company-wide concentration on every service and facility, from courtesy to cleanliness, is the order of the day. Our organization is looking for TOTAL customer satisfaction."

Now, this kind of sexy-sounding sop might please or at least pacify shareholders, but divisional managers were not taken in. They felt from the demands placed upon them that the primary objective of A&P management in 1965 continued to be the satisfaction of the dividend demands of Ralph Burger and the Hartford Foundation. Burger still actively controlled the Foundation, and the Foundation voted 40 percent of A&P's stock. New managements were selected and could only remain in office at the pleasure of their old bosses who now sat as trustees of the Foundation. Any management that embarked upon a bold or decisive course of action which might imperil current earnings might well not remain in office long enough to implement such action, particularly if success was not immediately assured. Indeed, A&P had become impaled upon a cross of its own making.

During the final seven years of Mr. John's life, A&P's sales had increased by 142 percent to $3.4 billion, and during the subsequent seven years, almost on sheer momentum, sales increased an additional 50 percent to $5.1 billion. However, during the following nine years through 1967, in a period of consistent food price inflation, while Safeway, Kroger, and the supermarket industry increased sales by over 50 percent, the A&P Tea Company sales increased only a miserly 7 percent to $5.5 billion. Confronted with such grim statistics, remembering that A&P had not previously expanded into 38 states and Canada based upon policies of timidity, and understanding full well that the Hartfords wanted them to preserve a vital organization and not a mummified cadaver, A&P's management continued on its course of administering only aspirin tablets while maintaining the death watch over the company.

Each successive year profit budgets were increased in the more successful divisions to compensate for the profit erosion in those divisions suffering the greatest sales declines. The gallant spirit of "He's not heavy, he's my brother" lasts only until the carrier gets overloaded. When the "higher retail price" virus infests the healthy partner, the sales infection spreads and the problem is compounded.

Repeatedly, executive expense committees were urged to effect new and better cost controls and reduce expenses. These committees, comprised of accountants, statisticians, merchandisers, warehouse and transportation specialists, invariably came up with new ways to effect savings in their sectors of operations, but most often these proposed savings were achieved by reduced levels of service to stores, resulting in further deterioration of store conditions and reduced sales and profits.

In a grotesque effort to improve results, management's sales planners forced many additional superfluous company-manufactured items into an already excessive product line, aggravating an existing serious problem of inadequate shelf display space. As a consequence, important fast-selling items were left with totally inadequate shelf space, which resulted in lost sales due to frequent out-of-stocks. Meanwhile, the new "junk items" gathered dust and accumulated price changes until their shelf expiration dates finally arrived.

This shelf stocking problem was compounded further when management accelerated expansion of the drug and non-food lines. Merchandising specialists designed attractive shelf schematics for these non-food displays to fit the size and sales volumes of different stores. These were sent to stores with orders for immediate implementation. Unfortunately, no one sent along a shelf-stretcher or any guidance as to where the store manager might display the truly important food items being displaced by these new non-food lines. As might be expected, management left such minor details to local discretion.

It would add nothing to detail any more of the lachrymose litany of misguided efforts by well-intentioned people trying to help get the aging "Grandma" back on her feet. Suffice it to say that the more aspirin and ice bags were applied, the sicker "old Grandma" became.

Lest the reader think the entire company had gone mad, it must be noted that some operating units did continue to generate increased sales and profits. These more successful areas were less intimidated by the upper level efficiency experts and were given more latitude to implement only those programs they believed beneficial to their operations.

So it was that The Great Atlantic & Pacific Tea Company continued to come apart at the seams. The decline was not random but spread insidiously location by location until the plague had infected sufficient stores to threaten seriously the growth and profitability of an entire unit, which typically comprised some 100/150 stores in a radius of approximately one hundred miles from the unit supply center and office.

An A&P unit chief executive was given the title Vice-President. His was by far the most important and challenging operating assignment in the company particularly in times of corporate management vacillation. In those troubled times, every interim position between corporate CEO and unit vice-president was a staff assignment attempting to implement indecision.

The successful vice-president required leadership talents, a broad background in retailing, and a continuing interest in consumer trends and competitive activities in the marketplace. Most importantly, the job called for the judgment and capacity to select, train, and motivate the most talented people available to carry out the unit plan. Finally, the vice-president needed the conviction and persuasion to sell effective ideas to upper management to help formulate their conclusions, rather than simply enforce without question all manner of dubious instructions from every higher source.

Unfortunately, during the 1960's, A&P had more units than it had unit heads qualified to operate successfully in that time-frame environment. Most vice-presidents of that era had completed thirty or more years of service with A&P and had been highly successful at every prior job level. Most also had been highly successful vice-presidents in earlier years when the strength of the A&P price program dominated the marketplace and competition was comparatively much weaker. However, since their talents and training were adapted primarily to executing, without deviation, a rigid corporate policy program, most lacked entrepreneurship qualities.

With the abandonment of the corporate low price policy after the death of Mr. John, many unit heads became ineffective because of an inability to formulate alternative retail strategies and execute programs that would revitalize their operating units. Without the accustomed firm corporate policy strategic support, many were simply unable to cope in the fast track environment of the technically advanced, highly competitive 1960's.

It has often been said that A&P was brought down by a massive infestation of middle management problems due to a "promotion from within" policy and management's relative lack of formal education. The simple fact is, A&P had only one major management problem—the company was unable to replace Mr. John, his dedication to a single corporate policy, and his unquestioned authority. His successors, however valiant, did not possess his ownership control, and either did not comprehend or could not persuade shareholders that A&P's enormous empire was supported by a single keystone policy premise—quality foods at lowest prices; and without this or an alternative keystone policy support the entire corporate enterprise would lack stability and soon crumble.

The abandonment of central corporate policy was the major contributor to A&P's failure in the 1960's. A clear, unswerving corporate policy was then, and is today, a paramount requirement of every successful major retail operation, and evidence of such policy direction is readily apparent to customers of Sears, K-Mart, McDonald's, Kroger, and many other successful chain operations.

Most successful conglomerates, or holding companies, have grown by acquisition of divergent businesses, each of which grew separately with its own policy control and entrepreneurship, and each tends to maintain its own policy identity. However, it is most difficult, if not impossible, to reverse the process and find within a single entity, no matter how large, the management talents and entrepreneurship to diverge a single entity successfully into a multiplicity of differing retail forms, each with its own discernably different, yet effective, policy control formulas. Certainly, all of A&P's efforts to date in this direction have failed.

Surely, the failure of the board and management to correctly diagnose the causes contributed to the erosion of A&P. If by some wondrous turn of events, or by some stroke of nepotistic good fortune, a powerful leader with clear purpose and persuasion had come forth this might be an entirely different story being told today. But that did not happen, and realistically it could not have happened because the board and management of the 1960's would not have recognized such talent. They seemed isolated and often defensive, apparently convinced that the booming prosperity was about to go bust. Some believed, with Kennedy in the White House and liberalism rampant, that this was a time to build a moat around the castle, guard liquidity, watch and wait. Many, lower on the corporate ladder, regarded such stewardship as indolent irresponsibility masquerading as conservative management.

But, some argued, why should there be real concern? Is not A&P still the world's largest retailer by far, with annual sales over $5 billion, profits over $50 million, over $100 million cash on the balance sheet, and no corporate debt? One smart-ass even remarked, "If things don't get better, we just could go broke in a couple of hundred years."

However, a realistic closer examination revealed that many very serious problems already existed. For the most part, A&P's operations were all east of the Mississippi River except for token representation on the West Coast and a successful retail unit in Canada. By 1967, all profits and most of the company's meager sales growth were generated in Canada, New York, New Jersey, Pennsylvania, along the Atlantic seaboard to Florida and west across to New Orleans. The remaining retail units, in the aggregate, produced little or no profit and were suffering sales declines. Results were particularly poor in former A&P strongholds such as Chicago, Milwaukee, Detroit, St. Louis, Buffalo, Cleveland, Dallas, Houston, and Boston.

Even more ominous, the lack of development and management direction combined with growing pressures for increased profits were negatively affecting sales growth in those profitable areas.

The Tea Company's share of market was declining in almost every trading area as competitors continued opening new, bigger, and better stores at an accelerated pace. Profitability was being sustained in many healthier A&P units through the unhealthy practice of raising margins to non-competitive levels.

As sales declined, the company continued proportionate layoffs of employees. By now most of the younger people representing A&P's best hope for the future had been discharged. Fortunately, most were immediately hired by the competition. Other outstanding young employees, sensing the trend, departed for greener pastures on their own volition. Ironically, A&P was running training programs for competition unwittingly and without remuneration.

Successful retailers require volume increases in excess of inflation rates. A&P per-store volume was now failing to keep pace with inflation or competitive sales growth. This aggravated problems further because markets with declining volumes become increasingly difficult to operate profitably. As sales volume deteriorates, balanced work schedules are harder to maintain and perishable products can expire on display. In an attempt to offset such product losses, stores tend to order and display lesser quantities and varieties. Before long, the store is losing money, not only because of uncompetitive pricing and poor service levels but also because prospective customers cannot find adequate displays of fresh products.

Now it was New Year's Eve, Sunday, December 31, 1967, and all A&P operations were shut down for the long holiday weekend. Warehouses and offices had been closed since Friday night. Suddenly, just before dawn, without warning or eyewitnesses present, the huge, relatively new grocery distribution facility in Elmsford, New York, exploded into flames and disintegrated into smoldering ruins over the next twenty-four hours. Fire experts could produce no reasonable explanation for the intensity of the inferno that literally levelled this modern one-story complex. A&P lost millions in inventory and fixture costs, most of which were self-insured.

Three months later, on April 6, 1968, a watchman reported a roaring fire on an upper floor of A&P's grocery warehouse on Decatur Street, in Brooklyn, New York. Moments after the fire department arrived, they discovered a second, separate blaze on another floor of the building. The fire department verdict was arson, and product and equipment losses again totalled in the millions.

Worse, A&P's distribution capabilities in its prime New York and Westchester marketing areas were now badly crippled, and despite valiant efforts to supply over 300 stores from out-of-state A&P facilities, sales and profits were severely depressed for months until the company was able to open a temporary facility in Secaucus, New Jersey, to service these stores.

Who was behind these devastating attacks on A&P, and why? No explanation was ever forthcoming and no suspect ever charged for the Elmsford disaster, which authorities were convinced was the result of arson.

The district attorney's investigation did bring forth a suspect in the Decatur Street fire. This young man's actions were suspect at the time of this fire and police files indicated his involvement in drug traffic. Police also alleged that his mother lived with a long-time employee of the Elmsford warehouse whose duties included contracting for A&P with rubbish removal contractors in the New York area.

Law enforcement officials had long been suspicious of West-chester County rubbish removal contractors' connections with the Catena family of the Mafia, and these law enforcement officials had reason to believe this long-time A&P Elmsford employee was actually a "soldier" in that Mafia family. However, sufficient hard evidence was never found to warrant an indictment.

The district attorney, after presentation of evidence to the grand jury, was successful in obtaining an indictment of the suspect in the Brooklyn warehouse fire, and stated publicly that he consid-ered this suspect merely a pawn of the Mafia in their continuing attacks upon A&P. However, much to the chagrin of the district attorney, the court later found the evidence inconclusive and dismissed the charges. It now appears almost certain we shall never know for sure whether all these violent and costly incidents were indeed the work of the Mafia—or, perhaps the work of other independent hit men attacking A&P on behalf of unknown cli-ents—or, possibly just sheer coincidences.

Byron Jay, a widely respected individual who understood store operations thoroughly, who possessed sound merchandising in-stincts, who had earlier achieved remarkable success in the Louisville, Kentucky, unit, had now completed three years as chief executive officer of A&P. After a noticeable improvement in 1966, sales and profits declined to very disappointing levels in 1967, and this downward trend continued into 1968. The A&P board, at a June meeting, expressed grave concern and alarm over these results and obviously wanted a change in leadership. Sensing their mood, Jay decided, perhaps with relief, to accommodate their wishes. He calmly and quietly announced his resignation as of that moment, bid the group "Good day," and walked out of the meeting and out of A&P. He had not succeeded in turning the company around, but given different circumstances, without the domineer-ing pressures of the Foundation and the family heirs, and given sufficient time, he might have accomplished a great deal more. He never lost the respect of his fellows as a merchant, teacher and man.

The board immediately elevated its chairman, Melvin All-dredge, to the position of chief executive officer, and elected William J. Kane to the office of president. Alldredge had been hovering around the top spot since 1963 when he was elected president. He became chairman in 1964 when Ehrgott retired and Jay was named president and chief executive officer. A board member since 1961, Alldredge was fully exposed to the problems confronting A&P, and was eager to take the helm and effect change. At age 57, he was the youngest chief executive of A&P since the 1929 crash when Mr. John was already 57 years of age.

Many hoped that perhaps now, at last, The Tea Company would be turned around.

Eight

How Big Is an Elephant Supposed to Get?

Things started with a flourish from an unexpected source. Nathan Cummings, the retiring chairman of the board of Consolidated Foods, assembled a group which included Henry Ford II, several Rockefellers, and an heir to Britain's Rothschild family, Colonel Henry Crown, and submitted an offer to the Hartford Foundation to purchase all of its A&P stock at $34 per share, or $284.3 million. With the Foundation's 34 percent of A&P, and purchase of shares from Hartford heirs who had expressed interest, Cummings's group would gain control of the company. At the time of the offer, A&P stock had been trading in the $26 per share range. Formal reply came from the Hartford Foundation one month later, stating, "It was not in the Foundation's best interest to accept the offer." Cummings later said the offer "was rejected in a matter of hours," inferring that Burger and the trustees had been hostile from the start. Asked later by a reporter whether he considered A&P a desirable acquisition, Cummings responded, "Why else would I be interested."

While the takeover did not come to pass, it created considerable interest and excitement in the financial community with respect to A&P as a potential target for takeover. Wall Street had followed the continuing progress of the Safeway chain since its takeover in the late 1950's by a Merrill family interest, headed by son-in-law,

119

financial-whiz Robert Magowan. Safeway, which had also appeared stalled at the time, had expanded rapidly in the prime growing areas of the western United States. Safeway's sales during the ten-year period ending 1968 increased some 64 percent as against a 9 percent increase for A&P in the period. On an annual volume of only 67 percent of A&P's $5.436 billion, Safeway earned $55 million in 1968, an after-tax return of 1.5 percent on sales. During that period A&P earned $45.2 million, or .8 percent on sales. The financial community saw in this comparison the potential for A&P to double profitability if it could match the steady Safeway performance of 1.5 percent after-tax profit on sales.

Despite the disappointing performance of 1968, Alldredge's 1969 message to A&P's shareholders was optimistic. It read in part as follows:

"The beginning of change is the story of A&P in 1968. It started with nine of the eleven officers assuming new positions during the year. This new management team set to work at once examining the change that is occuring in the wants, needs, education, buying power and life styles of A&P's millions of customers.

"A major development to date is the decentralization of the company into 33 autonomous retail divisions, effective February 24, 1969. Each division is headed by a vice president-general manager and is supported by an executive committee and supervisory staff. This administrative structure places authority, and all of the positive factors that go with authority, closer to the point of sale. A&P is becoming, with this arrangement, the equivalent of 33 individual companies operating in local areas, each enjoying an average of more than $150 million per year in sales. These 33 profit centers will draw upon the central administrative organization for certain common resources and services.

"A&P's course is clear: to assist in feeding America with wholesome and nutritious foods in a variety and quality second to none, at prices the individual can afford, and to do this efficiently.

"We are programming for modernization, for growth, for expansion into new and wider vistas....

"A&P is expanding, upgrading and updating its manufactured products...."

This was indeed an exciting agenda served up to an organization that had been waiting anxiously for new positive direction. The announced decentralization, eliminating the previously existing layer of administrative management between the units and head-quarters thrilled the 33 entities that now became "divisions" rather than "units."

In what some considered a master stroke, Alldredge has actually reduced administrative expenses and at the same time convinced the organization and the industry that great and positive change had taken place.

To add to the dynamism of change, the company arranged a series of formal meetings between each of the major national brand suppliers and the headquarters' merchandising executives. At these meetings, the long-awaited peace pipe was lit and passed between the astonished suppliers and the A&P executives present. The suppliers were told of A&P's new attitude of working together with suppliers for maximum mutual advantage. Suppliers were advised that their visits, advice, promotions, and products would be welcomed with open arms in the 33 newly formed and autonomous retail divisions.

The trade press was brought in and was encouraged to proclaim the "good news" throughout the land. *Chain Store Age* had a cover story and feature article in June, 1969, which said in part: "Most Wall Streeters and food industry execs agree that A&P's decentralization move, spearheaded by the affable, 57-year-old Alldredge, is the keystone in a major sales and profits rebuilding program."

Progressive Grocer published a 150-page hardcover book titled, *A&P, Past, Present and Future*. More than half this book was devoted to the new decentralization, the new relationship with suppliers, the new younger management team, demographics of the A&P customers' buying habits, and the company's plan for bigger and better new stores in the seventies.

On the surface it appeared that Alldredge had worked wonders: sales for 1969 totalled $5.75 billion, up almost 6 percent over last year, and profits surged 18 percent to $53.3 million. Enthusiasm ran high. What a closer examination revealed, however, was that 1969 was a 53-week year, and adjusted to an average weekly basis, sales had only increased 3.8 percent, and after adjustment for the 6 percent inflation in the period, actually tonnage sold was down over 2 percent. The profit increase from $45.2 million to $53.3 million was the result of a fixed-overhead-free 53rd week together with a substantial reduction in pension funding costs.

The annual message to shareholders again promised: "We plan to pursue an aggressive modernization program of larger new stores, enlargements and major remodeling."

The annual message glossed over the fact that during 1969, the number of new stores opened declined to a record low of 99, while more than 200 older supermarkets were closed. During the previous ten-year period of inadequate development, A&P had consistently opened over 200 new stores per year. The report dwells at length, however, on the capital investments in support facilities, describing a new delicatessen plant, an addition to a canned milk plant, an addition to the Terre Haute pet food plant and a new fluid milk plant in North Carolina. Also mentioned were new distribution facilities in Toronto, Atlanta, and New Orleans.

Here was a company, mired in a state of continued serious stagnation because of constantly declining retail sales due in great measure to failure to keep pace with competitor store modernization; a company whose top management could not deny knowledge of that failure to keep pace, but who nevertheless limited capital investment to little more than those funds made available by depreciation and amortization; a top management with a stone-age aversion to borrowing to finance growth, but an inbred conviction that 65 percent of profits must be distributed as dividends; and this same management spent half the $63 million capital budget on expanding support facilities serving an aging retail store network experiencing steady sales declines. In 1969, Safeway invested $131 million in new growth.

The annual message dated May 14, 1970, goes on to describe four new acquisitions the A&P had made during 1969. Three were manufacturing plants and the fourth was a wholesale health and beauty aid operation.

Clearly, the management of A&P was consciously, or under some strong hypnotic seizure, turning its back upon the failing retail business and building an enlarged manufacturing and distribution system to service that shrinking retail system. What was motivating this calamitous turn?

The hard fact is that decentralization did not work all that well in all areas. Many of the 33 units had suffered prolonged sales declines and were operating at a loss when decentralization became effective. Turning these units loose on their own devices, too often under the command of an unqualified "president," was like tossing a bird with a broken wing out of the nest. And that is precisely what happened. Turned loose without warning or sufficient preparation, the weaker units' position deteriorated rapidly.

Without question there was merit to loosening unconscionable controls which headquarters and the divisional offices had maintained over almost every aspect of store merchandising. This age-encrusted bureaucracy, desk-bound in New York or the divisional headquarters, visited stores mostly on ceremonial occasions. Many couldn't tell a prune from a pork chop, but most could report finding some fault with the operation even if it were their perception of the manager's poor attitude should he have not bowed profusely and eagerly made notes of their every pronouncement during the store visit. This unreasoned, unappealable authority had stifled initiative and, over time, dulled the merchandising talents of the local divisional sales personnel. But there is danger in unleashing a lion; danger to the lion as well as the trainer if there are no fences inside which the young lion can run free.

A national chain, be it corporate like Sears or franchised like McDonald's, must retain central core policy control or risk losing the identity which brings it success. Management's job is to provide maximum local autonomy over pricing, selection, promotional appeal to local ethnic or income differences, flexibility to match local competition of varying strength, etc., while never permitting alteration of the essential corporate policies, or the national image the corporation is trying to project. Policy is the heart without which a multi-limbed corporate being cannot sustain life.

It makes as much sense to permit 33 divisions to alter and set their own policy as it would for those divisions to permit each of their stores to create its own policies. In merchandising, as in all other human endeavors, freedom requires fences to distinguish it from anarchy.

Prudent judgment urges that even the best of new ideas be tested to make certain not only that the idea itself is sound, but also to be sure its application is functional and practical for present implementation in the intended environment. Surely, this decentralization should have been tested first in some stronger units in different locales, and then more carefully in selected weaker units.

Fairly soon, particularly in the weaker divisions, the local management discovered that its own merchandising schemes were not working as well as they had expected; either they did not get the planned sales response, or the sales response was terrific but they lost a fortune on the promotion. Then followed a rapid series of "let's dump that, and try this" sales plans. Soon the management confusion spread to the stores and before long even the faithful customers were involved as advertising formats changed, prices went up and down without reason, store hours expanded and contracted, product displays were moved within the store, etc. It was not uncommon to hear a question like: "Where did you guys hide the napkins now?" And the clerk to respond: "They're up on top of the frozen food case, lady." Customers tolerated some temporary confusion, but before long many took their business elsewhere.

Gradually, continuing sales declines resulted in profit shortfalls from budgeted levels; in time, an increasing number of divisions were losing money on an operating basis. Eventually the operating losses in the failing divisions offset profits reported by the remaining divisions, and the entire company was struggling to break even on store operations.

Historically, the Hartfords had a philosophy that the retail stores made the profits, and the manufacturing subsidiaries made enough to pay the taxes on the store profits. In other words, store operating net profit would approximately equal total after-tax net profit of the company.

In the 1960's, management's concern about the growing inability of divisions to meet budgeted profit projections encouraged their pumping up manufacturing profits as insurance against expected shortfalls in the divisions.

When an A&P manufacturing subsidiary was asked by management to increase profits, it could simply increase billing prices to stores, or arrange shipment of additional quantities of product to stores, or do both. At the end of each quarter a statistical distribution of manufacturing profits was made to stores on the basis of shipment volumes. This profit allocation quieted the complaints and eased the pain, particularly for those divisions which would have experienced net losses had it not been for manufacturing profit distributions. Headquarters sustained enthusiasm for company manufactured products by means of this statistical magic wand which gave both the manufacturing and the retail divisions full credit for earning the one manufacturing profit.

By the late 1960s, the manufacturing subsidiaries were producing, at least on paper, more profit than the total amount reported by the entire company. Management had become addictively dependent upon the manufacturing division as a source of profit, and as a consequence continued to allocate inordinate shares of an already inadequate capital development budget to the manufacturing arm of the company. Unable to reverse continued declines in retail divisions, some in A&P's top echelon foresaw an evolution after which A&P would emerge primarily as a manufacturer and wholesaler of A&P brand products.

The real beneficiaries of decentralization were those national brand suppliers who reported increases as high as 40 percent in shipments to A&P. Unfortunately for A&P, these national brand shipment increases did not translate into added business for the stores. Suppliers' salesmen became regular visitors in A&P divisions, performing two primary functions, the first of which was bringing the latest trade rumors and gossip. Next, came a few of the latest jokes making the rounds in the trade, a selection of product samples, an invitation to lunch, and maybe even a little sales pitch.

Meanwhile, on a parallel but much higher line, the national brand suppliers used their "first team" for cementing relationships with the Tea Company's "A" team in headquarters. Before long, the national brand suppliers sold the Tea Company's headquarter's group on the idea of national chain-wide promotions with this pitch: "It's a fantastic idea! With your skill and experience you can organize the format for all divisions, pick the appropriate week, arrange national TV spots and supply ad formats. We guarantee, our field people will get behind it a thousand percent, decorating stores, supplying sign material, helping with displays, etc." Pretty soon came the chain-wide A&P gala promotions of major national brand accounts. Divisions were overwhelmed with "hype" and countless tons of product were shipped to stores. All of it was sold—eventually.

Cleverly, the national brand people soon had headquarters scrapping its own idea of "decentralized marketing." Soon A&P's national sales department was issuing a model merchandising plan for each of the thirteen weeks in every quarterly period. This package, containing perhaps one hundred pages, included details of one or two national brand gala's, and suggested theme-music for all of the other weeks, with ad formats, holiday ideas, summer cook-outs, back-to-school programs, etc. Much of this was helpful and eagerly received by the divisions, but the "decentralization" idea was slowly fading into the sunset.

In 1969 management reached a decision Mr. John likely would have opposed because it further reduced potential for market expansion. A&P's strongest markets historically were in the larger cities from the east coast to the mid-west, whence the population exodus started after World War II. Failure to follow those consumers into the suburbs and the sun belt states drove the first nails in the coffin of A&P's growth.

Now, apparently through a myopic vision of the nation's economic future, A&P's board of directors nailed the lid down further by its 1969 decision to abandon all A&P operations in California. While it was true the Los Angeles division had been somewhat of a step-child since its establishment during the 1930's, the Tea Company had an organization, customer acceptance, and a solid 31 store core to build upon. Instead, "Grandma" abandoned what was then clearly recognized as the fastest-growing market in the nation. Admittedly this was a marginal foothold, but some of the 31 stores were very successful, others could have been, and a few were obviously obsolete. Surely, with A&P's resources, expansion of this market would have been relatively simple. The problem was management inertia and timidity, choosing to stay and throw good money after bad trying to survive in closer-to-home and more familiar but dying mill towns of the Northeast, rather than to get off their butts and go after the booming business in the growing West. Several years later, to permanently seal the lid on the Western coffin, A&P closed a more successful 40 store-operation in the Seattle, Washington, area. The board of directors, however, did not have the guts to change the corporate name to "The Great Atlantic & Mississippi Tea Company," which would more properly define its new territorial boundaries.

Nineteen sixty-nine also marked another passing. Ralph Burger, who had dominated the company and the Hartford Foundation since 1957, passed away. As he had chosen his successors in management, he also chose his successor to head the Hartford Foundation. Harry George, a career A&P employee and a good friend of Ralph Burger's, who had retired in 1962 as A&P's purchasing director and was then elected as trustee, now became head of the board of trustees of the Hartford Foundation. Like Burger, Harry George had little retail experience, and had little or no relationship with the field organization; however, in the Burger mold, he assumed that the Foundation's 34 percent vote of the A&P stock entitled it to dominate the company.

Nineteen sixty-nine was apparently a long and difficult year for Mel Alldredge. All dreams of conquest and of turning A&P around were fading, and in fact becoming nightmares. Something had to be done to stem the pervasive quickening pace of the sales decline, or the board would soon be back to the bullpen looking for a new leader. It was decided to re-activate an old bromide, a low-price discount operation under a new name, "A-Mart." By year's end A&P was operating some 150 A-Mart stores. All were conversions of larger than average size A&P supermarkets.

There was no clearly defined national format for "A-Mart" operation, other than conversion of existing stores of 18,000 square feet, or larger, to a discount price operation. Divisions took it from there, deciding price levels, marketing strategies, etc. As might have been expected, results were mixed. Most "A-Marts" enjoyed the usual initial sales spurt, but after the dust settled, relatively few had achieved substantial sales improvement and improved profitability. As also might have been expected, the more successful conversions were in the already successful divisions. The program was of little help to troubled divisions. As the "A-Mart" banner was starting to droop, a convenient excuse was found for dropping the whole idea. The K-Mart chain threatened a lawsuit against A&P, charging "A-Mart" was an infringement on their K-Mart name and identity. A&P quietly took down all of the costly "A-Mart" logo sign material, and while a rather feeble attempt was made to continue the basic operation under the name "A&P Discount" stores, the operation soon faded into oblivion.

As 1970 came to a close, optimism had again given way to pessimism, and the same old "graffiti" started appearing on the same old walls. Sales for the year were down again; converted to a tonnage basis, sales for 1970 were actually below 1952 volumes. More and more divisions were operating in the red, and the $50 million profit level was maintained only through squeezing excessive profits out of the remaining divisions and manufacturing facilities.

In February, 1971, just before the close of the fiscal year, Mel Alldredge announced his intention to take early retirement and resign as chairman of the board and chief executive officer of A&P. Obviously, he had failed to turn the old ship around, and did not foresee a turn occurring in the near future. He had served A&P to the best of his ability for 40 years, in a variety of positions from store clerk to chief executive officer and succeeded in all but his last assignment. He believed it was in the best interest of the company, his family and himself that the reins of leadership now be turned over to someone else. While A&P's failure to turn in a more positive direction had to be most disappointing, Alldredge evidenced no personal air of dejection or failure. He left his office with the same down-home charm, wit and confidence as the day he took command. There were no alibis offered. In headquarter's offices, few expressions of regret were heard, and the corporate flag flew at half-staff, but only until after lunch. *Sic transit gloria mundi.*

In retrospect, the Alldredge era could only be looked upon as three more years of decline in the sagging fortunes of A&P. Sales volume adjusted for inflation continued on a steady downward course, and profits were lower by 8.5 percent despite the reductions in funding costs of the employee pension plan. In this period, pension funding costs averaged $16.6 million less than annual funding costs incurred during the prior ten years. Even more ominous, the development program had bogged down, resulting in a continuing shrinkage of the company's available retail selling space while the industry was in a period of rapid expansion. And, looking ahead a few years, the company had at least another 1,000 stores whose sales and profit results would not justify lease renewal

Later stores (circa 1910) emphasized an abundance of canned goods, as these well-stocked windows in a New Brunswick, New Jersey, store show.

The inevitable anniversary sale—this one in 1913—in a typical store.

Caveat emptor! It certainly wasn't A&P's fault if you bought inferior merchandise from its competitors. Here is the front and back of a card gladly supplied by your local store.

1887.

BE CAREFUL what you Drink! Use only Pure Articles.

BEWARE of the VILE MIXTURES that are sold for TEAS and COFFEES. They are Dangerous and Detrimental to Health—Slow Poison. BUY DIRECT from FIRST HANDS and GET GOOD GOODS.

We don't advocate the buying of CHEAP GOODS, more especially in articles of food. The Medium or Best Grades are the CHEAPEST.

THE GREAT ATLANTIC AND PACIFIC TEA COMPANY.

THE LARGEST IMPORTERS AND RETAILERS IN THE WORLD.

PIONEERS in the Business, and ONLY IMPORTERS dealing DIRECT with Consumers.

HEAD-QUARTERS, 35 & 37 VESEY ST., (P. O. BOX 290.) NEW YORK.

SULTANA MILLS, 126 & 128 East 13th St., NEW YORK.

BRANCH HOUSES IN THE UNITED STATES.

Akron, Ohio,..........150 So. Howard St.	Greenpoint, N. Y.. 363 Manhattan Ave.	Springfield, Mass..............500 Main St.
Albany, N. Y..........114 So. Pearl St.	Grand Rapids, Mich ....108 Monroe St.	St. Louis, Mo........ 712 North Fifth St.
Allegheny, Pa.........178 Federal St.	Harrisburg, Pa.........221 Market St.	St. Louis, Mo.......1256 South Fifth St.
Atlanta, Ga...........75 Whitehall St.	Hartford, Conn.........427. Main St.	St. Louis, Mo........2208 Franklin Ave.
Baltimore, Md.... 27 W. Baltimore St.	Hoboken, N. J. ....58 Washington St.	St. Louis, Mo........611 Franklin Ave.
Baltimore, Md....41 North Eutaw St.	Hudson, N. Y.........283 Warren St.	St. Paul, Minn.......47 East Third St.
Baltimore, Md.... 281 North Gay St.	Indianapolis, Ind ....4 Bates' H Block.	Syracuse, N Y...78 South Salina St.
Baltimore, Md......142 South Broadway.	Indianapolis, Ind.164 E. Washington St.	Syracuse, N. Y........4 Granger Block.
Boston, Mass...........99 Court St.	Jamaica, N. Y.........48 Fulton St.	Trenton, N. J...........Greene St.
Boston, Mass.........694 Washington St.	Jeffersonville, Ind........90 Spring St.	Troy, N. Y............342 River St.
Boston, Mass.........1078 Tremont St.	Jersey City, N. J.......55 Newark Ave.	Utica, N. Y..........87 Genesee St.
Bridgeport, Conn.........290 Main St.	Kansas City, Mo.........927 Main St.	Washington, D. C......502 Seventh St.
Brockton, Mass..Winter's Bl'k, (Main St.)	Lancaster, Pa.........114 N. Queen St.	Waterbury, Conn.........19 E. Main St.
Brooklyn, N. Y.........215 Fulton St.	Louisville, Ky..S.E. cor 4th & Jefferson Sts.	Williamsburgh, N. Y.......163 Grand St.
Brooklyn, N. Y.........268 Columbia St.	Louisville, Ky.........1104 W. Market St.	Williamsburgh, N. Y.......329 Grand St.
Brooklyn, N. Y.........205 Court St.	Middletown, N. Y........6 E. Main St.	Williamsburgh, N. Y.......525 Grand St.
Brooklyn, N. Y.........794 Myrtle Ave.	Milwaukee, Wis....109 Wisconsin St.	Worcester, Mass.........528 Main St.
Brooklyn, N. Y.........598 Fifth Ave.	Milwaukee, Wis....313 Chestnut St.	Yonkers, N. Y..........32 Broadway.
Buffalo, N. Y..........405 Main St.	Newark, N. J.........738 Broad St.	**NEW YORK CITY.**
Buffalo, N. Y.... 188 East Seneca St.	Newark, N. J.........107 Market St.	196 & 198 East 13th St.......near 3d Ave.
Buffalo, N. Y.........193 Genesee St.	Newburgh, N. Y ....79 Water St.	316 Bleecker St........Cor. Grove St.
Buffalo, N. Y..........469 Elk St.	New Brunswick, N. J........11 Peace St.	97 Carmine St........Cor. Bleecker St.
Chicago, Ill..........91 North Clark St.	New Haven, Conn.........386 State St.	308 Spring St........Cor. Renwick St.
Chicago, Ill........945 West Madison St.	Norfolk, Va.........39 Market Square.	318 Bowery........Cor. Bleecker St.
Chicago, Ill.... 168 Twenty-second St.	Oswego, N. Y.........592 W. First St.	774 Third Ave........Cor. 48th St.
Chicago, Ill........421 Milwaukee Ave.	Paterson, N. J.........127 Main St.	1425 Third Ave........Cor. 81st St.
Chelsea, Mass ....393 Broadway.	Paterson, N. J.........60 Broadway.	2004 Third Ave........Cor. 110th St.
Cincinnati, Ohio.... 44 West Fifth St.	Philadelphia, Pa.........1120 Market St.	2319 Third Ave....Bet. 125th & 126th Sts.
Cincinnati, Ohio....941 Central Ave.	Philadelphia, Pa.... 334 N. Eighth St.	101 Eighth Ave........Cor. 15th St.
Cincinnati, Ohio.........79 Court St.	Philadelphia, Pa....700 N. Second St.	497 Eighth Ave........Cor. 35th St.
Cincinnati, Ohio.........647 Vine St.	Philadelphia, Pa.... 621 S. Second St.	661 Eighth Ave........Cor. 42d St.
Cincinnati, Ohio.........455 Main St.	Philadelphia, Pa....1819 Ridge Ave.	887 Eighth Ave........Cor. 53d St.
Cincinnati, Ohio.... 57 E. Pearl St.	Philadelphia, Pa....2242 Frankford Road.	944 Seventh Ave........Cor. 24th St.
Cleveland, Ohio.........172 Ontario St.	Philadelphia, Pa.........1529 South St.	383 Tenth Ave........Cor. 33d St.
Cleveland, Ohio.... .6 Prospect St.	Pittsburgh, Pa.........34 Fifth Ave.	135 Chatham St........near Pearl St.
Cleveland, Ohio.........580 Pearl St.	Port Chester, N. Y.........Main St.	341 Grand St........Cor. Ludlow St.
Cleveland, Ohio ....31 Broadway.	Poughkeepsie, N. Y.........291 Main St.	543 Grand St........Cor. Jackson St.
Cleveland, Ohio.........31 Woodland Ave.	Providence, R. I........263 Westminster St.	5 Avenue A........Cor. 1st St.
Cleveland, Ohio.........2587 Broadway.	Reading, Pa.........519 Penn St.	260 Avenue A........Cor. 16th St.
Danbury, Conn.........111 Main St.	Richmond, Va.........709 Broad St.	176 Avenue B........Cor. 11th St.
East Boston, Mass.........109 Meridan St.	Richmond, Va.........1513 E. Main St.	68 Avenue C........Cor. 5th St.
Elizabeth, N. J ....91 Broad St.	Rochester, N. Y.........126 State St.	217 First Ave........Cor. 13th St.
Elmira, N. Y.... 117 E. Water St.	Rochester, N. Y.........119 E. Main St.	392 First Ave........Cor. 23d St.
Erie, Pa...............620 State St.	South Boston, Mass.....305 W. Broadway.	441 Second Ave..........Cor. 25th St.

N. B.—BEWARE OF MUSHROOM CONCERNS.

A&P was always justifiably proud of its advertising, not only because it presented its products truthfully, but also because it was always up to date. In its sixty-fourth anniversary (1923) edition, the company magazine pointed out the dazzling modernity of its recent ads as compared to an 1887 ad.

BOSTON WAREHOUSE

CHICAGO WAREHOUSE

BRONX WAREHOUSE

PITTSBURG WAREHOUSE

PROVIDENCE WAREHOUSE

HEADQUAR

NEWARK WAREHOUSE

CINCINNATI WAREHOUSE

SCRANTON WAREHO

ATLANTA WAREHOUSE

BROOKLYN WAREHOUSE

The proud centerfold of the sixty-fourth anniversary (

RICHMOND WAREHOUSE

WASHINGTON WAREHOUSE

BALTIMORE WAREHOUSE

ALBANY WAREHOUSE

MILWAUKEE WAREHOUSE

JERSEY CITY

BUFFALO WAREHOUSE

DETROIT WAREHOUSE

SPRINGFIELD WAREHOUSE

PHILADELPHIA WAREHOUSE

CLEVELAND WAREHOUSE

edition of the company magazine, *The Tattle Tale*.

One of Our West Bend Factory Buildings

General View of Br

Corner of Evaporating Rooms West Bend Factory

General View of West Bend Wis Factory

Brockport Factory, Plant B.

Glir
F
Outsid

Cheese Plant at Cuba., N.Y.

Automatic Macaroni *and* Spaghetti packing Machine
Brooklyn Factory No.1

Milling Cocoa Beans Brooklyn Factory No.2

Packing Box Candy Brooklyn Factory No.2

Factories in the A&P Products division were featured in the six

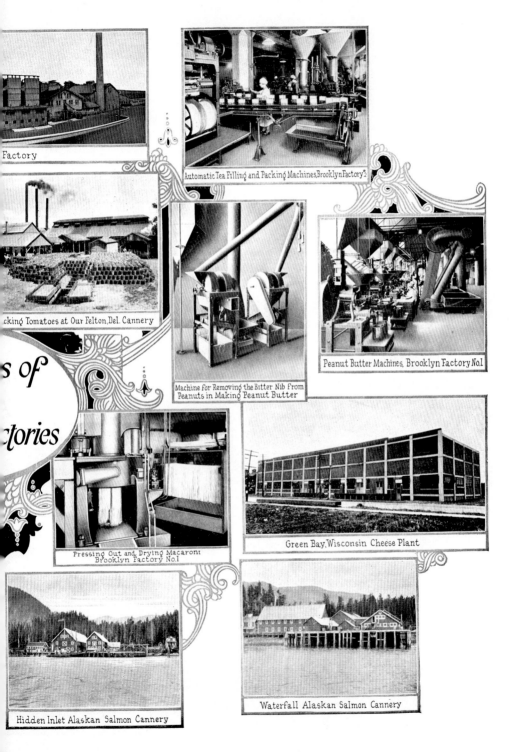

Factory

Automatic Tea Filling and Packing Machines, Brooklyn Factory

cking Tomatoes at Our Felton, Del. Cannery

Machine for Removing the Bitter Nib From Peanuts in Making Peanut Butter

Peanut Butter Machines, Brooklyn Factory No. 1

s of

tories

Pressing Out and Drying Macaroni Brooklyn Factory No. 1

Green Bay, Wisconsin Cheese Plant

Hidden Inlet Alaskan Salmon Cannery

Waterfall Alaskan Salmon Cannery

h anniversary (1925) edition of the company magazine.

An A&P combination store, *circa* 1929, which even has sides of beef hanging in the window. These stores were precursors of the modern supermarket, lacking only self-service and acres of parking space.

The familiar A&P suburban supermarket during the palmy days of the fifties and sixties.

as the current term expired, and no plans were on the drawing board to replace this endangered selling space.

Since A&P went public in December 1958, three different chief executive officers led A&P on three different courses. Burger's course was to squeeze as much profit as possible out of the favorable momentum he inherited when Mr. John died. This plan worked well for Burger, though not for the company, until after Mr. George died in 1957, and it was not until the early 1960's that it became obvious to all that A&P was on a collision course with calamity. When in 1962, the last vestige of momentum expired, Burger mistakenly believed that he could put wind back in the sails using the promotional hot air of a trading stamp program. It did not work at all.

Byron Jay chose more effective and aggressive promotion of A&P labelled products, and the loosening of some of the strictures and rigid controls of the Burger regime, as the course to regain vigorous sales growth momentum. Alldredge chose to loosen controls further in hopes that the decentralized divisions knew best how to make their own course corrections. All three saw a need to turn a ship in a new direction. None seemed to recognize that the aging ship needed more than a rudder correction... it had to be fully overhauled from the keel to the top of the mast. No one pressed the need to grow with the times, to follow America's families out of the big cities into the suburbs and the newly developing Sunbelt areas. None pressed the need to invest sufficiently in upgrading retail facilities to compete effectively for America's new generation of consumers.

While most of its customers were signing long-term home mortgages, A&P simply refused to make a reasonable financial investment in the nation's future. All of John's preachings on high volume and low prices seemed to be forgotten, and management seemed mesmerized only by George's warnings to hoard liquidity as the hedge against the depression that was sure to come again soon.

Nine

Desperation Breeds Discount Mania— WEEeeeeeoOOO!

In an effort to get things going in the right direction, the board of directors turned to William J. Kane, who was elected chairman and chief executive officer in February 1971. Kane went to work for A&P as a full-time clerk in the Philadelphia area in 1934. The son-in-law of a division vice-president, Kane was promoted to store manager within one year. Subsequently he was promoted to district supervisor, area superintendent and later served as vice-president of the Scranton, Baltimore and Philadelphia divisions before becoming president of the eastern region of A&P in 1963. Kane had been elected president of A&P in 1968 when Alldredge became the chairman and chief executive. During the three years of his presidency under Alldredge, Kane travelled extensively visiting retail stores and support facilities throughout A&P's vast network of operations in the United States and Canada. He came to the position of chief executive thoroughly acquainted with the problems facing A&P in each of its retail markets. With his depth of personal experience in retailing, and his recently gained comprehensive knowledge of A&P's problems, he was deemed to be

130

fully qualified and prepared to provide long-term solutions and lead the Tea Company back from its many difficulties experienced since Mr. John's passing.

Kane often asserted his conviction that the Great Atlantic & Pacific Tea Company was nothing more than the sum total of its parts, those 4,000 retail stores. Therefore, he said, A&P was not a big company but only some 4,000 little companies, in common. Carrying decentralization to its extreme, he argued that if the 4,000 stores did well, A&P enjoyed great prosperity. He seldom mentioned that if top management did well, those 4,000 stores might enjoy greater prosperity in sales and profits.

Kane was the "ultimate store manager" risen to chief executive. He wanted perfection and would agree to settle for nothing less than Ivory Soap's 99^{44}/$_{100}$ percent purity. More at home in the stores than in headquarters, he seemed to delight in inspecting every square inch of a store, including the storage areas, and then quizzing the store manager of his knowledge of retail prices. In addition to checking for freshness rotation of fruit and vegetable displays, he would usually open a number of meat packages to see what the customer would actually see if that package had been sold and opened on the customer's kitchen counter. Too often, the opened package embarrassed store personnel. Kane believed better store management would add $5,000 weekly volume to the average A&P store. Extrapolating that assumption over 4,000 stores provided the simple solution of A&P's problems. Sales would increase by 18 percent or $1 billion annually, and profits would rise at an even higher rate.

Kane's game plan for turning A&P in a positive direction was based essentially upon implementation of his expressed conviction that chainwide upgrading of store operations was necessary, and that such improvement, of itself, would generate the sales growth needed to insure satisfactory profitability. To support his argument, he pointed to numerous specific instances where a change of store manager brought about immediate improvement in store conditions which, within several months, resulted in substantial sales increases and improved profitability. To any skeptical vice-president who believed the stores in his division were well operated and above such criticism, Kane offered to lead an inspection tour to point out how much room for improvement existed in the best of that division's stores. There were no takers to Kane's invitation.

To a large degree, Kane was right about the extent of sub-standard store operating conditions existing at that time. And he was right in assessing the negative impact this had upon total company sales and profit results. After almost twenty years of steady decline and cutbacks, a debilitating paralysis had overtaken most stores in a growing number of divisions. The symptoms were visible and similar. These stores had few customers and did little business, but were open long hours, often seven days and six nights. These stores were obviously short of help, shelves were poorly stocked. What carriages were on hand were usually out in the parking lot. Only one of six checkstands was operating, with no bagger to help shorten the checkout wait. Advertised sale features were often missing from the shelves, dairy, produce and meat cases. Most times, and particularly at night, no employees were available to assist customers seeking a cut of meat not available on display, or to check back room stock for sales items missing from shelves, or even to scale and price produce items or grind A&P's bean coffees. Cleanliness and courtesy standards, freshness and quality control standards, shelf stocking and checkout standards, and store employee morale all deteriorated at the same grinding steady pace.

Stores, in desperate need of help and support, considered themselves as leper colonies of their divisional office as more and more of the wrong medicine was shipped in. Maintenance standards deteriorated as divisions cut back on store painting, purchase of new customer carriages, purchase of store use supplies, replacement of obsolete equipment and even burned out ceiling light fixtures.

The frequency of warehouse deliveries was reduced sharply, trucks were often a day late in arriving at the store, increasing numbers of important items, including advertised features, were missing from deliveries. Division's efforts to further reduce trucking expense by combining grocery, produce and fresh bakery items on a single truck delivery resulted in sickeningly high damage costs at stores.

Drowning stores, crying for help, were thrown another anchor. To improve profitability through better product-mix, new company brand products and additional non-food items were forced onto already inadequate shelving, adding to confusion. Soon the biggest complaints became: "I can't get what I want at A&P," "You don't have what you advertise," and "My family can't eat a rain check!" Desperate to maintain some level of profitability, the office computer, rather than local marketing conditions, determined store retail pricing, resulting in gross overpricing on many important commodities.

Things got so bad that many managers refused to put on the custom fitted "manager's jacket" which the company provided, because it would identify them and subject them to vocal complaints for which they had no sensible answer. Some managers, when asked why they weren't wearing the prescribed manager's coat, would reply: "It doesn't look right mopping the floor, putting out the rubbish, stocking shelves, or operating a checkstand wearing a manager's jacket." In many cases, area store supervisors had long since given up protesting to the divisional office about stores' need for better warehouse support, more competitive pricing, and merchandising authority to properly service neighborhood needs within the limits of available store space. The inevitable result was that many supervisors became sympathizers. Comments such as, "Yeah, Jim, I know you're right, but this is the way they want it done, so do the best you can," simply placed the stamp of approval upon despair.

The division vice-president, in too many cases, didn't know or didn't want to know, or face, the gory details. He often would limit his store visits to pre-arranged guided tours.

The vice-president and divisional dignitaries were invariably on hand at openings of new or newly remodelled stores where some degree of optimism could be found. Such openings were rare events, and just cause for excitement and new hope. All strictures were temporarily lifted, and the new store was carefully stocked, fully staffed, provided special service from the warehouses, and proclaimed to the surrounding world with an exciting "Grand Opening" program. However, company policy prohibited zone pricing, which would permit across-the-board pricing competitive with the new store's trading area. And, almost invariably, after the rituals of initiation, staffing was cut back, delivery schedules curtailed, advertising programs were modified.

Basic weaknesses in A&P's price structure were exploited by aggressive competitors seeking to recover their lost business. Before long, the store achieved the divisional norms of poor service and store conditions, and A&P had another new store failure. All sorts of glib excuses were forthcoming: "The local economy is way off." "We need a traffic light at the corner." "The rest of the shopping center hasn't opened yet." "The new highway has changed traffic patterns." "We need a deli and a fresh fish department." "The competitor enlarged his store just before our opening." Etc., etc. In actual fact, adding new stores into a sick environment only compounded A&P's problems, and constituted throwing good money after bad.

Most of these ailing divisions, ignorant or blind to the depth and the real causes of their problems, tended toward over simplification and pointed to their poor price structure, and competitors' below-cost selling, as the single ill to be remedied. They consistently proposed lowering prices across the board, which would admittedly result in losing more money for an indefinite, but longer, period of time. They insisted that only this course of action would eventually return the division to a position of growth and satisfactory profitability. Any objective, competent supermarket merchant, looking at this situation, would quickly realize that some weakness in the basic price structure was only one of a number of serious symptoms. The real disease was poor management at the top levels. Dramatically lower prices might force more business through the system, but a great deal more improvement was needed to effect constructive, lasting change.

Kane, more than any A&P President before or since, had seen first hand these deteriorating store conditions during countless visits to A&P stores, and their competitors, in every division of the company prior to his being elected chairman and chief executive officer.

Upon assuming command, he was convinced the fault was not primarily at A&P's headquarters' level, but in a great measure lay out in the field and was caused by poor store conditions. Mr. Kane accepted the office of chief executive with confidence. He had three years to study the entire company and assess the cause of the problems. He had taken full advantage of that opportunity. He believed he understood the problems and could correct them without undue delay.

He was determined to set the course and stay at the helm to prevent any deviation. Since he understood the organization so well, he insisted on approving personnel changes or salary increases above store manager levels, and each new lease, renewal, or capital expenditure for store or support facilities also required his approval. His rise through the ranks had been based upon success in dealing with store problems, and he was going to put that talent to work. He seemed less inclined to spend time wrestling with abstract future strategies and planning. It appeared that he saw A&P's problem as a retail store operating problem, and he was going to make managing that problem the function of the chief executive officer.

He monitored all important field activities, including labor contract negotiations, and he had the final say in negotiating strategy. Over time, A&P's negotiating posture had been seen as weak and transparent, based on avoiding strikes at any cost. This resulted in the Tea Company's being party to many of the toughest contracts in the industry. Based upon the shortsighted idea that almost any kind of new contract language was preferable to additional cents per hour wage increases, A&P contracts had introduced many innovative clauses into the business, among which were: no staggered starting times, guaranteed weekly overtime at the employee's option, double time and one-half pay for Sunday work, and guaranteed job security, with no lay-off before retirement, for full-time employees in certain areas.

In those areas where bargaining was not done on an industry-wide basis, A&P's contract penalties, combined with its high proportion of long seniority employees and lower-than-industry-average percentage of part-time employees, added up to too much weight in the saddle, and resulted in wage cost disadvantages of up to 1 percent on total sales, in an industry where that 1 percent equals the total profit expectancy.

In such circumstances, A&P struggled to overcome this labor cost handicap through attainment of proportionately higher productivity than the supermarket industry was reporting at the time.

Unfortunately, that "higher productivity," which looked so good on charts, was illusory, and in the real world could be more accurately described as a shortage of help. Since it penalized sales growth, it hurt rather than helped profitability.

Bill Kane was right in his conviction that many A&P stores were operating below acceptable standards of cleanliness, product availability, perishable presentation, customer service, and courtesy. He was right that huge sums were being wasted on elaborate promotions and deep cut pricing which added up to nothing more than futile attempts to con customers into loyalty to poorly run stores. And Kane was right that visible improvement in store operating conditions was the *sine qua non*, the quintessential prelude, to any further costly investment in lower pricing.

However, he was wrong to believe that these unsatisfactory conditions could be corrected instantly, without cost, or by the force of command. This was much more than a surface problem curable in the space of days or weeks. There was no magic, or long-term benefit, gained from the surface solution of bringing in an outside crew from other stores to transform each ugly duckling into a model "show store" overnight, because without making necessary improvements in that store's staffing and warehouse support services, reversion to the old unhappy operation happened within a very short time. And the continual threatening, firing and replacing of management personnel produced few positive operational results.

The basic problem reflected by unsatisfactory store conditions could not, in all fairness, be blamed upon store personnel. This responsibility rested with much higher levels of management, and the prevailing weakness at middle and upper levels of management was the sole responsibility of A&P's top management. Store personnel cannot be expected to operate at consistently higher performance levels than their supervisory and divisional executive staffs demonstrate. This was demanding of stores what management could not deliver in similar circumstance. It was unreasonable to ask stores to overcome the ineptness and deficiencies of upper management.

Unfortunately, no quick-fix solution was possible. A substantial investment in personnel training and upgrading, in reestablishment of adequate store supply service standards, in re-enunciating corporate sales policy priorities and in investing the necessary resources to insure full implementation of those corporate policy standards were all among the necessary prerequisites to honest-to-God improvement in store operations. And most division budgets had no provisions for such cost investments.

Many divisions faced a quandary. They were catching hell from headquarters both because of shortfalls in their sales and profit budget projections and also because of unsatisfactory store conditions reported in customer letters of complaint, or reported by visiting dignitaries from headquarters. Sales and profit results were compared weekly with budgeted projections agreed to by the unit vice-president. Achieving budgeted results was his responsibility and any serious shortfall threatened his job. Self-preservation being a most powerful human force, monies which should have been invested in longer-term improvements in store conditions and service levels were often diverted in efforts to pump up short-term sales and profits. Advertising media space was expanded beyond the value of the message. Feature sales item prices were often cut below the unit's capacity to meet demand. Still things kept getting worse. All these hastily designed strategies backfired because the stores did not live up to the promise of the ads, supplies of sale items quickly ran out, and disappointed customers felt victimized by bait ads and some never returned. Thus it went exactly opposite to headquarters' stated goals.

Meanwhile, Bill Kane was facing his own dilemma. Neither the board nor the Foundation fully understood how bad conditions in the field had become. They seemed convinced that A&P's deterioration was merely a surface problem which could be corrected readily by a competent chief executive officer. Now, results for the first quarter 1971 had been terrible, and the second quarter was worse. Despite all the sweet talk and assurances of the board, Kane knew the clock was already ticking on his reign. While he understood the scope of the operating problems facing A&P, he also knew that, with results continuing to worsen without any evidence of a turnaround in the near future, the wolves were becoming restless and could not be held at bay much longer. What was the proper course of action?

At that time this writer, then executive vice-president and board member, suggested something more positive than fixing blame and raising hell needed to be done. First, headquarters must own up to the scope of the real problem. Second, headquarters must design and, more importantly, implement a logical long-range plan to correct each of the serious administrative, supply, and store-level causes of customer dissatisfaction. Third, corporate assets must be employed productively in salvageable locations and new store development in viable marketing areas. Locations realistically appraised as beyond salvage must be abandoned.

Kane argued that immediate improvement was both necessary and possible. He disregarded long-term solutions in favor of his firm conviction that better operation would quickly add volume and profit to every store, while accelerated closing would increase corporate losses, reduce the sales base, and exacerbate the problem. He remained committed to achieving a speedy turnaround through divisional insistence on improved store conditions.

Early in 1971, the executive committee of the Philadelphia division was considering whether to recommend closing or renewal of the lease on a store whose option date was six months off. This store, once in a successful high volume market, had lost volume even more quickly than its neighborhood had deteriorated. It was now down to $15,000 per week. The lease had several five-year options remaining, but the landlord had agreed to change the first five-year option to five one-year options in order to encourage A&P to stay on. The Philadelphia division at that time had suffered sales losses to the discount-priced warehouse stores which the Penn Fruit Company had operated, before its demise. With little to lose, they decided to recommend a low-cost experiment with warehouse-type, low-price operation in this old market in Pennsauken, New Jersey. They asked headquarters for approval to exercise a one-year option on this basis.

At that moment in time, any reasonable idea to increase sales with a minimum investment would have received a full hearing. Approval was granted to go ahead with the experiment.

The Philadelphia division assigned their best talent to the task and during the last week of May 1971, the first A&P warehouse store opened. To avoid the embarrassment, the A&P name was removed from the premises and the words WAREHOUSE ECONOMY OUTLET appeared over the canopy on the front of the store, smaller parking lot signs used the abbreviation WEO as identification.

The week prior to the closing, the store had sales of some $15,000. During the first week of the WEO operation, sales reached almost $300,000, and exceeded that sum some weeks later.

The division had taken out the grocery shelving and thousands of slower moving items and set up displays of fast-selling grocery items on the floor in original cases, cut open so customers could select product. Produce variety was similarly reduced with fast-moving items also sold out of original shipping containers. The meat department offered a limited variety of fast-moving bulk items, smoked hams, beef roasts, whole chickens, pork loins, and packaged items such as bacon, canned hams, frozen turkey, whole or half bologna and liverwurst and similar bulk items. Everything sold was top quality. Customers had to do their own bagging or boxing of purchases.

The major attraction of course was price. To make certain the word got around about WEO's bargains, gross margins in those early weeks were cut to approximately 8 percent from a previous average of about 21 percent. Sales after the opening averaged slightly over $200,000 on the slow weeks, and up to and over $300,000 on the first of the month pay weeks. Sales volume reacted to the number of circular advertising distributions and the price impact of the feature items advertised.

At the end of a month, operating losses in the store were nominal and somewhat controllable by advertising cost expenditures and feature price reductions. The overhead absorbed by the new volume created a positive profit factor for the division.

The experiment created a great deal of excitement in the area and caught the full attention of the old "Aches & Pains" department, as some used to refer to headquarters. As word got around the company, other divisions were anxious to initiate similar experiments. Approval was granted for a number of such conversions in various divisions and each new WEO opening produced outstanding sales results. Bill Kane had a tiger by the tail, and may have come across the solution to A&P's problems without a huge capital investment in new larger stores.

As seemed inevitable, A&P incurred losses in both the third and fourth quarters of 1971. At year end, sales totalled $5.51 billion, down 3 percent, tonnage was down an additional 7 percent, profit totalled $14.6 million, down a rousing 71 percent. Despite these results, Kane recommended and the board approved dividend payments of $29.23 million, or 200 percent of earnings.

More distressing, the downward flow was picking up speed like a canoe approaching the falls. The commanded improvement in store operations either did not occur or did not produce desired results. Complete disintegration was inevitable, sooner than anyone thought possible, unless something was done quickly, and headquarters had run out of quick-fix ideas.

The WEO idea was recommended by Bob Jordan, vice-president of the Philadelphia division. Although profitability in the WEO concept was still uncertain after numerous experiments, each store had produced outstanding sales results.

Kane was convinced positive action was urgently needed now, and after re-appraisal of available options, and perhaps more through desperation than inspiration, he decided "WEO was the way to go." And, he promptly announced A&P was expanding its conversions to the WEO store concept.

Let us read the explanation in the chairman's own words in the annual report to shareholders covering the year 1971:

"During the past year, we went a step beyond discounting to experiment with "warehouse stores." The first of these was opened at Pennsauken, New Jersey.

"To further test this merchandising approach, a number of other Warehouse Economy Outlet stores were opened during the following months. These were located over widespread areas. The majority of these stores also have enjoyed excellent sales results and favorable consumer response. This careful experimentation led to a new merchandising thrust for the Company. Utilizing some of the proven merchandising approaches from these warehouse stores in conventional A&P stores, resulted in the creation of the A&P WEO store. WEO now stands for "Where Economy Originates." The WEO store is a hybrid, combining the best operating principles of each of the former stores with lower prices for the consumer.

"The first A&P WEO stores were opened in January of this year. Sales results have been most encouraging. Thus far, more than 1500 stores have been converted to A&P WEO operations."

Rather than being saddled with double advertising costs, and being in competition with itself, A&P made the decision to go WEO area by area, division by division. Obviously, the typical A&P supermarket did not have the size or the available business in the trading area to increase volume from the company average of $25,000 per week to several hundred thousand. The solution was to find the proper compromise between the existing low-volume supermarket in a city neighborhood, and the high-volume warehouse discount store which drew customers from an eight-to ten-mile radius. It was decided to strip junk merchandise from the shelves and reset available shelves to maximize sales of faster selling items. Next, prices would be reduced beneath the general price structure of the leading low-price competitor. Finally, the excitement of WEO media material would be broadcast heavily throughout the market, supported by in-store ad material, bumper stickers, etc.

At that time, the so-called "typical" A&P had an average weekly sales volume of about $25,000. Gross margins and expense rates were both close to 21 percent, and company profits were marginal or non-existent.

Based upon earlier conversions of selected stores to the WEO concept, gross margins needed to be reduced an average of 3 percent, or, in the case of this typical store, to 18.0 percent in order to project the lowest price structure in the typical trading area. In earlier tests, the WEO conversion with its lower prices, resetting of store shelves to assure adequate stocks of the most popular items, and the heavy WEO advertising resulted in sales gains averaging 50 percent over the base period. In other words, prior tests indicated that the average store volume would increase from $25,000 to at least $37,500 after conversion to WEO.

Earlier tests also showed that increased operating costs could be limited to 10 percent of the weekly dollar sales pick-up. Where volume increase was budgeted at $12,500, a weekly expense increase of $1,250 was expected and projected. Most of this increase went to hiring additional part-time help and added supply costs. The chart below illustrates projected results of the typical A&P store converted to the WEO operation:

| | Typical A&P | | WEO Market | |
	(dollars)	(rate)	(dollars)	(rate)
Weekly Sales	$25,000	—	$37,500	—
Gross Profit	5,250	.2100	6,750	.1800
Expense	5,250	.2100	6,500	.1733
Operating Profit	—0—		$ 250	.0067

This of course, was the classic illustration of Hartford's original theory of building business strength and making higher profits by selling more food to more people at lower prices. While it appears overly simplistic, it proved fundamentally sound in the pilot WEO experiments. The critical issue remained, that while the above figures were "typical" of the entire chain they were not necessarily typical of any individual stores. Store conditions varied greatly from excellent to putrid. Competitive price posture also varied greatly; in some areas a minus .0150 in gross margins was sufficient, in others, minus .0500 might be needed to achieve a "lowest" price structure. And, competitive reaction to WEO was another unknown which might vary greatly in different markets.

Prudent management recognizes that "test experiment successes" often result as much from the careful selection, preparation and supervision they receive as from the validity of the idea, and therefore they don't always reflect accurately the probability of success in mass application.

Despite the ranting and raving of competition about insane pricing that would lead to industry-wide genocide, there was a great deal of potential merit for A&P in the proper application of this idea. In almost every early test it produced exciting sales increases, enormous reductions in expense rates and the potential for improved profitability. In some instances increased profitability had been attained. For whatever inexplicable reason particular promotions succeed and others fail to catch the public's attention, WEO caught the public eye and ear. Media personalities, children on the streets, bill boards and bumper stickers were all yelling "WEEEEEeeeeeeeeeOOOO!" What was even more important, WEO created a tremendous flush of enthusiasm and energy in an organization which, in many areas, had been mentally down and discouraged with A&P in recent years.

The pluses and minuses, and the alternative options to stop A&P's losses of sales and profits, were discussed in detail. The WEO idea, properly applied, was sound in principle. Under any name, it was really only a modern update of the proven principle of Mr. John's 1913 Economy Store in Jersey City. There has never been a better merchandising idea than "sell more for less." WEO was potentially capable of improving A&P's sales and profits in existing stores and providing necessary time for sound and orderly new development.

The critical question for A&P was, how do we apply the WEO principle? Can we wait until we are sure all the fundamentals of store conditions are operative at standard? Such wait is certain to produce additional sales declines and substantial increases in the losses presently being incurred. Will the foundation and other shareholders tolerate further losses without positive signs of sales progress?

Or should we move ahead boldly and stop the hemorrhaging now? There is no reason for delay. Most of the store problems are the result of lost volume and will correct themselves with new-found volume.

The decision to turn A&P back toward the policy of "more good food for less money," upon which the company was founded, was eminently sound.

The decision to convert the entire chain to WEO on a crash program was a chaotic blunder.

All A&P stores did not meet WEO's requirements. Half of the 4,000 stores had less than 8,000 square feet of selling area. Many were in small country towns, or city neighborhoods where the potential for a 50 percent sales increase simply did not exist. The rest of these small stores were pitted against competition almost twice their size. All other things being equal, no small store stocking primarily fast-selling food items can profitably sell such foodstuffs cheaper than a larger competitor who can reap compensating higher profits from an additional extensive line of products, which the smaller store doesn't even stock—unless of course, the competitor, for whatever reason, permits it to happen.

There was no question that a sensibly modified, low-price, WEO concept properly implemented and supported did, and would continue to, work very successfully in up to 1,500 competitively sized and equipped A&P stores, particularly in those areas where the Tea Company enjoyed strong market share. But to arbitrarily reduce prices in stores already losing money, where there was little or no potential for attracting compensating new sales volume, or to order hundreds of poorly operated small stores into battle in price wars against larger competition with much higher shares of local markets seemed to challenge reasonable odds and reduce chances for success of the WEO program.

There is not the slightest doubt that Kane wanted to do what was best for the A&P Tea Company. There is little doubt that he struggled with this decision. There will always be the question as to what tipped the scales. One morning he came into the Graybar and said his mind was made up, A&P was going WEO all the way. His staff accepted the decision, and promised and delivered full support to the best of their ability.

All concerned were aware that the changeover would require enormous start-up costs which would translate into a substantial corporate loss during the first year. Discontinued slow-moving merchandise had to be reduced to move out of warehouse and store stocks. Additional carriages, interior and exterior WEO signs, necessary painting and repairs would add to costs. Stores would be closed briefly to reset and re-price merchandise. The program would be supported by heavy promotion in all media. And, of course, the major unknown, the cost of reducing regular merchandise stocks and maintaining those retail prices at totally competitive low price levels, while not precisely calculable, had to be underwritten by the company.

The company was in a loss position and sales were continuing to decline when, in January 1972, Kane told the board of directors that, based upon success to date, he planned to convert the entire company to the WEO formula as quickly as possible. The board concurred. Let us read how Mr. Kane summarized events in the annual report to shareholders for that year 1972:

"One of the most significant developments in the 113-year life of the Great Atlantic & Pacific Tea Company was the winning back of customers in huge numbers last year through the A&P WEO program.

"The success of this effort is demonstrated by the favorable impact of the WEO concept on A&P sales, on a quarterly basis as well as for the full year.

Quater ended	Sales gain vs 1971	Percent increase
May 1972	$122,966,000	9.0%
August 1972	214,413,000	15.6
November 1972	239,284,000	17.5
February 1973	283,705,000	20.3
Full year 1972	$860,368,000	15.6%

"A&P's WEO concept is now a proven part of our merchandising policy and will be of continuing importance in A&P's future.

"Against the background of all these positive developments, there is the fact of the $51,277,000 loss last year, in contrast to net income of $14,619,000 in 1971. However, the trend in our profit and loss picture is encouraging.

Quarter ended	Loss
May 1972	$20,540,000
August 1972	21,108,000
November 1972	8,371,000
February 1973	1,258,000
Full year 1972	$51,277,000

"In judging A&P's performance last year, it is important to consider what our future might have been if we had not taken decisive action. A&P operated at a loss during the second half of fiscal 1971, and there was every reason to expect the declining trend to continue unless we took bold steps to turn our entire system around in the shortest possible time."

Kane's decision to convert the entire chain to the WEO operation had been vindicated, or so it seemed. In any event, the board of directors, the foundation and shareholders were pleased that the seemingly endless sales decline had at last been reversed.

It is difficult to analyze results accurately in a year of conversion. Gross margin reductions appeared to be reasonably on the target established for the WEO program. The expense rate was reduced only slightly, but the admittedly high one-time cost connected with the conversion to WEO clouds this issue. We would have to wait until 1973 to determine the real effectiveness of the WEO program.

During 1973, A&P recorded sales of $6.7 billion, up an additional 6 percent over the record high 1972 sales performance. Also in 1973, A&P reported a rather modest net profit of $12.2 million. However, following the previous year's loss of $51.3 million, this modest profit came as welcome news to shareholders.

But let us analyze these 1973 results more closely. During that year food inflation soared to a record 16 percent so that even with the 6 percent dollar sales increase, A&P real unit sales, on a tonnage basis, actually dropped over 9 percent, all the way back to the dismal levels of 1971. The expense rate declined further in 1973 but not sufficiently to attain profitability without an upward adjustment of gross margins. The following compares A&P store results with the composite earnings of all chains in the Super Market Institute for the 1973 year. The comparison shows the stark reality of A&P's position.

	A&P	S.M.I.
Percent of Sales Increase 1973	6%	14%
Average Weekly Sales per Store	$33,974.00	$58,000.00
Average Weekly Sales per Sq. Foot	$ 3.51	$ 4.71
Gross Margin Reported	21.08%	20.90%
Store Labor Costs	9.00%	8.30%
Sales per Employee Hour	$ 51.63	$ 42.63
Sales per Customer Transaction	$6.67	$ 7.47
Net Profit Rate on Sales	0.25%	1.30%

Sales growth continued far behind the 14 percent growth rate of the industry. Most revealing is A&P's higher store labor cost, which trickles down to become the major part of the difference in the net profit rates between the industry and A&P.

The only A&P statistic which shows to advantage is employee productivity, where A&P's $51.63 sales-per-employee-hour results reflect a 23 percent higher productivity level than the industry composite. In fact, however, this statistic also provides some measure of A&P's poorer service and "lack of help" that customers complain about. As shown above, A&P suffers a labor cost penalty versus the industry of .7 percent on sales despite the apparent advantage in hourly productivity. This .7 percent penalty, of course, varied widely by divisions of A&P, and its impact also varied from little or none, to severe penalties exceeding 1.0 percent on sales. The severer the penalty, the more divisions try to offset it by forcing productivity improvements, sometimes to excess, which results in further loss of sales volume.

While many factors influence a labor cost comparison, the principal villain is below-average store volume, and the problem will persist until A&P can match the industry average per store volume.

The more deeply one digs and the more one understands the problems confronting A&P, the clearer it becomes that there is no quick-fix patent medicine prescription that will get the company well overnight. While A&P had always dominated the industry in total sales volume, that position of dominance did not prevail universally. The fact is that, by 1973, A&P had become a very badly fragmented selling machine. It dominated less than a handful of its more than thirty divisional markets, and held third or fourth position in market share in most trading areas. Share of market and high per store sales volume are the two most important levers influencing control of advertising costs and most fixed expenses in the supermarket business, and A&P was in serious trouble on both counts, in too many of its markets.

As 1973 came to a close, A&P's store count had shrunk to 3,614. Of that number, more than half were less than 10,000 square feet in size, and more than half that total number were generating sales volume of under $30,000 per week. Thus, more than half of A&P supermarkets simply could not compete effectively in the $60,000 per week sales environment of the 1970's supermarkets because both their physical size and volume levels were each only 50 percent of industry norms.

Also at year's end, another sad bell tolled for A&P. Safeway had finally surpassed the Tea Company in total annual volume. This fall from preeminence after 114 years really did not impact on the balance sheet, but it hurt real bad in the gut of many old-timers.

The WEO price program had to be compromised shortly after its introduction company wide. Competitively, it turned out to be a meek little lamb dressed in wolf's clothing. This was particularly true in the weaker divisions, where it neither frightened competition nor generated sufficient increased volume to provide the help needed. Simply put, in most areas reducing retail prices to competitive levels, or slightly below, did not offer sufficient inducement for customers to put up with problems of product unavailability, poor service, and the smaller, less attractive store conditions which customers did not encounter in competitors' stores. And, on the other hand, slashing retail prices to levels sufficiently low to induce customers to shop at the A&P despite the poorer service and other inadequacies produced gross margins far too low to generate net profits within the volume limits the store was capable of handling.

In an increasing number of smaller stores, A&P faced the stark reality that, even with competitive pricing, it could not compete effectively with the larger, more attractive competitors who also offered a broader product selection and better service.

The one obvious solution of abandoning such locations was considered abhorrent, as the moral equivalent to surrender. Further, any closing added to losses, at least near term, and eliminated all potential for sales and profit improvements.

The second solution often suggested and easily adaptable was repeatedly brushed aside as though it, too, was some form of surrender or weakness. Many of A&P's smaller stores that could not compete profitably at competitive supermarket price levels had no need to try and match all price competition. Many were, in reality, local neighborhood convenience stores which served a good purpose and were sorely missed when they finally closed. They easily could have offered local consumers many supermarket special features, and compensated with slightly higher pricing on non-sale items sufficient to maintain a measure of profitability. They could also benefit by featuring lower retail prices on items with special local or ethnic appeal. The right combination of convenience, quality, service and price is often more appealing to consumers than the trip, out of the neighborhood, to that big supermarket in order to save a few more pennies.

Whenever the viability of smaller stores came up, Kane would point to some little store out there somewhere, continuing to defy gravity by doing business and making money, and suggest that that would be the rule rather than the exception if all stores were run properly.

Ten

Lots of Internal Combustion—Still No Forward Movement

A&P had closed an average of slightly over 200 stores in recent years, but in 1973 this number was increased to over 400 stores closed, due to replacement by new stores, landlords requesting unreasonable rent increases, or because of profit losses or obsolescence. A&P has seen many many instances where such stores continued as independent food stores, often with the ex-A&P manager as owner. In many cases volumes increased under the new ownership, and the stores became profitable because they catered more attentively to the special needs of the community and offered improved service at prices higher than A&P's but acceptable to the consumer.

While the WEO banners floundered somewhat, a new problem confronted Mr. Kane. On February 1, 1973, *The Wall Street Journal* reported that Gulf & Western was making a tender offer to purchase 15 percent of A&P's stock at $20 per share, and reserving rights to purchase additional shares tendered. The report also disclosed that G&W, during the past year, had acquired 5 percent of A&P's stock under a street name at a cost of $18,405,269. A&P stock was trading at $17 on the date of the tender offer. The tender offer, if accepted, would bring G&W's investment in A&P to $90 million and represent its largest holding. The news caught Bill Kane completely by surprise. He immediately called in the attorneys to take whatever action was necessary to thwart Charles Bluhdorn's attempt to take over the management of A&P. Kane also approved release of the following statement:

"William J. Kane, Chairman of the Board of the Great Atlantic & Pacific Tea Company, stated today that the Company will vigorously oppose the Gulf & Western Industries tender offer to purchase a block of A&P shares. Quite apart from the fact that the tender offer of $20 a share is inadequate and not in the best interests of our shareholders, it would seem that the acquisition of a large block of A&P shares by Gulf & Western raises most serious questions under the anti-trust laws. We have instructed our attorneys to take whatever action is proper to protect the Company and are preparing to communicate with our shareholders promptly."

Gulf & Western promptly filed suit in Federal Court, claiming the above press release was false and misleading and violative of S.E.C. rules, first, because no basis was given to support the claim that the tender offer price of $20 per share was "inadequate," second, because there was no basis to the claim that the tender offer raised serious questions under anti-trust laws. The Gulf & Western action asked the court for an injunction against A&P for these alleged violations.

A&P responded, denying G&W's charges and seeking its own injunction to prevent the tender offer acquisition of more A&P shares, claiming it would violate anti-trust laws and the Security Exchange Act. On February 13, 1973, the district judge ruled for A&P on the grounds that preventing the tender offer would bring little or no hardship to G&W, whereas permitting the tender offer to go forward "could" have serious detrimental effects on A&P and "might" involve A&P in violations of anti-trust laws.

Gulf & Western filed an immediate appeal, and extended the date of the tender offer to March 16, 1973. The Second Circuit sustained the opinion of the district court in favor of A&P and the tender offer was blocked. Excerpts from the briefs of this action reveal the positions of the two combatants, Bluhdorn and Kane, and belong in any history of A&P.

First, the A&P position represented by Bill Kane. Here are excerpts from an affidavit signed by Kane:

"The threat manifested by the tender offer and its sudden disclosure of Gulf's clandestinely acquired holdings of A&P stock has caused grave concern and had an extremely unsettling effect upon all levels of A&P's management. In large measure this impact is due to the well known propensity of Gulf and Bluhdorn to take over or dominate the management of companies in which Gulf acquires even a minority interest, and to the well known opposition of the Bohack-Bluhdorn-Gulf group to the WEO program of A&P. Since the success of the WEO program requires the wholehearted and unqualified effort of A&P's management (uninhibited by any fear of future reprisals by this takeover team which represents conflicting competitive interest), the mere threat posed by the tender offer, coupled with its disclosure of Gulf's prior secret acquisitions, have already had an injurious effect on the management commitment needed for the WEO program which I believe is essential to the continued competition vitality of A&P."

He later testified about the impact of the tender offer on A&P management: "It's had an effect on the morale of our organization, particularly through our middle management. They don't know what is going to happen. They have never been through this before and it has a disturbing, unsettling effect."

While this tender offer caused some grave concern in top management, many at lower levels would have welcomed any change at the top. Kane was further disturbed to learn from depositions and testimony things he believed he should have been told first hand.

Mr. Ed Toner, a representative of Mrs. Carpenter, owner of 7.9 percent of A&P's stock, allegedly initiated a private meeting and met with Bluhdorn to discuss the tender offer on behalf of Mrs. Carpenter. At that time, Toner was also a member of A&P's board of directors, but apparently did not advise Kane beforehand of his meeting with Bluhdorn, nor of Mrs. Carpenter's intention with regard to the tender offer. In his deposition Bluhdorn stated, "Mr. Toner said he was here as personal lawyer, representative of Mrs. Carpenter, a very large shareholder of A&P stock, and she wanted to know who the new entity was that was going to become a stockholder in A&P."

Testimony also revealed that in November 1972 Bluhdorn had met with a partner of Kuhn Loeb & Company for the purpose of arranging a personal meeting with the senior partner of that firm, Mr. John Schiff, who was also a member of the board of directors of A&P at that time. Bluhdorn, at that November 1972 meeting with Kuhn & Loeb partner, John S. Guest, revealed that he was considering the purchase of all or part of the Hartford Foundation's A&P stock and understood that John Schiff was a trustee of the foundation and he thought it would be appropriate to introduce the subject through him. Mr. Guest later testified that after his discussion of the matter with Mr. Schiff, he (Mr. Guest) called and advised Bluhdorn that a meeting with Mr. Schiff was not feasible, but another partner would be glad to meet with Mr. Bluhdorn to discuss the topic. Mr. Kane was upset that John Schiff had not informed him of these events earlier.

Finally, testimony revealed that the trustees of the foundation were meeting to consider whether to tender some or all of their shares. Kane was most unhappy to hear that the foundation was even considering the tender offer and reminded Harry George, then head of the foundation, that, as he (Mr. George) should remember, one reason the Hartfords established the foundation was to protect the organization from such outside control. The relationship between Harry George and Bill Kane had been cool, and the foundation never did reveal what they would have done had the court not blocked the tender offer. To that time, Kane was the only chief executive officer of A&P who did not serve simultaneously as a trustee of the foundation.

Perhaps the unhappiest blow of all came from "family members" who were unhappy with the current state of affairs. One part of the family, the McIntosh Foundation, not only tendered a portion of its shares, but had an attorney file an amicus curiae brief supporting G&W's position against A&P.

Excerpts from Charles Bluhdorn's deposition are not only interesting but also prophetic. Talking about A&P he said:

"I think that everybody on Wall Street is condemning this as a lost cause. You can't imagine how I have been attacked, never before in the history of this conglomerate as in this one, for having made the purchase. Not for any reasons of this litigation at all, but from the point of view of the fact that this is a company that is not turn around, that is run down, that is over-priced, that is an adventure that is hopeless from the point of view that it cannot succeed as an investment, it cannot succeed at all because the company's going down hill and it's too late.

"And, they say, 'Well, Charlie, you're crazy to invest in a company like that.' I mean, can't you see what the record is? Show me another company with a record like that. They have said to me: 'This is going to cost you personally, Charlie. You're the biggest stockholder in Gulf & Western, do you know what this is going to cost you personally?' And I say that you've got to have faith. And, maybe, listen, it could be that I'm crazy, you know."

Talking about A&P stock as an investment, Bluhdorn said: "If I were looking upon this from the point of view of an investment banker, I wouldn't have bought one share. If I were looking upon it from the point of view of yield, I wouldn't have bought one share. If I took any of these ingredients into consideration, Counselor, I belong in a nut asylum, right?"

Talking about the grocery business, he said: "The significance of the A&P brand is that a brand name that is well known, if it is projected in the right way to the buying public, is a great asset."

He went on: "In the last decade look at what A&P's competitors have done and what has happened in terms of their sales increases, their closing down unprofitable units, they're moving where the people are going. Their opening of big new shopping centers. They're making their stores more at home for housewives so the housewife would be interested to go into them, because that's the kind of business we're in today, where we have to serve people. We have to make them want to go someplace.

"Obviously that had to be a fact or their [A&P's] competitors would not have been in a position to mushroom up all around them in the last decade. Now, that seems very evident. But if you want to lay it next to the record, Sir, of Safeway or Jewel Tea or a number of other companies I could outline, that . . . I think, would speak for itself.

"The customers have got to want to go there and to feel that this is where they want to buy, not just that we're getting cheaper prices, which is important, but also that we are going to get good service. I think one without the other is not sufficient. In other words . . . you're asking me purely for an opinion, because I'm not a specialist, per se."

In reference to Mr. Kane, Bluhdorn added: "Nobody would need a board of directors if they thought that they were God."

About Graybar Building management: "However, I did not feel that a breath of fresh air coming into the Graybar building will do anybody any harm, neither the foundation, nor the management, nor anybody associated with that great and proud company."

About the possibility of the tender offer being blocked: "Listen, if we don't succeed with the investment, maybe you are going to make all your shareholders happy. They'll all be redeeming their shares in the near future at $10 a share. Maybe he'll [Mr. Kane] make me a rich man. Our G&W stock will go up and his [A&P] will go down. Maybe a great adventure. Maybe one of the greatest things Mr. Kane has done for us. According to Merrill Lynch, we ought to go up $5 or $6 a share if the deal doesn't go through and if you prevent it."

At any rate, it was now over, the tender offer had been blocked. A&P had won another victory, or had it? Judging from the history of the following ten years, maybe Charlie Bluhdorn's last comment was right, maybe blocking the tender offer did help G&Ws shareholders more than A&P shareholders. At any rate, Charlie's G&W progressed nicely without A&P.

While the battle with Charlie Bluhdorn had been won, the fear of similar takeover attempts was now stronger than before in Bill Kane's mind. Consideration was given to possible defense mechanisms that might be instituted to prevent their future success. One area was given special attention.

Kane had been fortunate when he took over to find that the Employee Pension Plan was heavily overfunded. During his entire regime he was saved the expense of making any contribution toward funding that plan.

Management believed any prospective raider, friendly or otherwise, before announcing his tender offer, would have his experts check not only the balance sheet but also the funding status of any pension plan trusts, to make certain there was no serious underfunding position in such trusts. Such underfunding, while not a balance sheet liability, might impose future heavy obligations on the company that would make any takeover undesirable. Conversely, substantial overfunding in a trust, not appearing as a balance sheet asset, might indeed provide the best reason for a takeover attempt. By terminating such plan and diverting residual assets to the company, the raider could, in effect, employ the assets of the pension plan to purchase, or enhance the value of, the targeted company.

During the 1971/72/73 years, surplus balances in A&P's Pension Plan trust were used to underwrite annual funding liabilities, and Mr. Kane intended to continue this practice until the surplus was depleted. This use of funds already in the Plan trust, for funding annual benefits of members, was not in conflict with the promise implied by John Hartford's words that all monies contributed to this Plan would remain in the Plan for member benefits. Mr. Kane himself had expanded this sense of assurance. Many members recall his addressing their groups when, as Chief Executive Officer, he assured them how he was protecting their pension funds from seizure by unprincipled raiders who would try to buy A&P with those same pension funds. People don't forget such stirring promises. The summary booklets, distributed to employees to explain the Plan, further supported this belief with a forthright statement which said: "The Company hopes and expects the Plan to continue indefinitely," and, "However, if the Plan should end, all plan funds must be used for the benefit of members and their beneficiaries."

The termination language of the official Plan text, however, contained additional wording: "except that such excess funds as may exist because of 'erroneous actuarial computation' shall be returned to the Company." A&P management knew the 1973 surplus, in excess of $30 million, was not the result of some vaguely undefinable "erroneous actuarial computation," but was the clear and sudden consequence of the transfer of many thousand A&P Plan members into union pension plans, while funds contributed to the Plan for benefits earned by those members, prior to their transfer, remained in the A&P retirement trust. It was this knowledge which made contract language, requiring union retirement plan benefits for members, palatable and acceptable to management.

Regardless of the source of the surplus, it was decided to make certain that such surplus did not become a lure easily accessible to a successful raider through the mechanism of Plan termination. In August 1973, A&P amended the termination section of the Plan by inserting a provision which said simply: "The Board of Directors may terminate the Plan at any time, in which event all the funds of the Plan shall be used solely for the benefit of Members."

Mr. Kane never advised the full board nor the Plan members that a literal interpretation of this lucid provision was unwarranted because he only intended the language as "shark repellant" to thwart unfriendly raiders. The full board approved this amendment as assurance that pension assets would remain safe for members and permanently out of reach of any future corporate raider. Members accepted this new provision in the Plan text at face value.

Nine years later, a retired Mr. Kane submitted a sworn affidavit to the Federal District Court in opposition to members' rights to residual assets of the Plan under the terms of this 1973 amendment. In the 1982 affidavit, Kane claims that consultants, in 1973, assured him the proposed amendment would provide an "anti-raid weapon" that "seemed to shut the door" on surplus but permitted management to keep the key. If a threatening raider was hostile, A&P could terminate the Plan and surplus would be distributed to members; however, if the threatening raider was friendly to management, the Plan would not be terminated. After the successful takeover, the friendly raider would then be given the key to divert surplus through termination of the Plan after the re-amendment of this 1973 provision.

It is not surprising that retirement plan members were shocked by this belated admission of a management plot to trade pension trust assets as pawns in the corporate raider power game. It is not surprising that Plan members feel betrayed and defrauded by what they consider a criminal debasement and misuse of their retirement plan contract.

If Mr. Kane's affidavit is correct, then he, as chief executive officer, approved this provision lucidly codifying members' unqualified and exclusive rights to all residual assets of the Plan:

(a) when he, on behalf of management, intended no such unqualified benefit to members;

(b) when he instead intended the language for use merely as shark repellant against unfriendly raiders, and when plans existed for reversing the provision at the moment it was published in the official Plan text.

By September 1973, when this anti-raid weapon took effect, A&P's stock for which Bluhdorn had offered $20 in February, had already fallen to the $10/12 range. Management believed this made the company more attractive to a raider, and that another takeover was imminent; but apparently Wall Street concluded A&P was now a poor risk regardless of price.

Late in 1973, for a number of reasons which included a substantial proposed rent increase on the premises, and tacit agreement that maybe "a breath of fresh, clean air was long overdue," Kane initiated and approved plans to move A&P's corporate headquarters to Montvale, New Jersey, in the following year.

By the end of 1973, the trustees of the Hartford Foundation were angry and frustrated, as well as confused. A&P stock represented the bulk of the foundation's portfolio. They had received no dividends from A&P in more than a year; and the value of their A&P shares had dropped over $80 million in the year since Gulf & Western made its tender offer. It was becoming very difficult for them to defend their performance as fiduciaries of this large charitable foundation. They had recently opened their board to include trustees who were not former A&P employees. They now decided to demand that Kane, and A&P management, agree to hire a major outside consultant firm to make a thorough study of A&P, find out what in the hell was wrong, and make necessary recommendations for change. To make certain that they were not interfering in the operation of the business, and not abrogating management's authority, they gave Kane a choice of two consulting firms, Booz-Allen or McKinsey. Kane chose Booz-Allen. Shortly thereafter, a group of their clerical advance guard began gathering data from headquarters' records.

As 1973 came to a close, the company had lost all forward momentum and was adrift in a turbulent sea, rudderless, and without any power for propulsion. The air had come out of the WEO balloon, which had failed to generate projected sales and adequate profits. This failure was evidenced by the continuing increases in prices and margins to attain some small measure of profitability. The organization was thoroughy confused and rapidly losing confidence in management, which had absolutely no alternative backup plan to replace the failing WEO program except to repeat that survival at every level depended upon profitability. Some were awaiting the command: "Man the life boats!"

Among the poorest decisions of 1973, was the formal abandonment of the long-standing A&P Policy which John Hartford
insisted was the critical linch-pin, and key, to the company's
control over relationships between stores and consumers. The
substituted policy eliminated the following well established
dictums:

> "Do what is in the best interest of every customer."
> "Extend friendly satisfying service to everyone."
> "Give every customer the most good food for her money."
> "Assure accurate weight every time—16 oz. to each pound."
> "Give accurate count and full measure."
> "Charge the correct price."

Added to the policy was the provision for issuance of "rain
checks" whenever advertised items were unavailable in the stores.
Product unavailability had become the major complaint of A&P's
customers in 1973, and the Federal Trade Commission had attacked A&P's record on "truth in advertising" based upon complaints received and upon checks of advertised items' availability in
A&P stores. The inclusion of the "rain check" as an important part
of company policy provided an obvious recognition of the importance of this criticism. But, as customers will attest, a "rain check"
is a poor substitute for the real thing.

The 1973 policy changes did not include any loosening of
corporate insistence upon uniform pricing in trading areas covered
under one umbrella of the print or voice media. And below-cost
selling was still rigidly controlled and required the specific
approval of the division vice-president in each instance. Such
below-cost selling could be approved only to meet specific below-
cost advertisements by chains of five or more stores, and then only
if the vice-president concluded that failure to meet such competitive activity would result in measurable loss to the division.
Finally, detailed records, including copies of competitors' ads and
proofs of cost, had to be maintained in sales department files
subject to headquarter's audit.

The problems confronting A&P in February 1974 were substantially the same as the problems facing the company when Mr.
Kane assumed office in February 1971. A&P's ability to compete
successfully for shares of the consumers' grocery purchases had

deteriorated over a prolonged period of years during which competition had achieved far more effective store development and modernization, and had learned to recognize and respond far more effectively to the changing needs and desires of consumers.

Back in 1971, this writer, then executive vice-president, summarized A&P's problems and their solutions, in part as follows:

The so-called development plan is worse than non-existent, it is negative, resulting in an average shrinkage of retail selling space of over one million square feet per year. More than half of the new stores opened subsequently failed because the A&P new store prototype managed to stay three years behind the industry, or they were opened in divisions whose support systems, merchandising programs, and customer service levels were below competitive standards. Organizing a sound development program is a necessary long-term proposition which may not produce measurable results for several years.

Short term, a reasonable potential for significant sales increase and improved profitability is achievable through improved operation of existing stores. In many respects the cry "new stores will solve our problems" is an over-simplification. This prioritized summary of customer complaints analyzed the problem more accurately:

1) I can't get what I want at A&P!
2) You too frequently don't have what you advertise!
3) Your perishables, particularly fruits and vegetables, are lousy!
4) You don't have enough help. It takes too long to check out!
5) Your stores are dirty and sloppy!
6) Your prices are too high!

These were the problems in order of importance to consumers. A new store itself will not necessarily eliminate these deeply rooted operating problems, and the WEO concept is based upon the assumption that correcting the sixth most important problem will make enough customers forget the other five.

This 1971 report continued by pointing out that too often headquarters, confronted with the inescapable fact of poor store conditions, placed the blame upon the divisional vice-president, who in turn blamed supervision, who in turn placed all blame upon the store managers.

When thus confronted, the timid store manager passed the blame to the help and the unions, while the more astute manager indicted the warehouse, the office, supervision, and the whole damn company, and that manager was most nearly correct. Most poorly run stores are end products, just final repositories where the accumulated ineptness of corporate management finds itself upon display.

Retailing is not a high-tech business. It is a people business so simple, perhaps, that the source of its problems cannot always be uncovered through analysis of statistical data. "Big retail" is simply more of "small retail," the opportunities and problems are essentially the same, except that the communication link gets weaker as the size of the chain expands. In the 1970's, A&P faced the challenge of communicating with over 4,000 stores plus hundreds of warehouses, offices, and processing plants scattered across the U.S.A. and Canada.

Whatever the primary duties of the chief executive in any other business, the nature of A&P's problem required that the chief executive's primary function be formulation of company policy, and communicating in simplest terms the priorities for implementing that policy. If a test sampling of A&P's 140,000 employees were asked: "What is A&P all about?" or, "Can you describe the company game plan?" It is likely the same answer would not be given twice. The organization desperately needs policy re-affirmation, and the policy chosen must be based upon reasonable objectives in light of realistic evaluation of assets and liabilities of the Tea Company vis-a-vis existing competition.

The executive vice-president also pointed out that operating policy cannot succeed relying solely upon unrealistic, unaffordable "lowest prices" as its foundation. Many retailers succeed with moderately higher retails provided such pricing is complemented by better service, quality, and selection. Value, after all, is a composite of quality, service, and price. While it is true that the only logical purpose for business investment is profit, it is also true that broader operating purposes need to be explained to a business organization. As a suggestion, A&P's operating goal might be defined as: "Maximizing profit through higher volumes sales." This goal would be sought by employing a: "POLICY OF OPERATING CLEAN STORES, OFFERING A WIDE VARIETY OF QUALITY FOODS, PROVIDING HONEST, FRIENDLY SERVICE TO EVERY CUSTOMER, AT THE LOWEST PRICES POSSIBLE, WITH AN UNCONDITIONAL GUAR-ANTEE OF COMPLETE SATISFACTION OR CHEERFUL REFUND, FOR EVERY PURCHASE."

Policy affirmation is not for the purpose of reflecting standards achieved, but rather to provide the "game plan" for maintaining standards which will insure success. Policy establishes the order of priority and, in this instance, says: (1) A&P should not unlock the front door if the store is not clean. (2) Priority is on a wide variety of quality foods taking precedence over non-food type items, and freshness, proper trim, and presentation are essential to "quality foods." (3) Honest friendly service to all means that the rich, poor, pleasant, or crotchety customers are served equally well. (4) Lowest prices possible does not mean the lowest prices extant, but the lowest retails we can establish and still obtain a reasonable profit return for our labors, in clean, well-stocked, friendly stores. This policy demands our efficiency and control of waste and points us in the direction of return to the position of lowest prices in the industry.

Effective policy must apply equally throughout the entire support system of the chain. Processing plants, distribution facili-ties, and offices must accept the totality of company policy, and insure that each of their operating procedures complements the stores' efforts to achieve and maintain policy standards. Owner-operated stores are successful, in part, because everyone under-stands how the boss wants things done, and complies. Similarly, chains can be most successful only when everybody understands the company policy and complies, when policy is respected as the corporate flag, when it reflects bed-rock principles and not just this week's changes in management attitudes.

Policy takes time to implement effectively. It is not a quick-fix. It costs money and sometimes produces a painfully slow measure of return. Policy alone cannot turn A&P around, but without it no turnaround can be sustained. This executive vice-president's report concluded with the observation that: "The alternative to business based upon sound Policy is failure, as A&P has witnessed since the death of John Hartford." The message was heard and promptly forgotten.

Here, may be found a lesson. Perhaps too many loyal aides who succeed strong entrepreneurial executives advance more on their proven ability to execute short-term objectives than to formulate and administer policy. Unless our next generation of leaders comes equipped with that broader capability, in addition to a talent just to execute, we shall find ourselves led by photo-copies, mannequins who look and even speak the part, but are merely fair weather sailors of little use in troubled seas.

Now, on July 6, 1974, headquarters moved from the Graybar Building, and left New York, to move to sparkling new offices among the rolling hills and peaceful lakes of picturesque Montvale, New Jersey. The new environment lifted spirits, but unfortunately did little to improve the operating results of the company. That year's new sales high of $6.875 billion represented only a 2 percent increase over the prior year, and had to be considered a dismal performance in view of the continuing food-price inflation which rose over 15 percent during that same 1974. Worse, sales trend lines were pointing consistently downward from a 6 percent plus in the first quarter to a minus 4 percent in the final quarter. Substantial increases in retails and profit margins, although providing fuel for the sales decline, did generate a net of $22 million during the first three quarters, and $11 million of this profit was paid in dividends to shareholders. However, these sales, profit, and dividend performances did not appease the trustees of the Hartford Foundation who considered them much too little and too late.

Meanwhile, Booz-Allen's early findings were being communicated to Mr. Kane, a committee of outside directors, and, through unexplained channels, to representatives of the Hartford Foundation. By mid 1974, those Booz-Allen preliminary recommendations included hiring outside talent at upper management levels of A&P, and their services were enlarged to include such executive search activities. Kane was aware of, but not enthusiastic about, the "search" idea, and doubted that outside talent could contribute much to help him improve conditions at A&P.

Late on a balmy afternoon in August 1974, a telephone call from San Francisco caused a major earthquake in peaceful Montvale, New Jersey. Based upon a jury's verdict, a California Federal District Court had entered a judgment against A&P for damages which, including attorneys' fees, totalled $35,833,559, and these awards would bear interest at 7 percent during appeal. The action had been brought several years earlier by a Mr. Bray and five other cattle producers, charging that A&P, Safeway and Kroger had violated the Sherman Act by conspiring with other chains to fix wholesale meat prices at artificially low levels. Shortly after the action was filed Safeway and Kroger each settled separately out of court, without admission of wrongdoing, reportedly for amounts approximating $40,000. And, at that time, A&P's general counsel had brought similar settlement offers to Mr. Kane.

After explanation of the details of the case, the Kroger/Safeway settlements, and the similar settlement available to A&P, Kane asked his general counsel whether the company was guilty of any wrongdoing with respect to the charges. When counsel replied he knew of no A&P guilt in this regard, Mr. Kane rejected settlement and chose to have the matter go to trial rather than pay forty thousand dollars to parties whom the company had not injured. Again, prior to the start of the trial, Mr. Kane once more rejected settlement, this time in an approximate amount of $200,000.

Now, this $36 million court judgment struck like a bolt of lightning, and the stunned board demanded immediate and full explanation. During the board review, it became quickly apparent that Kane had made the decision to risk trial strictly on his own. He had apparently not discussed this decision with any of his executive staff, outside counsel, or members of the board. In the course of the review, several outside directors inquired whether Kane realized that pre-trial settlement involved no admission of guilt, and whether he had weighed the $40,000 settlement cost against the much greater cost of attorneys' fees for litigating the case through trial.

A&P's outside counsel advised the board after review of court transcripts that on the merits A&P might prevail on appeal, and they explained that plaintiffs' attorneys had done a masterful job convincing the jury of A&P's misdeeds based upon the flimsiest of evidence.

But the magnitude of this calamity, added to the multitude of other serious problems confronting the wounded company, was not to be easily dismissed. When the painful discussion finally ended, no one moved or said a word. The air in that board room hung heavy and grim, choking the awkward silence. Before anyone chose to speak, everyone in the room knew the bell had once more somberly tolled its ominous knell on another A&P management. The case was settled in 1975 at a cost of $7 million to A&P.

During the summer of 1974, Harry George, representing the Hartford Foundation, and Leonard Dahlsemer, first outsider to be elected trustee, visited the new A&P facilities in Montvale. The visit was much briefer than expected, and the tour included only the office of the chairman. After the curtest exchange of pleasantries, they advised Kane that the foundation wanted him out, and would not support his re-election; and they thought it would be best if he resign. Without waiting for an answer, or any response, they took leave to their waiting limousine and the trip back to New York City.

Bill Kane immediately related the purpose of Harry George's visit to his staff, and during that discussion suggested it would be futile to stand for re-election without the proxy endorsement of the foundation's 34 percent share of A&P's stock. He decided he would not be party to a proxy battle which would surely split and damage the company, its shareholders, and employees. He announced his decision to resign as soon as his replacement was selected and available to take over. The board, relieved at this decision, soon set about finalizing contractual arrangements with the successor already chosen; and arranged a severance contract that included enhancement of Kane's retirement benefits to the income level he would have received had he stayed on until normal retirement date.

The final days dragged slowly, the fire went out in the boiler, the good ship A&P was temporarily tied at the dock, momentarily secure in safe harbor, resting, waiting once again for a new captain to chart the new course, and set out to sea again. Within headquarters, the days were given to speculation, did Bill Kane

really dislike his replacement, or did he just dislike being replaced, or was it both? In any event the two sat in offices at
opposite ends of the hall, totally uncommunicative, during the so-
called transition weeks set aside for the orderly turning over of the
keys of command. Both were strong-willed guys, neither seemed
willing, or felt any need, to break the stony silence. Bill Kane was
not about to feign happiness, and the new man respected that, and,
knowing time was on his side, merely let the clock run out quietly.

Bill Kane never ducked the challenges, or controversy, that
marked most of his four-year term as chief executive. His office in
the Graybar Building had once been physically taken over by a
minority group after he had refused to meet personally with them
to defend what they considered to be unfair hiring practices of
A&P. His home was picketed on a Good Friday afternoon by
California grape picker sympathizers carrying a cross, because he
insisted A&P would continue to sell grapes and not join in the
boycott against the growers. He maintained A&P had no place
applying pressures or otherwise involving itself in the labor
disputes of other parties. The Gulf & Western tender offer, the
Bray case, the constant intrusion of the Hartford Foundation, the
final intrusion of Booz-Allen, and most of all the agony of being
unable to reverse the steady erosion and decline of A&P, all added
tremendous pressures to those four years. He had been unrelent-
ing, demanding that everything be done his way. He hated failure
even more than he loved winning.

Failure is merely an afterbirth of surrender and the admission of
defeat. Personal failure cannot result from outside judgment, it is a
private confession of despair, freely given. Kane was a scrapper
with strong convictions, who could hardly believe he had failed,
but likely remained convinced he had set the correct course for
the company, and if given adequate time and more loyal support,
he would have succeeded in turning A&P back on the course of
new growth and improved profitability.

In any event, he had fought what he perceived to be A&P's
dragons fiercely, valiantly, and with all he had. What more can one
ask? He walked out of A&P with his head high, and the ghosts of
the Hartfords walked out with him. It was the end of an age. The
old homestead was still standing, but Grandma was dead. The Tea
Company would never again be the same.

Eleven

Fresh Air at Last—In the Executive Suite

In November 1974, Booz-Allen submitted a 79-page progress report to the A&P board of directors. The "Introduction" of this report contained the following comments:

"After a long history of growth, profitability and leadership, A&P entered a period of decline, losing market share to more aggressive chains throughout the 1960's. In the early 1970's, the company utilized aggressive pricing (WEO) as its chief turnaround tactic. However, declines in market share were reversed only temporarily and profits are still substandard.

"This presentation deals with the current problems of A&P and what can be done to improve operations. However, A&P has significant strengths on which to build. These include:

A well-established consumer franchise for the company and its private label.
A strong balance sheet.
An experienced and loyal corps of field and middle managers.
A well developed manufacturing and distribution capability.

"A&P's traditional strengths have eroded substantially, and fundamental problems need to be addressed in a long-term plan. Food retailing in the last ten years has undergone a transition process which has caused fundamental changes in industry prac-

167

tices. Major challenges have developed from a continued shift toward suburban one-stop shopping, which has necessitated a rethinking of the nature and location of food markets. Shifts toward non-foods and increased emphasis on convenience and frozen items have impacted store layouts. Merchandising practices have changed: nearly every chain and many cooperatives now offer private label products; trends toward and then away from discount pricing have upset traditional margins; traffic builders such as stamps, games and continuity programs have come into vogue but are now infrequently used. During this period of fundamental change, performance in the industry has been mixed; a number of chains and regional operations have produced significant growth in volume and profitability while others have slipped in performance. A&P's sales growth has lagged behind that of industry leaders and profit performance has been poor. Lack of reinvestment in the business—both people and facilities—appears to have been a major reason for the firm's current weak position. Failure to concentrate in growing markets and move to the suburbs has caused A&P's market position and image to decline."

After some seventy-five pages of commentary and statistical data, Booz-Allen's preliminary conclusions included the following:

"A&P will have to undergo major change to achieve attractive returns. Fundamental weaknesses have to be overcome.

—The company's current market strength is in the least attractive markets.
—Facilities—stores and warehouses in particular—are either undersized or poorly utilized.
—Personnel development and training have been neglected.
—A large proportion of the company's assets are committed to unprofitable areas in the heart of the chain's geography.

"A lasting turnaround will take several years to implement.

"Large write-offs will result from consolidation and redeployment programs affecting stores, warehouses, division offices, and manufacturing facilities. Major borrowings will probably be required to support major facilities upgrades, particularly an accelerated store building program.

"A major personnel rebuilding effort will be required. The existing core of executives and middle managers needs to be augmented by a substantial number of outsiders. Training and development programs need to be expanded.

"Organizational development needs to emphasize a move to separate regional retail operations, reconfigured regions, and profit improvements. Retail operations need to be structured under strong regional executives. Regional and, in some cases, divisional boundaries do not now follow logical marketing or logistic lines. Reconfiguration is required to better recognize the importance of these factors. Based on regionalized retail operations, administrative support functions need to be restructured for maximum efficiency and minimum cost."

Upon conclusion of the progress report, the A&P board authorized Booz-Allen to develop its preliminary conclusions into firm recommendations. Shortly thereafter, Booz-Allen recommended that operations in stores not meeting certain business criteria be discontinued with dispatch in order to stem the heavy and apparently irreversible loss situations in those units and to avert possible ruin of the company as a whole. And the board of directors approved the Booz-Allen consolidation plan which involved the closing of several divisions and a total of 1,254 stores.

The Booz-Allen plan recommended closing 36 percent of A&P's 3,468 stores. These 1,254 stores accounted for slightly over 20 percent of A&P's total volume. The $1.4 billion in annual sales targeted for closing was tantamount to closing the ninth largest food chain in the United States at that time. And, as is the case with most profit improvement programs, this plan required a major one-time loss. By that time, such write-offs had become chic, and since all residual one-time loss reserves only add to future profitability, bigger tends to become better. In this instance, the nicely rounded sum of $200 million was considered to be adequate.

The task had been approached with antiseptic precision by skilled statisticians preparing for emergency surgery. All stores experiencing continuing losses, in excess of estimated 3 percent fixed overhead absorption, were targeted for closing. The stores targeted averaged 8,200 square feet in size, and $21,000 in weekly volume; however, the list did include some 50 larger and new stores which experienced continued heavy losses.

Some viewed this prescription as surgical over-kill. Such operations may, like an amputation to cure a runny nose, achieve the primary objective but leave the patient worse off than before.

However, this amputation did promise the immediate improvement in annual profit of $48 million, and the board agreed that such improvement coupled with a well-planned aggressive store development program, would more than cover the cost of plastic surgery in the event the nose did not grow back.

Not calculated was the negative impact of further fragmentation in market share by divisions losing substantial additional amounts of volume, nor the hidden costs resulting from contractual necessity to transfer higher-salaried, senior, union employees to remaining stores where younger, lower-salaried employees would be "bumped" and discharged. Not calculated either was the impact of additional tonnage losses on warehouses and manufacturing plants already underutilized.

The study did recognize the obvious, onerous burden created by continuing losses in large numbers of stores and the urgent need to stop this drain upon company resources. However, the store-closing prescription addressed only the *fact* of the losses, and not the *cause* of the losses. The closing program cured the illness by cremating the patients, but failed to treat, or even recognize, the very same operational deterioration illness spreading in many stores then above the 3 percent loss line but trending in that direction.

In a strangely different way, the closing program provided just another WEO type quick-fix, an aspirin that relieved the pain temporarily but never addressed the underlying illness which still remained: The once powerful, well disciplined A&P armada had broken formation and become badly fragmented, and was drifting, without compass or communication, plan or purpose, with the captains of each ship floundering helplessly because of lack of purposeful direction from the bridge of the flagship.

Still another corporate re-organization, this time to reconfigured regions and separate regional retail operations structured under strong regional executives, constituted another fashionable recommendation, in vogue at the time. In reality it represented only change for change's sake, creating new organization charts, and adding to the existing maddening confusion, during the six-month to one-year period of changeover and trial runs. A&P had been through every conceivable kind of reorganization, and if the company history proves anything, it is that drawing new corporate organization charts has never added a dime to sales or profits.

In February 1975 the study was completed and the board of directors approved the implementation of the Booz-Allen recommendations, co-incident to the resignation of Mr. Kane, and the election of Jonathan L. Scott as chairman and chief executive officer of A&P.

The election of the first outsider as chief executive of A&P was greeted with enthusiasm by the financial community and the shareholders. A&P's inner circle of top management shared this enthusiasm—outwardly. Inside there were mixed emotions and concerns. No one who had been part of top management could honestly deny being part of the failure. What hurt most was that they had wanted so much for A&P to succeed and had tried their best to contribute to that success. They had individually argued and disagreed with Kane in private session at times, but always joined to support company-approved programs.

But by now, they had begun to question their own convictions, the things they knew to be truths of retailing. They wondered what had gone wrong, where they had missed out. Deep down, they knew the traditional rule of in-house succession to chief executive had been given more than a fair chance, and had failed. They knew it was long past time for a change to an outside viewpoint. They knew it couldn't hurt, and perhaps a new set of eyes might see what they had so long missed. And, finally, they were concerned about the future, their own as well as A&P's. And, they were not too happy, but they smiled and greeted Scotty, warmly.

Hand-picked by Booz-Allen's executive search team, approved by the Hartford Foundation's board, and a committee of the outside members of A&P's board of directors, Scott demanded a free hand and a five-year contract at $275,000 plus incentive compensation guaranteeing a minimum of an additional $100,000 during each of the first two years, and both demands were granted.

Seldom has a major business appointment been greeted with more enthusiasm and expectancy by the financial community than was the election of Jonathan L. Scott as chairman and chief executive officer of the Great Atlantic & Pacific Tea Company.

Fortune magazine, in January 1975, said: "In a gesture akin to opening a long closed window, the Great Atlantic & Pacific Tea Company finally reached outside its ranks for a new leader. Next month Jonathan L. Scott, little-known chief executive of an Idaho based grocery chain, becomes chairman of A&P."—"As Scott recalls, it took him 'exactly thirty seconds' to say yes, he would go East"— "Scott is everything A&P executives are not. At forty-four he is the youngest by three years, of the dozen executives who make up top management. His predecessor, after forty-three years in the company, is still called 'Mr. Kane'; just about everybody calls Scott "Scotty."

A *New York Times* article, January 20, 1975, discussing an interview in A&P's Montvale headquarters, quoted Mr. Scott in reply to a question: "there were two events that proved to be of great significance in his life and career. 'One was in 1961 when J.A. Albertson, the chairman, had a heart attack and I was asked to take over supervision of the 200-store chain.' Mr. Scott said, 'it was a make-or-break situation because it was a matter of suddenly running the whole company. But I made out. It was what you might call a victory.' The other event, he went on, 'must be called a failure.' He had married Mr. Albertson's daughter in the early nineteen-fifties but in the early nineteen sixties the couple were divorced. 'That situation left me with lots of doubts,' he said, 'but I had to continue with my career and my work despite it.'"

The Wall Street Journal, February 7, 1975, said, in part: "'We've got to take steps to improve our image," said the 44-year-old executive. 'This is going to involve time, money and most of all an attitude change. We've got to start to lead and stick our neck out once in a while. We've got to get back the feeling that we're a winner.'" It went on to say: "Part of Scott's rebuilding program calls for establishing a corporate real estate department that will both stake out choice locations for stores and presumably abandon A&P's traditional policy of contracting mostly short-term leases."

The article added: "Some of the organizational changes at A&P are sure to involve a decentralizaton of merchandising and operations. 'I got the feeling that the . . . company has been run from the top,' said Scott, 'and this has to be changed. People are dying to grab the ball and run.'"

The article concludes: "The (Hartford) Foundation was instrumental in installing Mr. Scott as chairman and ousting Mr. Kane from the top slot. Although Mr. Scott said he hasn't any constraints on his five-year employment contract, he did say: 'I think it makes good sense to know the people at the foundation and make sure they're getting all the information they're entitled to.'"

All of this public press created great excitement and expectancy at all levels of the Tea Company, but also created anxiety and raised questions among some of the old guard. Scotty was coming from a small chain, founded by Joe Albertson, which throughout its history had gone almost straight up along with the population's increase in America's growing West and Southwest. Albertson's, although in the same food business, had never encountered problems of the kind now plaguing A&P. Within a month of arrival, Scotty would recommend closing out $1.4 billion in sales volume, which was 65 percent greater than the total sales of the Albertson chain. He was coming in cold without sufficient time to form his own judgments about A&P's problems, and their resolution. There was no one in the company he knew well enough, or whose judgment he valued enough, to exchange ideas and argue with. His introductory knowledge of A&P was based upon conclusions reached by Booz-Allen representatives, and consultants have no proven record of infallability. He was coming on board at perhaps the most critical moment in A&P's 116-year history. With all of his excellent personal attributes, did he possess the breadth of experience and tested "street smarts, retail smarts and people smarts," to manage this complex assignment single-handedly?

Later, an outside member of A&P's board was to confide that the board erred in "giving Scotty too much of a free hand when he was first elected," and in doing so the board had forfeited some of its responsibility.

At any rate, Scotty assumed command probably influenced by current prattlings of the press and business commentators that "inbred" A&P management was bad and "outside" management was good, and like the knight in shining armor he would drive off all the Tea Company's devils. No one in their right mind would deny that outsiders can and do bring a fresh viewpoint and ideas into corporate thinking. That is the justification for bringing qualified outside experience onto the board of directors of a corporation, and the strongest argument favoring the blend of "inbred-outside," or if you will, "outside-inbred," as the best management team possible. However, that was not to be the game plan for A&P.

And there was another questionable proposition receiving widespread attention at that time, namely: "Management is its own art form, and is a science on its own," meaning, "Any good 'manager' can manage any enterprise equally well." This odd notion lays claim to some validity so long as the company being run by the "generalist manager" is enjoying prosperity. But when an enterprise runs into serious trouble which bores deep into its loins, the person in charge had damn well better have some intimate knowledge of every part of that particular corporation, if only to prevent surgery on the wrong organs, which can never cure and just might kill the patient.

If a "house doctor" cannot be found who possesses the necessary skill, and the board is also unable to find an "outsider" fully qualified, then the board must involve itself in assembling an entire team with the proper qualifications and experience. A board should not delegate such fiduciary responsibilities to consultants or any one corporate officer.

Another popular misconception of the time was the notion that anyone who was a member of management of a successful operation necessarily made contributions to that success, or, that any member of a successful management could bring that success with him to a new job in another company. Indeed, evidence abounds that many "outsiders" later proved to be practicing discontents who had already attained the Peter principle's rung one step above their capability. Many are corporate driftwood, but most share an abundant talent for marketing the "Id." Selection, therefore, is extremely important in finding those outsiders who can truly make real contributions to a corporate turnaround.

Unfortunately, the fool-proof corporate executive-grader, over which you can run masses of candidates and retain only the U.S. #1 Fancy crop after the undergrades have fallen through the holes in the track, does not exist. All of this further complicated the enormous problems facing young Mr. Scott. Scotty had recruited a number of key executives from Albertson's before Joe Albertson threatened to sue. The balance of the outsiders had to be brought in from other competitors in the industry.

The annual report for 1975 included the following comments in Scott's message to the shareholders:

"In the twelve months since our last annual report, nearly every significant aspect of this very large organization has been touched by change.

"The plan announced over a year ago to close marginal and unprofitable stores, along with some support facilities, was completed ahead of schedule and well below estimated cost. (All told we closed 1,433 stores, including 137 units due to normal attrition, and are in the process of closing another 52.) Notwithstanding additions to the original plan, we were able to make a net reversal of $35 million from the $200 million reserve created to absorb these costs. This, together with an adjustment of deferred taxes amounting to $7.2 million despite operating losses in the first three quarters, produced net income of $4.3 million.

"In a broadscale construction and refurbishing program undertaken during 1975, we opened 91 large supermarkets. In addition to building entirely new stores ranging up to 35,000 square feet, we undertook a continuing program to repaint, relight and generally refurbish our stores. We also enlarged 32 stores. With improved layouts, new fixtures, revamped merchandising and a vigorous program to keep our stores clean and attractive, the customer response has been heartening."

Scott also commented on the success of the new "Price & Pride" advertising campaign which featured two grocery clerks. The clerk named "Price" appealed to the Spartan ethic, while "Pride" invoked the modern consumer's concern with quality, attractive stores and service.

To complete the image change, A&P introduced the new tricolor logo and initiated label and name changes on over 2,000 A&P private label items. The enormous expense involved was considered worthwhile and even necessary to complete the burial of the "old A&P image."

In 1975, Scott also reported still another "sweeping reorganization" of the vast field network. The year began with 3,468 stores operating out of 31 divisions centered in five regions. The year ended with the "new A&P" operating 2,074 stores out of 28 divisions centered in eight regions.

Assisted by more competitive pricing and new merchandising strategies, including 24-hour openings in many stores, sales for 1975 totalled $6.5 billion, down only 5 percent as compared to the previous year. While the 1975 fiscal period contained 53 weeks, this was still considered a strong performance in light of the fact that the 40 percent of A&P's stores which had closed accounted for approximately 20 percent of company volume in 1974.

Scotty, moving with dazzling speed and decisiveness, had completed in a single year the most dramatic "image change" in A&P's long history. The organization, gasping for breath at the speed of change, was exhilarated and proud of its new positive leadership. Scotty had done a great job in his first year.

Building upon this enthusiasm, 1976 became a year of celebration. A&P attained record sales of $7.2 billion, an increase of 10.7 percent over the 53-week fiscal period of 1975. The modest profit of $23.8 million was most encouraging, compared to the $4.3 million of the prior year and the negative results of recent years. By year's end, Scotty had his "top-three outside management" team in place. The first 55,000-square-foot Family Center store had opened in Greenville, South Carolina; and, the Supermarket Systems subsidiary had signed its first major contract overseas, to manage food distribution services and supply A&P brand products to Aramco, in Saudia Arabia. The business press and financial community were reporting imminent victory in the long-awaited turnaround of A&P.

Fortune magazine, in April 1977, ran a headline: "Price, Pride and Profitability," and said: "A couple of years ago the Great Atlantic & Pacific Tea Co. was on its knees. Then out of the West came Jonathan L. Scott, now 47, to be chairman and chief executive of A&P. One way and another, he has trimmed down, toned up, and reinvigorated the company its employees used to call "Grandma." After four profitable quarters, it is even free under its loan agreement to resume paying dividends if it chooses."

The *Fortune* article continues: "In the old days A&P was handicapped by the insularity of its management. Scott has built bridges to the outside, luring executives from other chains. Says Scott: 'I have a philosophy that you should surround yourself with people better than yourself. My strength is to provide the setting for the people to do their best.'"

Scotty cautioned *Fortune's* readers, saying: "We have not turned the company around yet, but we are in the process of turning it around."

Forbes devoted an entire "Special Situation Survey," dated March 11, 1977, to the Great Atlantic & Pacific Tea Company, Inc. This seven-page report said in part: "Only three years ago A&P's very survival was being questioned. Today the company is on a strong rebound, thanks to an impressive new team of executives, executives who all had records of outstanding achievement with other companies in the supermarket industry. They're making A&P a vibrant giant once more. A&P is one of this decade's great comeback stories."

The *Forbes* survey concludes and recommends, in part: "A few years ago, in failing health, A&P nearly committed suicide attempting to recover its lost grandeur. On the verge of catastrophe, A&P brought in Jonathan Scott, an outsider to save and restore this sick supermarket colossus. He quickly installed a group of brilliant, experienced supermarket executives. Result: Scott not only has saved A&P from the corporate graveyard; he has been successfully returning it to a point where A&P can make juicy profits once more."—"This is your opportunity. Don't let the stock's recent past close your mind to its brighter future. We think A&P's price will be *at least* 50 percent higher within the next 18 to 24 months. Buy this stock while it is cheap."

Despite all the glowing reports, a closer look revealed that A&P's skies were not all that blue. Certain light, but meaningful, cloud formations were again gathering on the horizons. The percentage of sales increases over 1975 trailed off badly each quarter from the strong 23 percent gain in the first quarter. Profitability also deteriorated badly as the year progressed. The final quarter contributed only $1.7 million to the annual total of $23.8 million, and was substantially behind the poor $2.7 million profit of the fourth quarter of 1975.

While the company did point out that the 1976 profit of $23.8 million included an extraordinary tax benefit of $10 million, it neglected to mention that most of the remaining profit could be attributed to a one-time bonanza enjoyed following the 1975 coffee freeze in Brazil. A&P had for many years been a prime purchaser of Brazilian coffee, and had signed lucrative contracts with Brazil whereby in exchange for loyalty to Brazil coffees, and advertising "Brazilian" on "Eight O'Clock" brand coffee, A&P enjoyed guaranteed below market pricing for projected annual purchases of all Brazilian coffees.

Wisely, A&P's coffee subsidiary had not scaled down maximum potential Brazilian contract purchase quantities for the 1975/76 period to reflect negative impacts of closed stores. In July 1975, an extraordinary freeze destroyed a major portion of Brazil's coffee bean crop waiting to be picked, and permanently damaged large numbers of coffee trees, signalling a serious long-term world-wide shortage of coffee.

Despite the immediate, exploding price escalation, Brazil scrupulously honored every part of its contractual commitment, allowing A&P to purchase maximum quantities out of existing Brazilian inventories at the old pre-freeze, discounted price, while others were paying higher prices which had skyrocketed after the freeze.

In-store sales of A&P private label coffees increased over 16 percent in 1975 to more than $83 million, and sales of these same A&P coffees soared by another 53 percent to over $126 million in 1976. From mid-1975 through all of 1976, A&P was in the coffee cat-bird's seat, selling more of its own coffees than ever before, at prices further below national brand prices than ever before, and harvesting an extraordinary profit bonanza above and beyond average coffee profits previously experienced.

Another unusual event occurred in 1976. Both A&P and the National Tea company had been long-time losers in the Chicago market. Each had significant investment in this market but dwindling market shares of available business. Each waited longingly for the other to drop out. Finally, National Tea announced its intention to abandon the Chicago market, and A&P, rather than leave bad enough alone, made a hasty decision, based upon a blitz executive inspection of National facilities, to purchase 62 National Tea stores, personnel included. It was correctly characterized as a bold move that would immediately strengthen A&P's market share to more competitive levels, but elementary logic has never concluded that two losers make one winner, no matter how merged. National Tea closed some 60 additional stores which A&P did not purchase, and during the intervening months, until independents or other chains reopened those closed stores, A&P enjoyed a six-million-dollar weekly sales gain in the Chicago market. This added strength to A&P's 1976 figures, but much of this newfound volume left A&P for those 60 new competitive openings, or to Jewel, or to others in the Chicago market by the end of the first quarter of 1977.

Most ominous of all indicators, the strong sales increase of 1976 did not produce anywhere near the normally expected reduction in expense rates, which is indicative that costs were out of control or

A&P was buying its new business with extravagant advertising or service costs.

A&P's report for the first quarter of 1977 announced sales and profit increases, both approximately 2 percent over the previous year, and as an expression of confidence in continued progress management recommended and the board approved renewal of cash dividend payments at the rate of five cents per share quarterly.

Chain Store Age magazine, in June 1977, described A&P as "halfway through its five-year recovery program." In that article, a top management A&P executive described some changes that had contributed to the success to date as, #1, the decentralization of buying; #2 the increase in average size of A&P's stores; #3 the doubling of non-food sales in the past two years; and #4 the new executive management who "know what it takes to be successful."

However, such optimism seemed unwarranted when one examined the published industry data, which disclosed that A&P's 2 percent sales increase was way behind the pace of the 6 percent food inflation rate, and further behind the supermarket industry's sales increase rate of 10 percent for comparable periods.

During the second quarter, A&P sales continued to stagnate at the 2 percent increase level but profits plummeted 81 percent to $1.3 million. Clearly, A&P was in trouble again, but this time it was being strangled by the razzle-dazzle of a cadre of outside management of all descriptions at every level, who had been recruited from both winners and losers in the industry, and who had been brought into A&P and turned loose, usually at at least one level higher on the management ladder than their previous experience, and told to go and do their thing. Management that was criticized as being too rigidly from the top down was being replaced by middle management anarchy. Strangely, most of such newly hired managers wanted a corporate "game plan" to embellish or follow, since they, in fact, had very little merchandising autonomy in their previous jobs. Before too long, corporate confusion and waste were rampant. The merchandising format became a continuing hodge-podge of games, gimmicks, and advertising slogans, hastily planned and introduced and as quickly discarded, which left both the A&P customers and the retail organization equally confused and disgusted.

The Montvale headquarters had to be enlarged to accommodate the 22 corporate officers and their staffs who sat where seven officers had sat in 1974. Management turnover increased, as one by one the old guard was weeded out, and then even some new arrivals began jumping ship.

Despite all the talk about margin improvement coming as a result of a better non-food mix, the sad fact was that A&P had higher retail prices than some competition in many markets. The Tea Company had now awakened after several years to find that, although the old wheels had been spinning furiously, the wagon hadn't moved an inch. The razzle-dazzle games and gimmicks, high-powered advertising campaigns, changes of personnel, and infusion of more non-foods onto the shelves had produced no measurable lasting benefits. Further, the store development program was dragging badly, not offsetting selling space lost by store closings and making little or no progress against continued new growth of competition. Eighty percent of A&P's 1,900 stores hadn't changed at all since Mr. Scott's arrival. It was important that management kept these facts in mind, and dealt with the realism that the Tea Company team still had a lot more "turtles" than "hares."

First, the sickening symptoms were obvious: sales growth not keeping pace with inflation, expenses continuing upward unchecked, retail prices higher than competition in an increasing number of markets, and disappearing profits. Next, the results of a recent market research study made in Chicago showed that A&P had remained extremely competitive price-wise in this troubled market in efforts to gain market-share improvement necessary to achieve and maintain profitability. But this independent research study told it like it was, dramatically.

Some 300 customer respondents, comparing A&P to its major competitors, Jewel and Dominick's, declared that A&P had:

1. The lowest everyday prices.
2. The best overall value.
3. The best specials on grocery and produce.
4. The freshest fruits and vegetables.
5. The friendliest and most helpful employees.
6. The best parking facilities.

7. Comparably good private brands.
8. Comparably clean stores.
9. Comparably conveniently located stores.
10. Stores that are reasonably pleasant to shop in.

While all of the above sounded extremely complimentary, the shock was that 90 percent of those respondents still considered A&P the poorest of the three. Ninety percent regularly shopped and spent most of their food budget in Jewel or Dominick's, and only 10 percent did most of their shopping at A&P, because:

1. A&P was judged poorest in the variety of the food products regularly stocked; poorest in shelf stocking with the most "out-of-stocks"; poorest in national brand selection, and poorest in selection of those "hard-to-find" food items.
2. A&P offered the poorest quality meats, and poorest meat specials.
3. A&P offered the poorest and slowest checkout service.

These Chicago stores scored better than A&P's average, on similar studies, in low pricing and fruit and vegetable quality, but poorer than A&P's average on meat quality and feature pricing; but the study pin-pointed precisely the two major faults plaguing A&P since the 1960s, obvious to all but continually ignored by top management, namely: "I can't get what I came for at A&P, and the service is lousy!" Before any turnaround can be achieved, management must face up to these problems and realize that further investment in advertising campaigns, or cutting prices deeply enough to force higher sales in poorly stocked and serviced stores, represents waste of corporate funds that achieves no retentive sales gain, and costs more than it would to correct the stocking and service problems.

Management must accept direct responsibility for any problems which create such widespread negative impact on their business. Management must temper its high-powered campaign to increase non-food sales by forcing additional products onto limited store shelving. Attempts to seduce customers into making impulse purchases of things not on their shopping lists look good on the boardroom charts, but in the real, small world of A&P, such programs force important food stuffs off the shelves, adding to the unavailability problem, and hurt the business they are trying to help. The unavailability problem first must be corrected at the purchasing, warehousing, merchandising and ordering levels, then the store manager can re-set his store's limited shelving to assure maximum availability of the items he knows his customers want most.

Next, management must accept responsibility for poor checkout service. The store manager, embarrassed by his poor checkout service but constantly taken to task for already excessive labor costs, and given no practical help or advice in solving that dilemma, is only further embarrassed by the mouthings of top management about "Giving our customers better service." Most middle level brass who understood the problem were unwilling to deliver the unwanted message that A&P's major investments in promotions, pricing, and administrative expense were being underwritten by poor service in stores, and thus wasted. It was easier to avoid the issue and to snow-job higher level brass with reasons for failure that cast all blame upon the store manager.

It is strange how even those who have worked in stores and should know better, when promoted to the white collar league, conveniently forget the additional labor costs and stocking problems inherent in trying to display one hundred items in space designed for fifty. The extra labor, inventory tie-up, and lost sales due to out-of-stocks more than offset any so-called advantage from better product-mix.

As a first major step to reducing administrative overhead, A&P announced in September 1977 another sweeping reorganization of field operations. This time it centralized the existing eight regions into three groups, northern, southern and eastern, with six operating divisions in each group reporting directly to a corporate executive vice-president. Thus an entire layer of regional management was eliminated.

The results for the third quarter of 1977 confirmed the seriousness of A&P's problems. Quarterly sales of $1.8 billion were dead even with the previous year but 6 percent behind last year on a tonnage basis, and the company reported a net loss of $5.02 million.

The business press which had been so kind and optimistic in 1975 now looked upon A&P with a much more jaundiced eye. *Time* magazine, in a December 12, 1977, issue, headlined their story: "Price and Pride on the Skids" and asked, "Can anyone revive A&P? When Jonathan L. Scott was brought in as an outsider in 1975, he appeared to be the man to shake up the insular A&P. Chairman Scott, now 47, swung a cruel ax on "Grandma" as employees sometimes call the venerable food chain. He closed 1,700 stores, released 10,000 employees, borrowed heavily to revamp and enlarge the remaining 1932 supermarkets. Now, more than halfway through Scott's "five-year plan" for making A&P solidly profitable, the results are dismal."

For the full year 1977, sales totalled $7.3 billion, a new record high although less than 1 percent above the previous year, and 5 percent behind last year on a tonnage basis. For the period, profits plunged by 98 percent to $0.6 million, equal to 2¢ per share. Cash dividend payments of 15¢ per share exceeded earnings by more than 750 percent, but following this report dividend payments were suspended.

A profile of A&P's new management disclosed a phenomenon not noticed or commented upon by the business press. All outside management recruited into A&P came from the smaller, secondary chains. Remarkably, and for reasons never explained, no important A&P management position was filled by executives recruited from either Safeway or Kroger.

Safeway and Kroger are the two largest, and certainly two of the most consistently successful, operators in the supermarket industry. While one can argue that a store is a store is a store, there is no experience available to an executive of a regional chain to match the expansive complexities existing in the Goliaths of the industry, Safeway, Kroger, and A&P at that time. Safeway and Kroger were, and are, even more disciplined and more effective than A&P at promoting private label brands. Surely, their executives recognize the important competitive advantage gained by developing mother-to-daughter generations of lasting customer loyalty to their specific house brands which consistently offer uniform high quality at savings over comparable national brand products, and they also appreciate and protect the extra profitability which becomes available through promotion of house brands.

Safeway's and Kroger's operating officers are also primarily "inbred," and are not habitués of the convention, seminar and country club set, and thus are seldom recruited for other firms. At any rate, most of the new outside management recruited into A&P

came with an apparent fixation, probably based upon gossip from national brand salesmen, since they had little or no extensive personal experience, that A&P was strictly a private label house, that this was an important part of A&P's problem, and that the private label in general and A&P manufacturing in particular must be dismantled.

While it is indeed true that all A&P's problems were not just retail problems, and every part of the operation—purchasing, merchandising, warehousing, administration, manufacturing, and top management—shared major responsibilities for corporate failures, it was a tragic mistake to hastily condemn manufacturing without in-depth study. The manufacturing division came under criticism for heavy-handed, overbearing attitudes toward retail, and continued efforts to push unwanted, unnecessary products onto store shelves. This criticism more properly should have been leveled at top management who created this environment by their constant pressure on manufacturing for increased profits. Many of A&P's manufacturing problems were correctable, but the pervasive attitude of the time was, "If it's broke, write it off."

Sales to outsiders and billings to stores by A&P's manufacturing arm exceeded $1 billion annually in the early 1970's, and most plants were not operating close to maximum capacity. A&P manufactured, processed, and packaged over 1,500 grocery store products, some of which, such as candy, were seasonal and holiday items; some others were realistically unnecessary slow-moving duplicates that admittedly were added to increase production.

Since the turn of the century, the Hartfords had developed the manufacturing arm to the point where John used to boast: "The stores make the profit, and Manufacturing pays the tax." In other words, A&P's operating profits usually equaled its after-tax net. Over the years, private label products were billed to stores at prices which permitted divisions to offer retail prices 10 percent below comparable national brands, and at the same time to generate a 10 percent higher operating gross than was obtained by pricing national brand products competitively. Then, at the end of each quarter, manufacturing would turn in its own profits averaging 6 percent of total billings, and thereupon headquarters statistically distributed these profits back to each division on a proportionate shipment basis. Thus both manufacturing and retail each received credit for the same manufacturing profit, and the Hartfords smiled all the way to the bank.

Now, starting in 1975, the manufacturing subsidiaries were in a defensive position, and in fact were doomed. Almost a century of product development, and the investment of over $100 million, were in peril as divisions were permitted to treat "Manufacturing" as just another supplier.

Division operating budgets were submitted without inclusion of estimated subsidiary profits. This foolishly unnecessary practice rendered subsidiary profits meaningless to a division struggling to meet budget commitments and save its jobs. To pump up operating profit, some divisions actually substituted cheaper outside-label brands for well-known A&P labels. Such short-term idiocy only added to the confusion of both the store organization and customers. Later, as outside management came into the manufacturing arm, competitive billing became the all-important factor to survival, and quality and sales both suffered as customer loyalty evaporated.

It must be reported that the majority of the old inbred divisional executives fully supported and joined the new chorus excoriating A&P's old manufacturing subsidiaries. Some of this mis-directed denunciation represented the long-awaited opportunity to lash out at what had been, in reality, a headquarters malpractice of continued forced over-shipment of the regular items, and insertion of unnecessary company labels duplicating slow-moving national brands. Most of the denigration was simply the result of divisional personnel seizing an opportunity to divert blame for their own failures. It must also be noted that some of the most vociferous critics never turned in a nickel in operating profits during their entire management tenure.

Decisions to close A&P warehouses and service the stores through outside wholesale suppliers added significantly to A&P's manufacturing demise. Most wholesale suppliers claimed that they were not in a position to add several hundred items to their inventory to serve only one customer, A&P. Obviously, their profitability would be enhanced by distributing their house brand private label to A&P stores in place of A&P's label. Most agreed to stock a limited number of the fastest-moving A&P items, and the remainder of private label merchandise was supplied from the wholesalers' house brand stock.

The avowed purpose of this entire effort was not intended to hurt manufacturing subsidiaries, but rather to put all profit up front at the retail level where it was "earned," and where presumably it would do the most good. Let us see how it all came out.

	1974	1977
Manufacturing Profits	$60,104,000	$37,376,000
Retail Losses	(26,674,000)	(36,807,000)
Total Operating Profit	$33,430,000	$ 569,000

The above results show that just about all manufacturing profits sacrificed to enhance retail operations fell through the corporate cracks and were lost. Worse, retail profitability, in its own right, declined 38 percent in the period.

Admittedly, hindsight is always much superior to any immediate confrontation viewpoint. The purpose here is not "I told you so," but rather an effort to highlight the enormity of the decisions thrust upon Scotty co-incident to his arrival at A&P. In so many ways, Scott was as well, if not better, equipped than his predecessors to run A&P. He had the brains, the guts and the talent to get the job done. . . . If only he had come at a quieter time. If only he had some more time up-front to size up A&P on his own, to form his own judgments on the problems and personnel.

If only Scott had more time to develop his own strategies, against which to compare the Booz-Allen restructuring plan for A&P. But such was not to be, and "if onlys" don't help things now.

In January 1978, the board engaged the "other consultant," McKinsey, at a fee of $100,000 per month, to study and make recommendations helpful to A&P's turnaround. The study took most of the year.

For the 119-year-old Tea Company, 1978 was "the pits"; nothing seemed to go right. Annual sales totalled $7.5 billion, another new record high, but only 2.5 percent ahead of the prior year, and adjusted for the runaway food cost inflation, sales, on a tonnage basis, were down 9 percent. In 1978, A&P reported net losses of $52.2 million, or $2.10 per share, including a net reserve of $40 million to cover further McKinsey-recommended "restructuring," which was the nice way of saying "closing more facilities." In this instance, Cleveland, Pittsburgh and the Milwaukee divisions were closed along with several manufacturing plants. At year's end A&P operated 1,771 stores, having closed 186 and opened 52 new supermarkets.

This writer, the last of the old-guard corporate officers, enjoyed an excellent personal relationship with Chairman Scott despite frequent voicing of dissenting business philosophies. In 1978, to resolve the inherent conflict, Scott assigned the writer to the presidency of Supermarket Systems, a newly formed subsidiary whose purpose was marketing food distribution expertise, operating management, and consulting services world-wide.

As the year began, the last vestiges of old "inbred" top management had been cleaned out of operations, the new crew of outside executives had completed the orientation stage and their training cruises, the Booz-Allen recommendations had long since been implemented, the board of directors had been expanded to include such distinguished names as Agee of Bendix, Dodd of Owens-Illinois, Dance of General Electric and others. Still the "Old Queen Mary" was not turning forward, in fact the damn thing was turning backwards. All of which raised some disturbing questions.

What was wrong? Why did this new management appear to be floundering? Why were they relying upon such trade-worn merchandising gimmicks as "Action Prices" and, of all things, "trading stamps"? Did they have no more constructive ideas than scrapping the huge "Price and Pride" advertising program and introducing a substitute advertising theme which joshingly advised customers, "You'll Do Better at A&P"? Was there nothing more?

To a seasoned food operator, one thing was crystal clear: A&P's drift in all directions resulted from management's failure to fix a single firm corporate direction, and from management's belief that a firm underlying corporate policy was not an imperative for success in a huge retailing enterprise.

Obviously, without a flag, a game plan, or corporate policy to rally round and build upon, this new management was not a team at all, but just a "gang of hopefully talented anarchists" running amuck. In the absence of the corporate game plan, each manager created his own plan. And, with each frequent change of managers, his game plan gave way to the new man's plan. Often, the same manager changed his own plan, when it didn't work fast enough. Down below, the organization became completely frustrated, confused and disgusted with its management. It is, and it always will be, impossible for the captain to move the troops forward while the corporals are ordering: "Left turn, Right turn."

Negative is the absence as well as the opposite of positive. When there exists no positive policy direction, the organization begins to be managed from the bottom up, and the old familiar negative norms formulate a plan which says: "They're nuts," "What's the use?" "Why the hell should I care?" "Do only what you have to," and, "Protect your own butt!"

Management sometimes tends to think of the business it leads as some cold finite object, be it a bank, a factory, a mill, a mine, or a retail chain. Agreed, the organization, which makes it operate, is the most important component, but the enterprise itself is the "thing." The Hartfords, however, believed they were managing an IDEA, called A&P. They were determined to take whatever management action became necessary or helpful to the furtherance of that IDEA, which was: "To provide the most good food for the money, and to do that honestly and in the best interest of every customer." To the Hartfords, the IDEA was much more important than the pot it grew in. They used little stores, big stores, wagons, and factories, all to help that IDEA flourish and grow.

During the 1930s, the company was shaken to its roots because the IDEA became inoperative and impossible to achieve in 16,000 little stores competing in a new supermarket era. But rather than surrender the IDEA, the Hartfords simply closed the 16,000 stores and opened their own 4,000 supermarkets wherein the IDEA could continue to flourish better than ever.

A&P only began to flounder when the IDEA, unfortunately, was buried with the Hartfords. It would have been sad had the Hartford IDEA been replaced with another "idea" for doing business; but what happened was even worse, the IDEA was never replaced at all, and the company was trying to run without an engine or a heart.

To the consumer, A&P's steady deterioration was just as dramatic and shocking as if today customers walked in and found individual K-Marts or McDonald's markedly different than they were, strangely different from each other, and each following inconsistent merchandising routes. It was utterly amazing that this void created by lack of policy control escaped the notice of top management and the board. It appears that management, out of touch with consumer realities, had become so convinced that A&P's solution lay in better ambience, advertising, price and product-mix that they scoffed corporate policy need as nonsense after it had been suggested as a necessary ingredient to success.

In 1978, A&P management was faced with three policy options:

(a) Attempt to resurrect the policy upon which A&P was founded and flourished for so many years. This would be difficult because A&P was no longer the "low price" merchant, and enormous costs and considerable time would be required to re-claim such position in the market. However, that policy might be restored if predicated upon commitment to the eventual goal of "lowest price," because what matters most in policy control is the organized pursuit of a sound goal. Many goals are distant, some are never reached, and that matters little, it is the organized effort that counts.

(b) Clearly define a new and different game plan and corporate policy by establishing a sensible order of priorities of various elements which contribute to retail success, such as: product selection, quality, price, store ambience, service, and special departments. Many chains succeed with higher price policies provided service, selection and store ambience warrant the higher prices. The important thing is assessing the market available, defining that share you seek to capture, and putting together an effective program to accomplish that purpose.

(c) The third option took little thought. It was to simply discard as trivial the idea of policy importance. This option, which appeared to be cost free, was the one followed. In reality it cost the most.

At the annual shareholders' meeting in June 1978, A&P disclosed its first-quarter operating results. The stock plunged, and the business press reacted accordingly.

An article in *Supermarket News* reporting on the annual shareholders' meeting said in part: "The last time A&P stock closed below

$7 per share was December 13, 1974—when it hit 6½—the day after the board elected Jonathan L. Scott to replace William J. Kane as chairman and chief executive. Shortly afterward, a $200 million reserve was set up for closing 1,600 stores. It was the beginning of Scott's turnaround campaign, the failure of which was acknowledged at the annual meeting in Detroit 10 days ago. It's hard to say whether last week's stock plunge reflected general dissatisfaction or the maneuvers of some financial interests."

The article continued: "Scott and his team are working on all manner of operating improvements—improving customer service, reducing out-of-stocks, working up a more positive advertising campaign to replace Price & Pride, introducing a line of generic products and improving the balance between grocery and perishable merchandising. But they are working without a general business and investment strategy, which is McKinsey's responsibility, for the time being."

Fortune magazine devoted their November 6, 1978, cover and feature story to an article captioned: "A&P Shrinking the Supermarket Giant." The six-page article began: "When Jonathan Scott took over as chairman almost four years ago, the company was in desperate straits. It still is. On the record so far, Scott's performance at A&P has been one of the most disappointing management failures of recent years."

The article goes on to criticize not only the disappointing results of the closing program but also the lackluster results of the planned new store, enlargement and remodelling program to date. After detailed discussions of personnel changes, employee morale and newly planned merchandising and advertising programs, the article adds: "Scott has spent a considerable amount of energy overhauling the organization—bringing in new people, building a sound real estate department, putting in tighter financial controls, improving the company's cash management, and installing information systems. But it remains to be seen whether these management-manual improvements at the corporate level will translate into better performance where it counts—in the operation of A&P stores. A&P's future depends on increased sales and lower operating costs in the stores, and in these nitty-gritty matters, Scott's record so far has been grimly disappointing."

Twelve

Hartford Heirs Sell Out to Haub

By mid 1978, the trustees of the Hartford Foundation were at wit's end and frustrated with Scotty, as he no doubt was with them and their wailing for more dividends. Over the years, the foundation had put off major diversification of its portfolio which still relied heavily upon A&P stock as the primary source of income and asset growth. Now, once again, they were without dividend income, and without realistic prospects of such income. The per-share value of A&P stock had dropped from a high of $70 in 1961 to less than $7 in 1977. This represented a market devaluation in excess of $440 million on the more than seven million shares still held by the foundation. Thus, it became impossible to defend their posture as fiduciaries of this charitable trust any longer. Unhappy with the present performance, and unwilling to embark upon another five-year-plan with some new management, they decided to bail out and dump their A&P holdings for the best price available.

In retrospect, the foundation failed the long-term purposes for which it was established by John Hartford, and to which George had also bequeathed his entire A&P holdings. The brothers had frequently expressed their hope that this foundation would provide a continuing source of generous charitable contribution, while at the same time preserving the A&P Tea Company and its organization in the original charter established by their father George Huntington Hartford.

The Hartford Foundation trustees wielded the voting power to make and break the succession of chief executives who succeeded John and George Hartford. The mere existence of the foundation exerted powerful pressures for continued dividends as the guarantee of management's tenure during periods when such dividend payments were contrary to the best interests of the company, its shareholders, and the desires of the brothers who funded the foundation to perpetuate A&P as a great company in tribute to their father. These trustees had no direct corporate management responsibilities, or sufficient retail expertise to aid in solving company problems. However, from an investment viewpoint, they considered any reduction or cessation of dividends the result of inept management, because the alternative conclusion was that they had failed their fiduciary responsibilities through unwise investment decisions and failure to diversify asset holdings.

History has shown that such publicly disguised dominance contravenes the best interest of a company and its shareholders and suggests consideration of SEC rules under which trusts, foundations, and other institutional entities can vote only a limited percentage of shares of a publicly held company.

Having made the decision to dispose of its A&P stock, the foundation, in the fall of 1978, started discussions in the appropriate financial circles. Three of the Hartford family heirs, Mrs. Carpenter, Mrs. Bryce, and the McIntosh Foundation, advised of the Hartford Foundation's decision to sell, decided to join in and offer portions of their A&P stock, with the result that more than 40 percent of A&P's stock now became available in a single offering.

Within a very short time, negotiations began between representatives of the foundation-family heir group, and representatives of a prospective purchaser in West Germany. After discussions had progressed to a serious stage, Scotty was invited to West Germany so that he, and the interested buyer, could get to know each other and agree upon the nature of the working relationship that might exist if the deal was consummated. Scotty's visit to West Germany and his discussions with Erivan Haub apparently were mutually satisfactory, because the deal was finalized shortly thereafter.

Erivan Haub is an enormously wealthy and important man in West Germany. Most of his business holdings are privately owned. He appears to have a passion for privacy, and avoids the public

The author, at far left, briefs the Soviet delegation that visited the United States in 1979. At the head of the table are CEO Jonathan Scott (left) and Vadim Lazko, Deputy Minister of the Food Industry, U.S.S.R.

Vladimir F. Promyslov, Chairman of the Executive Committee of the City of Moscow (in other words, the mayor), presents the author with a souvenir during his visit to Moscow in 1980.

A&P's Supermarket Systems, Inc., had the capability to desi
construct and manage the operation of a food distribution

network large enough to support efficiently the retail food needs
of a city, a state or an entire nation.

Ralph W. Burger, Chairman of
the Board and President,
1951–1963.

John D. Ehrgott, Chairman of the
Board and President, 1963–1965.

Chairman of the Board John D. Ehrgott (right) reviews the
company's operations with Byron Jay, President.

Byron Jay, Chairman of
the Board and President,
1965–1968.

Melvin W. Alldredge,
Chairman of the Board and
Chief Executive Officer,
1968–1971.

William J. Kane,
Chairman of the Board
and Chief Executive
Officer, 1971–1975.

Jonathan L. Scott, Chairman of the Board and Chief Executive Officer, 1975–1980.

Erivan Haub, chairman and chief executive of West Germany's
Tengelmann Group, the owner of the A&P, attends the opening of
the first Plus store, in Plainfield, New Jersey, August 1979. Mrs.
Haub is in the center, and Tengelmann director Rosemarie
Baumeister at the right.

James Wood, Chairman of the Board and
Chief Executive Officer, 1980–

A wintry day at A&P's Montvale, New Jersey, headquarters.
Many of the executives who occupy the building at the left may
wish that they had heeded the groundskeeper's advice.

spotlight with a Howard Hughes-like fervor. In his A&P dealings, he operates behind the name "Tengelmann Group," which he privately controls. Born in Germany in the early 1930s, he was too young to have had any personal involvement in World War II or its politics. He inherited a family-owned grocery business from his mother. The family business traces its origin back to the mid-1890s, but like most German enterprises was reduced to near rubble by World War II. Since that time it has enjoyed remarkable growth, and in 1979 Erivan Haub was sole owner of a 2,000 store chain with annual volume exceeding $2 billion, under the name "Tengelmann Warenhandelsgesellschaft."

The New York Times, on January 19, 1979, on its front page announced: "A major West German food retailer announced plans yesterday to acquire 42 percent of the Great Atlantic & Pacific Tea Company, the supermarket giant whose initials have long been a household term in American retailing. The Tengelmann group, a privately owned company, said it planned to buy some A&P shares from the John A. Hartford Foundation, which has held a major interest in the chain for many years, and from several other major shareholders." The *Times* article also noted that observers believe the long decline of the dollar against the deutsche mark has made such investments attractive to increasing numbers of overseas companies.

The Wall Street Journal article of January 19, 1979, pointed out that the West German retailer agreed to pay $75 million for the 42 percent interest in A&P, and it outlined the details of the 10.4 million share purchase as including 6.3 million shares from the Hartford Foundation, which at the time represented their entire holdings; and 4.1 million shares still held by the Carpenter, Bryce and McIntosh family heirs. Under the terms of the deal, Tengelmann agreed to pay $7.375 per share in cash, or a total of $53.8 million for 70 percent of the 10.4 million shares, and hold a one-year option, which included voting rights, to purchase the remaining 30 percent of the shares at $7.50, or an additional $23.4 million. The article reported the Tengelmann representative as saying the group would seek proportionate representation on A&P's board but would leave the day-to-day management to A&P's management, in which it had strong confidence. A&P's chairman, Jonathan Scott, was quoted: "A&P welcomes this expression of investment confidence from the Tengelmann Group. Their financial strength and broad experience in operating a highly profitable, rapidly growing chain of some 2,000 supermarkets and (other) food stores in Europe could prove beneficial to our company in its redevelopment program."

After 120 years, the Hartford family name was no longer a major force in the control of A&P, as the family heirs sold 42 percent of the company's stock to the new West German owner. The next largest block of stock was the estimated 7 percent held by the A&P Thrift Plan. This stock was voted by members who were primarily non-union employees, normally compliant with management's wishes.

Supermarket News, in an extensive article dated January 22, 1979, reported that Leonard Dahlsemer, the retired executive of International Paper Company, New York, the first outsider elected as trustee of the Hartford Foundation, and who in 1978 succeeded Harry George as president of the foundation, had been the prime mover behind the proposed takeover. The article said that Dahlsemer reportedly was convinced the foundation had to rid itself of its interest in A&P and had hired Dillon Read & Company to find a buyer, shortly after he took over as president of the board of trustees. The details of the Tengelmann purchase were reported to have been handled by Nicholas Brady, Abram Claud and Willard Webb of Dillon Read.

The *Supermarket News* analysis reported: "The consensus on Wall Street and in food trade circles was that supermarkets rarely have gone as cheaply as the 1,800 A&Ps are going to Tengelmann." Later, the article added: "In short, it is clear that Tengelmann is getting control of the 1,800 A&Ps for a fraction of what supermarkets have been going for. The 75 or 80 stores A&P has built in the past two years alone cost more than Tengelmann is paying for the control of the entire company." The article concluded with the humorous speculation that the Tengelmann takeover might possibly involve the name change to "Die Grosse Atlantik und Pazifik Teegesellschaft," but even that would be a name to conjure with.

Erivan Haub was a West German native with his business headquarters at Mulheim an der Ruhr, Germany, but he was not entirely foreign to the United States. As potential heir to the family's grocery business, he had been sent to America as a young man to study the U.S. retail food business. In this pursuit he had spent a number of months as a trainee-observer of the Jewel Tea

Company operations in Chicago. His family had also purchased a home in the Tacoma area of Washington State where his three sons happened to be born, and where he normally spends a part of each year.

Nothing in Haub's history suggests that emotionalism or anything but coldly calculated, meticulous business judgment decided the purchase of A&P. His demeanor was viewed by some as more of the super cautious business type than as the "riverboat gambler." Many people have been invited to come alone to see Mr. Haub regarding business proposals, but few have ever seen Mr. Haub alone. He made it a point always to have an aide as witness to verify any possible future question that might arise concerning what was said at such meetings. Mr. Haub, like many prominent Europeans, was quite security conscious. He usually traveled with a security person and, when in Europe, preferred to ride in armored automobiles.

Haub's decision to take over A&P was based upon a carefully considered appraisal of the realistic values involved, after his financial experts had meticulously pored over, not only the balance sheet numbers, but the market value of assets, and had assured themselves there were no potential non-balance sheet liabilities, such as under-funded pension plans, that might detract from the value of the purchase. When Erivan Haub wrote his first check to purchase A&P, he knew precisely what it was worth.

Back at Montvale headquarters, Scotty expressed optimism about the prospects for 1979. He called the Haub investment a most significant development and a welcome expression of confidence. In his 1979 message to shareholders, Scott said: "Tengelmann, one of the most successful European food retailing organizations, has an excellent track record of growth and profitability and has pledged to take an active and enthusiastic "partner-investor" role in our collective efforts to restore A&P to sustained profitability."

The year 1979 turned out to be an unmitigated disaster; the results were dismally disappointing but the growing corporate confusion was even more ominous. The year started out poorly with sales behind 8 percent in the first quarter and continuing downward to finish the year 10.5 percent behind 1978 despite record high food-cost inflation. On a real unit sales, or tonnage, basis, annual sales were down an incredible 20 percent. During the year, A&P opened 20 new supermarkets, six new large Family Center markets, and converted 32 former A&P's to PLUS stores, but ended the year with 229 fewer stores due mostly to the closing of the Pittsburgh, Cleveland and Milwaukee divisions. Pre-tax operating profits started poorly at $3.4 million for the first quarter, and deteriorated each quarter thereafter, culminating in a net loss for the year of $3.8 million.

Scott's hoped-for opportunity to manage A&P without the constant heckling from the stands by the foundation and family heirs was finally realized, but things got worse because the heckling from the stands was now replaced by Haub's forces, who had joined the team and were giving orders from the bench.

First, Haub invited high-ranking corporate officers of A&P to visit Germany for orientation into the Tengelmann ways, and to see how things were done in a successful organization, and also no doubt to stand appraisal by his home organization.

Second, Haub increased his ownership interest to 45 percent, and, prior to the annual shareholders' June meeting, the character of the board of directors changed dramatically. Five of the nine outside directors quietly departed; they were Dodd, of Owens-Illinois, Agee, of Bendix, and Detmar, Dunn and Toner. The board was now expanded to include seven Haub selections, Rosemarie Baumeister, vice-president of Tengelmann and Haub's personal confidante, Helga Haub, his wife, and Sidney Kohl, Paul Nagel, Eckart Siess, Fritz Teelen, and Henry Van Baalen, trusted acquaintances or Tengelmann employees. Four of the outside directors, Hauptfuher, Berry, Dance and Taylor were renominated and elected, and the composition of the board was completed with the re-election of Scott, and the two other corporate officer-directors. Haub also insisted upon the election of four corporate officers including Eckart Siess, a long-time friend, who was elected vice-chairman of the board, and assistant to the chairman and chief executive.

One of the outside directors before resigning submitted a report containing what he considered important priorities requiring management resolution. The first priority listed in the report was: "Development of a charter. What is A&P trying to be? What are the primary objectives?" The second priority was the development of an organization plan and structure for accomplishing the first priority. Later, he outlined the need for policy review, resolution, documentation and communication in areas such as pricing, merchandising, private label, buying and labor relations. Discussing corporate environmental factors, he cited the need for a "settling down period"; too many changes were coming too fast for the organization to absorb, due in part to Tengelmann studies, visits, suggestions, etc. He noted: "Tengelmann needs to concentrate on basic policies, practices, and/or changes required. Presently too much emphasis is on form over substance." The report also said: "The chain of command is presently being weakened by [Tengelmann] observations to lower level personnel that may impact on other components. Morale is therefore adversely affected. Consideration needs be given to avoiding organization indigestion with the result that little basic improvement is realized." His final note called for review of "Board responsibilities to minority shareowners." This report was clear evidence of board members' real concern about confusion growing in A&P and its impact on the company's future.

On Haub's instruction, Fritz Teelen was brought from Tengelmann in West Germany and elected vice-president of A&P, and president of the PLUS store Discount Foods, Inc., subsidiary. During 1979, PLUS opened 32 new discount stores. The annual report to shareholders covering 1979 described the PLUS store concept as a low-price, no frills approach which "has tremendous appeal during this time when rampant inflation continues to be the number one economic problem in the United States. The country's highest inflation level in 33 years stimulated price competition among food retailers throughout 1979, causing us to accelerate our strategic move into limited assortment stores. While the strategy of introducing PLUS stores in the U.S. has proven to be successful, the initial start up costs together with the time required to build volume and develop earnings had an adverse impact on overall profits. This affected our results in the last half of 1979 and will continue during 1980."

PLUS was an importation of a successful, bare-bones, German retail operation, the only concession to strict Germanic style was of course English labels and American products. Many millions of A&P dollars were spent in efforts to foist this formula upon customers. It proved to be a lot easier to set up these marketing standards in American stores than it was to get the American consumer to dance to the "Ump-Pah-Pah, German-Band" Music. One look at the sparse selection, the fruit and vegetables withering in unrefrigerated cartons, and the stark store atmosphere was enough to dissuade most consumers from further patronage. The PLUS store idea was ill-conceived and added nothing to the turnaround of A&P. It has quickly faded into oblivion.

The annual report to shareholders covering the year 1979 described the current multi-directional aims of A&P as "Diversification," the report said:

"An essential part of A&P strategy for the 80's will be to build on our capabilities in other segments of food distribution. Our expertise and experience in the supermarketing field has led to the development of four independently-operated subsidiaries. Each of these organizations has important growth potential during the next decade as each initiates programs appealing to the related but separate segments of the food distribution business." The four subsidiaries were:

Family Center, Inc., the combination store subsidiary which then operated twenty 55,000 square-foot stores in the Southern States, and which, after a prolonged start-up period, met with moderate success.

PLUS Discount Foods Inc. Describing the 32 stores opened in 1979, the report said: "This rapid growth is indicative of the strong customer attraction to these highly efficient, low-price operations. PLUS stores provide a remarkably flexible approach to modern food retailing. We believe the PLUS store concept has great potential in any viable market area." Time has proved this belief in PLUS potential was misplaced.

Compass Foods, Inc., formed to pursue opportunities in export and other outside sales of the company's extensive line of private label products. It serves companies in non-A&P domestic markets as well as overseas clients. Compass was started as a means of expanding production in A&P's underutilized manufacturing plants, but it continues long after those plants have been closed. The first receptive world market was the Middle East, where in the 1970's, A&P brand products with Arabic labelling soon became national brands. Compass, a dependable export supplier, has the ability to offer an almost limitless variety of consumer products, combined in a single delivery, to any world destination at competitively fair prices. While the present strength of the American dollar works against export growth, Compass is founded upon a sound independent principle and can continue to grow even independently of A&P.

Supermarket Systems, Inc., was founded in 1976 to oversee A&P's contract to manage food distribution services for Aramco, which had recruited many thousands of U.S. engineers, and their families into Saudia Arabia to assist in the development of the vast oil and gas reserves. Later the subsidiary was expanded to assist in improving food distribution systems throughout the world. Contracts were signed under which Systems agreed to develop, manage and supply supermarkets in Saudia Arabia under the ownership of Prince Talal, brother of King Fahad. The first such store was opened in 1982. Systems was progressing with extensive negotiations in the U.S.S.R. when, without ceremony, A&P's new chairman, in July 1980, withdrew from further pursuit of this project. Nineteen eighty was the year of President Carter's boycott of the Moscow Olympic games. On the surface, U.S.A.-U.S.S.R. feelings were tense. Therefore, it seemed possible that A&P's new German interests planned to pursue this venture directly from Europe, free of American-Russian tensions. It didn't work because, at that time, the U.S.S.R. was interested in the U.S.A. food distribution system because America's vast size, climatic differences and elaborate transportation systems more nearly paralleled problems facing the Soviets.

U.S.S.R.-Systems negotiations had proceeded for over a year, including discussions in Moscow and visits by their delegations to the U.S.A. Believing it totally improper to terminate these discussions by note, Systems management went back to Moscow to meet with Soviet representatives, and explain that A&P, faced with its present operating problems, did not feel it could adequately support a vast new undertaking at this time. The Soviets continued to express interest in the project, and the hope that A&P would continue to coordinate the undertaking. This is evidenced by the following letter dated August 21, 1980, addressed to Systems' management and A&P by J. Gvishiani, Deputy Chairman of the USSR State Council of Ministers for Science and Technology:

STATE COMMITTEE
OF USSR COUNCIL OF MINISTERS
FOR SCIENCE AND TECHNOLOGY

11, Gorky Street, Moscow

21st August. 1980

Dear Mr. Walsh:

This is to confirm our support of the Seminar sponsored by the State Committee for Science and Technology and the "A&P" Company to be held in Moscow on Food Processing, Storage and Distribution Systems, specifically in big industrial cities.

The meetings and discussions you have had this week at the Moscow City Council, the Ministry of Food of the USSR, the Ministry of Agriculture of the USSR and the "CENTROSOYUZ" Association indicate a definite interest on this subject matter among Soviet specialists.

It is our understanding that you would be main coordinator in charge of this Seminar on the American side and in the period to come before the Seminar takes place our staff will correspond with you on all organizational aspects.

To proceed with preparation for the Seminar the State Committee will send you within next week a list of specific topics to be included in the agenda. We shall take responsibility for an appropriate audience to participate and invite experts from the organizations concerned in Moscow and the Union Republics.

It is our feeling that such a Seminar could be a starting point for developing long-term cooperation beneficial to both sides and help find specific areas for joint effort.

My best regards.

Sincerely,

J. Gvishiani
Deputy Chairman

The USSR was fully aware of its serious and growing need to upgrade food processing, distribution and selling systems, and realized they were discussing a long term multi-billion dollar undertaking. They saw A&P as uniquely equipped to assist in this project due to its vast experience in all aspects of food and consumer goods, across America, in processing, storage, distribution, selling and administrative control. Systems thanked the U.S.S.R. delegation for the letter but expressed doubt A&P would change its mind. In August 1980, A&P's new management held to its position to curtail any further Systems expansion, and the Systems manager decided to underwrite the Moscow trip out of his own pocket and resign.

But to get back to our story, by late 1979 speculation was rampant in Montvale as to whether Scotty could endure much longer the clattering of Haub's lieutenants' heavy boots through the halls of A&P. Scotty was, and always will be, a free spirit. He was then in the fifth and final year of his contract, and although he never, through word or action, revealed any outward sign of dissatisfaction, those who knew and respected him believed there wasn't enough money in all of North America to get him to renew this contract. He had given five years of his life unstintingly to A&P. No doubt he hated to leave the job unfinished, and under different circumstances might have stayed on, but now it was time to leave, and he amicably advised Erivan Haub of his intention to resign at the termination of his contract, leaving Haub ample time to secure a replacement.

Reputations are often formed more by the events of mens' time than by their own contribution to those events. Many with lesser talents, and less effort, have comfortably ridden favorable waves to glamorous corporate success. For others the tides are not so favorable. Scotty's time can best be summarized by that ancient Chinese corporate proverb: "He who stands to get most credit for success, must also get most credit for lack thereof." The hardened crass financial community doesn't give a damn "how you played the game" or what the odds against you were; they ask only: "Did you win?" And all who cannot answer in the affirmative are bunched as losers. And Scotty was not about to risk losing, with someone else rolling his dice.

Is it possible to isolate a single cause for A&P's gigantic failures over the twenty-one years since George L. Hartford died and the Tea Company went public? Perhaps the failure of sales to keep pace with inflation was the primary reason for failure, but A&P's 1979 sales of $6.7 billion still represented the third largest chain in the U.S.A., and that ain't chopped liver. Lack of sales growth is a critical problem, but not *the* critical problem for A&P.

In 1958, A&P's expense rate of 12.56 percent of sales was far below the industry average of approximately 15.00 percent. Because of its dominant market share and higher per store volumes, the Tea Company enjoyed expense rate advantages on most fixed as well as some variable costs, such as advertising and store labor. A&P was also free of the debt-service cost carried by most of the industry's chains.

In the intervening period to 1979, the industry's expense rate increased 37 percent to 20.50 percent of sales, while A&P's expenses skyrocketed by 72 percent to 21.58 percent of sales. A&P's expense disadvantage now exceeded the entire 1 percent profit margin traditionally achieved by the industry.

Supermarkets' critical competition is in expense rate control more than in retail pricing. It is relatively easy to offer lower retail pricing when your cost of doing business is lower than the competition's. It is virtually impossible to earn a reasonable profit and enjoy a healthy sales growth when your costs are significantly higher than the competition's. The only exception to this rule can be found in those chains, mostly in more affluent areas, whose noticeably higher retail prices are offset by noticeably superior quality/service levels which balance the value equation in the eyes of the consumers.

Historically, the financial community has attributed A&P's decline to prolonged sales deterioration stemming from the failure of managements to follow population movements out of the big cities and into the suburbs and the sun-belt areas of America. In truth, A&P's deterioration can also be traced to management's failure to maintain effective cost controls. The higher costs resulting from this failure mandated the forfeiture of the noticeably "lower retail prices" which, over the years, had brought customers into A&P's smaller stores. Further, these higher costs, and resultant higher retails, were the primary cause of the generally dismal performance of those new, larger stores which A&P did open in the suburbs, and this dismal record of performance, in turn, discouraged more widespread, aggressive development, and thus further aggravated the company's decline.

Obviously, the primary focus must be on increased sales as the primary aid to "cost control," and at times a cost investment must precede the increased sales results; but when, after reasonable time and effort, sales results do not justify expense investments, management must choose between the pruning shears or the poor house. Since 1974, A&P had closed more than 2,000 low-volume unprofitable stores and increased its weekly store average to $83,000. It meant nothing because expenses were more out of line with the industry than ever before.

Managements of prominent German companies traditionally hold year-end news conferences. *The New York Times* reported a December 1979 conference in Mulheim an der Ruhr, West Germany. The *Times* headline read: "A&P German Owners Bullish." Referring to Erivan Haub, the man who bought what seemed to be the white elephant of American supermarket chains, the *Times* revealed Haub's current outlook: "It's not out of the woods yet, but we think that with our know-how and strength, we can bring it to long-term health once again." Haub was later quoted: "We don't want to sit on our investment like the previous owners, we have to make it work." He also said he had "utmost confidence" in Mr. Scott and would extend his contract when it expired in February (1980). *The Times* found Haub's statements of ownership participation newsworthy because, as they said: "there has been an apparent attempt to play down the German connection and Mr. Haub has refused all requests for interviews, remaining a mysterious absentee landlord."

Further evidence of Haub's dominance of A&P management is contained in a ponderous eight-page document printed on A&P's "Executive Offices" stationery, April 10, 1980, shortly before Scott's announced departure. The paper is titled: "Realignment of Management Organization." Following are two excerpts which explain that structural realignments are required to insure that all segments of the company "move efficiently in the same direction."

Article I began:

I. Concepts and Requirements to Be Met.
   A. The guiding principles of organization—as developed through the A&P/Tengelmann Coordination Committee with particular emphasis on strong policy and control systems.

   B. Corporate strategy—as developed through the A&P/ Tengelmann Coordination Committee, the Strategy Formulation Project, and in direct collaboration with Tengelmann representatives."

Article IV, "Organization Profile," discussing management, said:

> I. The Chairman and Chief Executive Officer, with the
> assistance of the Vice-Chairman [a Haub appointee and
> life-time friend], will manage the company. He will also
> have the advice and assistance of the Executive Vice
> President, Management Controls [another new Haub
> appointee imported from Germany], whose primary
> functions will be the overall monitoring and evaluation
> of progress in major programs and processes against
> established objectives, and giving direct assistance as
> required in implementation."

Haub apparently had been accustomed to exercising total control over all of his privately owned German enterprises, and it now
appeared as if his personal 45 percent stake in A&P bestowed the
singular right to dominate the widely held A&P Tea Company
without consultation with other shareholders.

It appeared increasingly evident that neither Scotty nor any
qualified, assertive American chief executive would long tolerate
this continued heavy-handed interference in management
operations.

The expected press release was dated April 29, 1980, it said:
"The Great Atlantic & Pacific Tea Company announced today that
Jonathan L. Scott, chairman of the board of directors and chief
executive officer since February 1, 1975, was leaving the company
to form a personal investment firm. James Wood, formerly chairman of the board and chief executive officer of the Grand Union
Company, has been elected chairman of the board of directors and
chief executive officer of A&P replacing Scott."

Thirteen

Terminating a Pension Plan Is Not a Capital Offense

To replace Scott, Haub had chosen an executive with a European background. An article in the Bergen *Record*, April 30, 1980, said: "Wood, a 50-year-old British subject who resides in Franklin Lakes, came to the United States and Grand Union after it was acquired by Cavenham Ltd., a British food conglomerate headed by international financier Sir James Goldsmith." During his six-year tenure at Grand Union, Wood was credited with acquiring two other supermarket chains and with raising sales from $1.5 billion with 531 stores to almost $3 billion with 840 stores. This impressive growth by acquisition now appears to have questionable long-term value to Grand Union, which has subsequently encountered serious profit problems and has been disposing of numbers of stores.

Over many years, Grand Union and A&P stores have been in direct competition in many markets, and over those years A&P always looked fondly upon Grand Union as one of the few competitors it could consistently best in most markets. One thing seemed sure, an infusion of Grand Union expertise would not bring any new marketing skills to the struggling A&P.

The business press normally monitors activities in major corporations for a period following changes in top management. *The Wall Street Journal* reported, in May 1980, A&P's announced plan to raise new capital through sales of an additional 12.5 million shares of stock, and the same article disclosed the sudden resignation of A&P's chief financial officer, commenting that "both moves reflect push by the Tengelmann Group."

The Journal, in the same article, described the fringe benefit's which Wood earlier said were the key attractions luring him to A&P. Wood "will receive phantom stock units whose number initially equal 10 percent of Tengelmann's shares after the rights offering. After April 1985, or earlier in certain circumstances, Wood may elect to be paid the value of all or part of the units credited to him. This will be done by Tengelmann rather than A&P." Here the real magnet is not A&P's lucrative contract but the phantom stock offer by Haub. The unit value will be the difference between $4 and the market price of a share on the cash-in date. This total package could be worth more than $20 million.

In due course, normal routines were again established at Montvale headquarters. In June 1980, Wood announced his first major move. Not surprisingly, A&P was scheduled to undergo still another reorganization. Under this restructuring the company was divided into ten geographic operating entities "directed toward achieving closer coordination and control." Wood's announcement included the customary line charts detailing the pecking order of who will report to whom. One would think that A&P's long record of costly unproductive realignments should have provided suffi- cient evidence to succeeding managements that while reorganiza- tion is still an acceptable first move after top level changes, it is no longer chic, because despite its high cost it is usually boringly unproductive.

The 1980 shareholders' meeting was held in Indianapolis, where Wood, addressing the stockholders for the first time, reported heavy losses in the first quarter 1980, and said he would be pleasantly surprised "if we broke into the black any time in the next two years, even for a quarter." At the same meeting Haub was reported to have shrugged off the sour earnings outlook by saying: "I never expected a meaningful return from A&P before five years."

If A&P's 1980 performance had been a motion picture, it would have been rated X as having absolutely no redeeming social value for the company, the shareholders or employees. Sales on a weekly basis were up 2.5 percent which could not be hailed as significant growth in a year of 9 percent inflation. Four successively poor quarters added up to a loss of $43 million. However, as we all know, a new management's first year poor results have come to be expected as the resolution of past management's unsolved problems. This is the "things must get worse before they get better" syndrome which almost guarantees marked improvement in second year results.

On the brighter side, Wood's 1980 message to shareholders stated that PLUS stores were showing promising signs of being successful, that 47 had been opened in Philadelphia and Baltimore, and a new division of PLUS stores would be opened in the current year in Chicago. Little else in the annual report could be considered encouraging.

Prior to his initial investment, and in even more meticulous detail since 1979, Haub's financial experts have carefully examined every monetary aspect of A&P. The board of directors systematically reviewed these charts, all of which seemed equally grim; all, that is, except for one chart which the board regularly reviewed and drooled over. The subject was not included on A&P's financial balance sheet and was not the property of the company, but A&P's board was responsible for the administration of the Employees' Retirement Plan, and under law had the fiduciary duty to administer this plan solely in the best interests of the plan members. This plan contained several hundred million dollars in potential termination overfunding.

Publicly, Haub appeared to be taking a hands-off posture regarding A&P management, but his appointed staff continued to exert dominant influence. An example is seen in the following memo sent to all officers down through department head levels on the subject of "Cars and Car Rentals":

The control of the expense statements has surfaced that we have to keep a much more critical look at the rental of cars and the excessive use of company cars.

If an employee intends to rent a car, he has to inform his superior who will sign afterwards his expense statement, about the fact. There might be ways to avoid to rent a car by using company cars at the specific place which, very often, are just parked the whole day and not used by employees who just need the cars to and from work. During the day, the cars may very well be used instead of renting a car.

Dated 10/29/80   Signed_____

Executive Vice-President, Management Controls

By the end of 1980, Mr. Wood completed assembly of his management team by recruiting two trusted assistants from the Grand Union Company into A&P's top management inner circle, one in finance and administration, the second in merchandising and sales. As the financial community once more turned its back and seemed to have given up on A&P as a lost cause, Mr. Haub continued quietly buying more shares, and by the end of February 1981, Tengelmann owned 50.3 percent of A&P's stock. Haub now held majority voting power over A&P.

Erivan Karl Haub's personal control over 50.3 percent of A&P's stock, and his power to vote that stock as he saw fit, gave him effective control over the selection and election of each and every member of A&P's board of directors. In this instance, one dominant shareholder can at his discretion negate the votes of all 31,110 other shareholders owning the total of 49.7 percent of A&P's remaining shares. Such absolute power to control boards of directors, to otherwise dominate management activities, and to influence market values of shares poses significant additional threats to the limited powers of minority shareholders in widely held, so-called "public" corporations such as the A&P Tea Company.

In keeping with his penchant for anonymity, Haub discreetly chose to sit with, but not become a member of, the board of directors of A&P. He did, however, effectively wield his power to elect each member of that board. The board he elected in 1981 included:

ROSEMARIE BAUMEISTER: Haub's assistant, confidant, and long-term Tengelmann official in Germany.

HELGA HAUB: Erivan's wife who, in the proxy statement, disclaimed any voting power over his shares of A&P's stock, or over other organizations which he controls.

ECKART SIESS: Boyhood friend of the Haub family, and recently elected Vice-Chairman of A&P.

FRITZ TEELEN: Chief of Haub's German PLUS Operation, brought to U.S.A. to run A&P's PLUS Operation, recently elected Senior Vice-President of A&P.

HENRY W. VAN BALLEN: Consultant of Haub's Tengelmann Group.

The annual shareholders' meeting was held in New Orleans on June 26, 1981. On that very same day, immediately following the shareholder meeting, Haub's newly elected board undertook as its first order of business a vital amendment to the A&P Employee Retirement Plan which would thereafter permit diversion of surplus assets from the plan trust to the exclusive benefit of the Tea Company and its shareholders. Having gained the 50.3 percent stock control earlier in 1981, Haub sat and nodded approvingly as the new board, at the earliest possible moment, sprang the trap eliminating the existing language in the official plan text which had promised plan members that all residual assets of the plan were for their sole benefit and could not be diverted to corporate uses.

For months prior to the June 26, 1981, board meeting, A&P's top command had been developing its strategic plan for the blitzkrieg upon the surplus in the Employees' Pension Plan. Initially two barriers existed blocking capture of pension trust assets by the management of A&P.

First: The Employee Retirement Insurance Security Act (ERISA) as enacted by Congress specifically forbids any diversion of any funds from any pension plan for any purposes other than the exclusive benefits of the plan members "during the life of" any pension plan. Further, the law requires that administrators of plans exercise their fiduciary duties solely in the best interest of the plan members. Thus, the law appears to have created a burglar-proof repository to protect and insure employee pension rights.

Managements, however, have found a glaring loop-hole in ERISA. Its back door has been left wide open by use of the words "during the life" of a plan. ERISA contains no provision prohibiting such diversion of residual assets after plan termination. Thus hundreds of American companies have crowded their way through this loop-hole and gained access to assets in their employees' pension trust by the simple expedient of terminating their pension plans completely. Here we have a tortured anomaly, under which the very law, intended by Congress to secure and protect the private pension plan system and the rights of its employees members, actually contravenes that Congressional intent and encourages the dismemberment of the system it was designed to perpetuate. And the Labor Department, the Internal Revenue

Service and the Pension Benefit Guaranty Corporation, Federal agencies responsible for the administration of pension law, stand by watching and approving the demise of the defined benefit private pension plan system. Members of Congress, aware of what's happening, and aware of the ultimate additional burden such plan terminations will add to the already troubled Social Security System, are looking into less volatile matters rather than tackling an issue so unpopular with many major PAC contributors, particularly in an election year.

A&P could easily circumvent the first barrier blocking access to the surplus funds in its employee retirement plan by following other major American corporations through the "termination loophole."

Second: A&P was faced with a more formidable additional barrier rarely encountered by other companies intent on seizing assets from employee pension plans. The A&P Retirement Plan Text, since 1973, contained a most rare and unusual provision that stated unequivocally that in the event of any plan termination, all the funds of the plan shall be used solely for the benefit of plan members and their beneficiaries.

This unique provision had been recognized as an effective barrier blocking management's access to the surplus funds in this plan. There also existed the untested legal question of whether such specific provision in the plan text constituted a contractual liability to members, and whether such provision could be amended unilaterally by the company, particularly as a first step, in a two-step scheme, to seize residual assets of the plan.

In any event, on June 26, 1981, Haub's management recommended, and the Board of Directors approved, an amendment changing the termination provision of the plan so that all residual assets thereafter would revert to the company in the event of termination.

Following that fateful June 1981 board meeting, it was decided to withhold information on this important change from the plan members. Thus, the apparently top secret scheme moved stealthily forward, culminating with an October board meeting at the Waldorf-Astoria Hotel in New York, and a high level final briefing with Haub in West Germany. Thereupon, the order "to execute the Plan" was given, and the formal invasion of the trust fund was announced to a stunned membership on October 16, 1981.

In sugar-coated terms, Mr. Wood's announcement disguised the primary purpose for the action, claiming it provided management an opportunity to offer members a better retirement benefit under a new form of plan. Believe it or not, the coarse word "termination" never appeared in this announcement. Instead Wood employed the more soothing terms: "The Company has announced a 'restructuring' of your pension plan," and "The Company will 'change the form' of its pension plan."

Later, Mr. Wood explained: "Your Company is making this change because it believes it can offer a better retirement benefit to most of its employees under the new form of plan and also because it wishes to make A&P a stronger and healthier company by use of excess funds now accumulated in the present plan."

The New York Times, on October 17, 1981, carried an article saying: "The Great Atlantic & Pacific Tea Company announced yesterday that it planned to close or sell unprofitable stores and manufacturing plants and would finance the ensuing write-off by drawing $200 million from an overfunded pension plan." A later comment, presumably not intended as whimsical, added: "An A&P spokesman said that the facilities to be disposed of were still under study with the objective of affecting the least number of employees."

A *Wall Street Journal* article on October 19, 1981, reported: "The Company also said that the $200 million from the company's pension fund will be offset by using the company's tax-loss carry forwards." This article also included an A&P comment that the cash from this fund, "along with the re-deployment of assets from the disposition of unprofitable facilities will provide the needed financial resources for the company's future expansion and operations."

On October 30, 1981, I, as plaintiff, filed Civil Action 81-3377 in the United States District Court, Newark, New Jersey, as a class action on behalf of all plan members to prevent A&P's seizure of assets from this pension trust fund. Thus, the issue was joined and A&P was barred, at least temporarily, from access to plan assets pending resolution of this suit.

At stake was the largest and single most important financial transaction in A&P's long history coming into direct conflict with plan members' rights to exclusive benefit from all funds in this pension trust. The precise amount of the surplus was never revealed to the court, but has always been expressed in vague numbers by A&P. This can be explained by the fact the total is subject to change with the vagaries of the investment markets, and the fund grows daily by income from those investments. As of early 1984, the surplus probably exceeded $375 million, and most estimate the amount will exceed $400 million when finally distributed.

To put this huge pension surplus into proper perspective, and to get a more accurate handle on its importance to A&P and the plan members, we should point out:

(a) The surplus, if distributed entirely to members, would more than double the meager annual benefits (averaging less than $2,000) now being received by members or beneficiaries.

(b) The surplus exceeds the total of all corporate contributions made to the plan since the company went public twenty-five years ago.

(c) The surplus exceeds the total of all other net profits reported by A&P in that same twenty-five years since 1959.

(d) The surplus exceeds total stockholders' net equity in A&P in 1984, adjusted for the $130 million extraordinary credit covering prepaid pension expenses, which is, in fact, part of the surplus.

Mr. Haub's 51 percent share of this pension surplus would exceed his total investment in A&P stock to date. Effectively, funds from this employee pension plan shall have underwritten his purchase of control of A&P. Ironically, the 1973 amendment allocating the plan's residual assets to members, was intended precisely to prevent such possible action by a corporate raider, and to assure the exclusive benefit of all plan funds to members and their beneficiaries.

A&P was not surprised that members instituted a class action to prevent such diversion of plan assets. Probably, management wanted such an action filed so that after court approbation of a modest pre-trial settlement with plan members, individual members of the board of directors would be relieved of any potential personal liability for malfeasance before the actual termination and diversion took place. Also, any such court-approved settlement would permit diversion of enormous sums to which the company had no other access. And, even if the suit went to trial and A&P lost, and no post-trial settlement was later reached, the company would have lost nothing it now possessed.

The official A&P position on this surplus diversion was best described in the sworn affidavit, dated June 14, 1982, submitted by Mr. Wood to the Federal District Court outlining the background and reasons for the decision to terminate the plan.

In paragraph (6) of that affidavit, Mr. Wood explains that write-offs required to effectuate A&P's revitalization program would have brought the company close to a default position under its outstanding loan agreements with creditors. Apparently a $200 million write-off, without any asset offset, would have left A&P at or below the minimum asset requirements of its loan agreements. However, this unhappy contingency had been averted without need for any surplus infusion when Deloitte Haskins & Sells approved the establishment of an extraordinary credit of $130 million as a prepaid pension expense which represented gains from the 1981 purchase of annuities covering all service credits, at rates far more favorable than the previous rate assumptions in the plan.

This $130 million paper asset removed the threat of technical default on provisions in long-term loan agreements, and since facility closing programs, with liquidation of inventories and sales of other assets, tend to improve cash positions, there was little subsequent likelihood of bankruptcy from other sources.

In paragraph (14) of this same affidavit, Wood describes the steps A&P's Board took to insure that the company would receive the entire surplus upon plan termination. He states: "This was accomplished on June 26, 1981, when Section 11.4 was changed to provide for the allocation of any residual (or excess) assets to the Company." Continuing with what appears to be a non-sequitur describing the mind-set of the board, he adds: "At that point, however, it was still hoped that the Company's bleak financial picture might somehow improve, and it was decided by our directors to defer the matter of whether to terminate the Plan."

With respect to the above referenced 1981 amendment, the simple admission of need to amend Section 11.4 to insure all surplus reversion to A&P is itself admission of a previously conflicting provision in the plan text. Further, while it is normal and expected that the directors "still hoped that the Company's bleak financial picture might somehow improve," one wonders whether this decision to defer termination was also intended to help portray this "amendment" and closely followed "termination" decisions as independent actions rather than two necessary and related steps in a single planned action.

In paragraph (18) of his June 1982 affidavit, Mr. Wood, at last, bluntly summarizes A&P's reason for termination, saying: "In sum, prompt access to the surplus funds in the plan is the only reason for any Plan termination." This testament starkly contradicts the explanation given members in the letter of October 16, 1981, announcing a "restructuring" of the Pension Plan. In that letter, Mr. Wood announced as first reason for the "restructuring": "Your Company is making this change because it believes it can offer a better retirement benefit to most of its employees under the new form of plan", and adding, as second reason, the wish to make the company healthier by use of excess funds then in the plan.

Thus, by October 1981, the die was cast. A&P had announced the termination of the plan to divert all surplus assets to corporate uses, and plan members had instituted a class action to prevent that diversion.

Fourteen

Anatomy of a Class Action

Prior to initiating legal action on behalf of all plan members, this author and his wife carefully reviewed every logical reason why they should not get directly involved in such activity. First, there was an abiding respect and gratitude toward A&P which had provided thirty-six years of prosperous employment, and was the sole source of income for our family.

Second, we had just recently retired on friendly terms with the company, and the almost inevitable consequence of such legal action would be accusations of bitterness and betrayal by a management with whom we had no other personal quarrel; perhaps also we would encounter complaints and dissatisfaction on the part of plan members who had different ideas on the resolution of the pension issue.

Third, we knew this was not a frivolous action and, once undertaken, would require diligent pursuit and high priority allocation of our time over at least several years.

Fourth, in addition to time demands, there was an incalculable personal expense certain to be incurred. Any plaintiff is just another "member of the class," and can receive no reimbursement other than his proportionate share of any increased benefit which all members may gain as result of the class action.

Fifth, such visibly overt, anti-corporate action would permanently muddy the reputation of the plaintiff and become a serious handicap should he ever desire, or need, to return to employment in the food industry. Finally, there was the ever-present possibility that it "might all be for naught," that after all the struggle and controversy the case could be lost.

On the other side of the equation stood the personal conviction that this A&P action was both morally and legally wrong, that A&P possibly was contriving an "impending threat of bankruptcy" as a plausible excuse to divert pension trust funds to which they had no proven right, nor any over-riding need. Also, there was the knowledge that most of the thousands of retired plan members were subsisting on sub-poverty level pension benefits of less than $1,800 per year after an average of over thirty years of loyal service to A&P. Next, there was the demonstration of raw selfishness on the part of a board which, despite knowledge of a bulging surplus in recent years, had steadfastly refused to increase benefits to offset the ravages of inflation on retirement benefits; and a board which was now determined to seize this entire trust surplus without sharing a dime with the plan members in whose name those funds were invested. Finally, there was the inevitable realization that no one had less excuse than I to duck the issue.

The critical legal issue was "ownership" of pension funds, specifically that of "ownership" of surplus assets. In recent years interest rate income has exceeded the rate assumptions applied to the plan. This generates termination surplus when annuities are finally purchased, upon plan termination, at prevailing interest rates much higher than previously estimated.

Specifically, in the A&P plan massive surpluses had also been created by the transference of thousands of plan members to various union pension plans without similar transference of their accrued credits. Finally, additional massive surpluses resulted from the various major A&P closing programs since 1975, under which thousands of then non-vested members were terminated and their accrued credits reverted to surpluses in the plan.

This plaintiff, petitioning the court on a pro-se basis, argued vigorously but in vain that such massive closings constituted "partial terminations" under the definitions of ERISA; and, consequently, those many non-vested members terminated were entitled to termination vesting and payment of then earned benefits as well as proportionate benefit increases to those proposed in the "settlement" for other members.

On the "ownership" issue, Chairman of the House Select Committee on Aging, Rep. Edward R. Roybal, of California, has labelled reversions of assets to corporations through termination of pension plans "pension piracy." Calling the Labor Department's policy on terminations "deficient," Roybal continued: "By drawing a sharp distinction between actions taken with regard to ongoing plans and those taken with regard to terminated ones, the Department has created the impression that actions by corporate officials that it would not tolerate under ERISA, in the case of ongoing plans, are legitimate and tolerable in the case of terminated plans. It should be apparent that if such a distinction is maintained, it will constitute an open invitation to plan sponsors, or their officials, to use terminations as a device to circumvent ERISA's fiduciary standards whenever it is convenient for them to do so."

Roger Thomas, counsel to this Committee, said: "ERISA states that the assets of the plan shall never inure to the benefit of any employer.... Even a village idiot can see that a lot of corporations are making a mockery of that law, turning the assets to the benefit of employers."

Pension & Investment Age magazine, which typically does not depend on the average plan member for circulation income, has covered this issue more thoroughly perhaps than any publication in the United States. In an article dated October 31, 1983, on the subject of ownership of the more than one trillion dollars presently invested in pension trusts, the author Nancy Webman writes: "Historically, discussion of pension asset ownership has often come down to an analysis of who bears the risk of those assets. Until recently the most popular conclusion was that the corporation owns the assets because the corporation bears the risks, that is, the corporation must make up any shortfall between the amount of assets and the promised benefits. Now, another conclusion is surfacing almost as often: the employee at least shares the risk, and therefore should at least share the ownership and control, because employees bear the inflation risk or the interest rate risk. That means that accelerating inflation has reduced the real values of the contracted pension obligation, so employees risk receiving less money unless they receive cost of living adjustments."

Corporations argue vehemently that they must not be held accountable for an inflation over which they have no control, then are faced with great difficulty defending the alternative position that somehow they alone are entitled to all benefits which spring from that very same inflation over which they had no control. Most private defined benefit plans provide no built-in cost of living provisions, but that does not alter corporate managers' "heads we win, tails employees lose" attitudes regarding inflationary impact on plans, and corporations' sole rights to assets generated by an inflation.

No doubt, strong moral and legal arguments can be made on behalf of members' claim to ownership of pension assets. An example is seen in the resolution of an ownership dispute involving plan members of the *Washington Star* newspaper after its new owner Time Inc. closed the paper and terminated its pension plan expecting to divert surplus assets to corporate uses.

It so happened, the *Washington Star* had two pension plans. One covered Newspaper Guild Employees and was administered jointly by management and union representatives. The other plan covered non-Guild employees and was administered solely by management. A dispute arose over "surplus ownership" between management and the employees of both plans.

In accordance with specific provisions in the text of the Guild Members' plan, the dispute over ownership was required to be decided in binding arbitration. Professor Walter Gelhorn, of Columbia University Law School, one of America's most distinguished legal authorities, was agreed upon by both sides as arbitrator. *Pension & Investment Age*, on December 26, 1983, reported Professor Gelhorn's decision.

His opinion explained: "The pension program was structured not to produce the possibility of monetary refund to the *Star*, but to produce assurance of retirement pay for the *Star's* qualified employees." Continuing, he added: "The pension fund's trustees did not seek advantageous investment opportunities in order to create a bit of extra cash for the *Star's* ultimate use; they did so for the sake of the Plan's beneficiaries. To impose on the fund's trustees an obligation to disburse money, not to the beneficiaries whose interests the trustees have guarded, but to the corporate employer.... would be a distortion of benefit design. As a result, any excess assets created by actuarial miscalculation should be used to further the Plan's basic purpose—the well being of pensioners." In keeping with this ruling, Guild members received all excess assets in the plan.

Meanwhile, in a class action brought by the non-Guild members of the *Washington Star* over the parallel issue of surplus in their plan, both the District Court and the Court of Appeals ruled in favor of management's right to divert surplus assets from that terminated plan. Addressing a Senate labor sub-committee, Robert A.G. Monks, then recently appointed by President Reagan as U.S. Pension Administrator, said of the courts' approval of a last-minute amendment by management to reverse a provision in the plan trust agreement which awarded surplus to plan members: "Every fiber in my body says that was an inequitable result." Without preventive legislation, the defined benefit pension plan may become an extinct species in the private sector.

Rather than further disrupt this historical narrative, we shall limit digression on the general issue of ownership and get on with the specifics of this class action and its importance to A&P.

As 1981 came to a close, A&P and the members of the retirement plan were locked in a struggle over ownership of surplus in that pension plan. The class was represented by Shea & Gould, New York, and Kalb, Friedman, Siegelbaum, New Jersey, as co-counsel.

A&P, through counsel, alleged the substitute savings plan was better for most employees, that the company needed the plan surplus for corporate survival, and that diversion of such surplus after termination was not in violation of law. The complaint of the class charged that the company had no moral or legal right to any plan funds upon termination because specific provisions in the plan text explicitly stated that in the event of any termination, all the funds of the plan shall be used solely for the benefit of members and their beneficiaries upon plan termination.

Within two months after the initiation of the class action, it appeared evident that A&P was becoming anxious to come to a settlement before trial. By mid-December, the plaintiff advised class counsel, based upon leaks emanating from A&P's corporate headquarters, that the company was prepared to offer $50 million of the surplus for the purchase of additional annuities with which to provide increased benefits to members as an out-of-court settlement of this action. At that juncture, the class counsel and plaintiff both agreed such proposal, if in fact offered, should be rejected as inadequate.

At their first meeting, class counsel and this plaintiff discussed goals and objectives. Before accepting the case on a contingency fee basis, counsel asked the plaintiff: "What do you want out of this?" Plaintiff replied he sought equity and justice for plan members, emphasizing that he particularly did not want to be party to any compromise involving a sellout of principle such as a settlement arrangement in an amount sufficient only to claim token victory and justify payment of substantial legal fees. Plaintiff acknowledged there would be no reimbursement for his personal time and efforts on behalf of this case, and he assured counsel he wanted no such reimbursement. On the matter of specific goals, plaintiff asserted his personal belief that: "nothing less than a 50 percent share of total plan surplus could be considered an equitable settlement to members in light of the stated provisions in the plan text." Counsel advised that such action was unlikely to ever come to trial, and that if the surplus totalled $200 million, $100 million was a reasonable objective for the class.

Plaintiff, as sole named representative of the class, readily accepted counsel's statement that in class actions the best interest of the total class must take precedence over the personal views of any member, or groups of members, including the named plaintiffs. Therefore, it would be highly improper to hold out stubbornly for some personal higher goal when such position might deprive the entire class of the opportunity to consider acceptance of a lesser settlement which they, in fact, might find unobjectionable and satisfactory.

At subsequent meetings, discussions ensued to reach agreement on the minimum settlement terms that might be deemed worthy, in light of the merits of our legal position, to warrant presentation to the entire class for consideration. Both plaintiff and counsel then agreed that any acceptable settlement offer should be expressed in terms of a percentage increase over current retirement benefits, since that was a measurable yardstick for individual members who would have no way of calculating what benefits would accrue to them from any lump sum settlement figure regardless of amount.

After considerable discussion, it was agreed to target a 20 percent increase in present member benefits as the minimum settlement acceptable for presentation to the class. While accepting this compromise, plaintiff repeated his strong personal feelings that an acceptable settlement must involve no less than half of the surplus, and reserved the right to campaign against acceptance of the 20 percent figure if it involved substantially less than 50 percent of the surplus.

At this stage no meaningful actuarial data was available to the Class counsel. A&P had announced the surplus as being approximately $200 million but had refused to certify a specific amount or provide actuarial data to enable the class to calculate what shares of surplus would be required to provide various percentage increases to members. Based upon flimsy actuarial advice then available, it was estimated a 20 percent increase in member benefits might cost between $80 and $100 million which would represent between 40 percent to 50 percent share of the announced surplus.

From January through March 1982, formal negotiations toward settlement were carried on by class counsel and A&P's attorneys. Plaintiff did not partake directly in these negotiations but was kept advised by class counsel as A&P's offers, starting with $10 million, increased rather quickly to $25, $40 and finally to the $50 million figure which plaintiff reported had been bandied around the halls of corporate headquarters in December 1981.

With each passing week, plaintiff grew more concerned that class counsel was attempting to hedge and lower the previously agreed upon minimum compromise settlement. More frequently counsel expressed concern about frailties in our legal position, and concern for A&P's counsel's warning that the company was on the brink of bankruptcy.

Plaintiff argued that the cry of "imminent bankruptcy" was a contrived threat which would impress lawyers more than analyzers of balance sheets, and if indeed such threat did exist it would work to the advantage of those negotiating on behalf of the class, because, by means of a prompt settlement for half of the alleged $200 million surplus, A&P's Board could avert any potential bankruptcy other than one intentionally contrived. While the discussions sometimes grew more heated, the plaintiff was repeatedly assured by counsel that no settlement would be agreed upon without his compliance.

Class counsel's most serious concern centered around A&P's threat to file a Motion for Summary Judgment asking the Court to dismiss the Class Complaint. Plaintiff was repeatedly advised of the possibility of such motion being filed but was given no logical reason to believe such motion could carry if filed. Further, if A&P

had confidence in such a motion, they would not merely threaten but proceed to file it, and thus save further court costs and settlement expense.

By the end of March 1982, negotiations between attorneys for both sides had apparently reached an impasse at the $50 million level. More accurate actuarial data, then available, suggested the 20 percent guaranteed increase could be purchased for somewhere between $60 and $75 million. However, class counsel stated that A&P was holding to $50 million as a "final offer" and recommended plaintiff agree to a settlement in this amount. Plaintiff, again contrary to his personal assessment of equity, agreed to submit a proposal to the class under which members would be guaranteed the greater of a 20 percent increase or the sum of $60 million, provided that A&P also agreed to pay all class counsel legal fees outside the settlement.

A&P responded by agreeing to the payment of legal fees outside the settlement but refused to budge off the $50 million sum previously offered. Class counsel urged plaintiff to now accept these terms explaining that $50 million represented an enormous settlement for which all concerned should be pleased. Plaintiff argued that $50 million represented less than 20 percent of the more than $250 million surplus which A&P now admitted was in the plan; that $50 million was quickly diluted when divided over 30,000 recipients; and finally, that the offer as stated provided no guaranteed percentage increase to members, nor did it provide for members to receive income earned on the settlement amount between the time of acceptance and the eventual distribution of increased benefits. Plaintiff, in short, refused to agree to the settlement proposed.

Following their own best judgment, class counsel accepted A&P's terms in a co-signed settlement memo dated April 1, 1982, without the compliance of plaintiff. Both counsel presented these terms to the District Court on April 2, 1982, as the basis of settlement of the class action.

A&P's press release of April 5, 1982, announcing the settlement came as a shock to the plaintiff and those members with whom he had been in constant contact and who shared his position on settlement terms. After expressing his shock and displeasure to class counsel, he immediately contacted *The New York Times* and *Wall Street Journal* to disavow the settlement reported in A&P's press release.

At a meeting on April 8, 1982, counsel assuaged the plaintiff by advising that the announced terms were not necessarily final but that by acceptance of these terms the class had now reached a "plateau" from which A&P could not retreat, and from whence we could now proceed upward in final negotiations. Numerous meetings were held during the next five weeks during which much was proposed but nothing changed. Finally, on May 19, 1982, class counsel advised that the District Court was expressing impatience and was anxious to move ahead with the case, and that A&P counsel was accusing the class counsel of reneging on a previous agreement. As frosting on the cake, he stated that A&P was threatening to have this plaintiff de-certified and removed from the case if his resistance and delay continued. After asserting that the present offer was the best we could expect to achieve, counsel urged plaintiff to agree to its acceptance.

Plaintiff responded that he felt the offer to be grossly unfair and he would not agree to it. He suggested that counsel follow their own judgments and proceed without compliance of this plaintiff if they felt so impelled. Counsel responded, stating their intention to proceed with the settlement process, and the plaintiff restated his intention to attempt to abort what he considered to be a grossly inequitable settlement. At that point the relationship between class counsel and the sole named plaintiff representing some 30,000 class members was severed, and no substitute class representatives were later named.

After class counsel had accepted A&P's settlement offer, a large body of the membership opposed to these settlement terms were effectively left without benefit of counsel to advocate their cause before the court. Further, the court had set July 9, 1982, as the date for the final hearing, which provided members their last opportunity to present opposing viewpoints.

On June 10, 1982, the plaintiff, acting pro-se without counsel, filed a motion to dismiss class counsel. The court promptly dismissed this motion but did approve a second plaintiff motion requesting a stay of the final hearing date, and the court set

September 21, 1982, as the new date for the hearing. This would provide more time for members to study and discuss the proposal, and provide dissenting members opportunity to attempt to hire substitute counsel to represent their views.

During this interval the court received approximately one thousand letters from plan members almost unanimously expressing objection to the proposed settlement. The plaintiff received several thousand letters and/or phone calls from members and beneficiaries across the country deploring the settlement as unfair and reasserting their belief that the company had no right whatsoever to any pension funds.

Convinced that these several thousand objectors represented an even much larger body of dissent, plaintiff and an ad hoc committee of members set out to attempt to engage substitute counsel. Meetings were held with a number of prominent law firms including such as Paul, Weiss Rifkind, New York, and Wolf-Block-Shaw in Philadelphia. These meetings followed a similar pattern. After review of case details to date, the firms usually expressed regret at not having been brought into the case initially, and there was general sympathy to the viewpoint that the proposed settlement seemed hastily reached and might well have been improved upon, both on the merits and on the belief that a defendant who so quickly offers $50 million would likely go higher to avoid a jury trial, particularly in light of the huge sum at issue.

Those larger firms with pension expertise on staff, and readily qualified to enter the case, foresaw legal costs quickly mounting into the high six figures. They also expected great difficulty in obtaining the court's certification as class representatives, which certification would be necessary to assure reimbursement of their fees out of surplus and thus enable them to take the case on a contingency fee basis.

When the matter of legal fee payment assurance was discussed, the plaintiff made it clear that he could not possibly underwrite such prodigious legal fees, nor would he guarantee their payment through voluntary contribution from plan members because he refused to become party to committing members, presently subsisting on poverty level benefits, to payment of such a bottomless pit of financial obligations. The discussions with major law firms ended at this point. A number of smaller firms, fascinated by the scope of the case, appeared genuinely eager to enter the case leaving fee reimbursement at risk, but after reflection all wisely begged off because they realized they were lacking pension expertise and were understaffed to handle a case of this magnitude, particularly on short notice.

Thus, after weeks of futile search, having spent most of the stay period in failed efforts to engage qualified counsel for this dissenting sub-class of members, the plaintiff found himself confronted with an enigma. Despite all the pontification from the bench about each member's right to engage counsel of his choice, the fact was that, in the brutally cold economics of today's legal world, these thousands of disorganized retirees scattered across the nation were effectively denied qualified counsel to advocate their position in court.

Given these circumstances, and with time running out, the plaintiff's only viable alternative was to attempt to carry on the advocacy of dissent in opposition to both A&P's attorneys and the class counsel.

As the records of this case suggest, class action can sometimes result in serious diminution of individual rights to due process. Class actions seldom go to trial because defendants tend to seek settlement in order to moderate legal costs and eliminate risks of huge jury awards. Valid voices of the class, commenting on settlement equity, are sometimes muffled and made subordinate to the fallible judgments of class counsels, upon whom the court places higher credibility. Some class action attorneys who pride themselves as litigating gladiators should more properly be classified as novice negotiators, since they are often easily duped by their basic ignorance of the defendant's business, and by their inability to correctly evaluate the economic worth of the business proposition which every settlement represents.

Courts, which sometimes callously dismiss the right of every individual member to adequate notice of class proceedings, and courts which, by precedent, routinely subordinate class judgment to counsel judgment regarding settlement equity, should remember they exist only to protect the rights of individuals, even those who have been herded wittingly or unwittingly into a class. Further, the law should insist that potential class counsel, in their frenzy to be hired, must stop salivating long enough to spell out the rules of the game, and advise class representatives of the rights which they, and all class members, are about to surrender to these solicitous solicitors. As matters now stand, a suspected felon is guaranteed more individual protection under the law than some class members.

While we agree that settlement is usually the most desirable and sensible resolution to controversy, we must remember that settlement merely for the sake of settlement does not necessarily serve justice. The misuse of settlement as a device to obtain court approbation for an illicit transaction can itself become an illicit transaction.

Getting back to the specifics at hand, the critical issue to be resolved in litigation was whether or not A&P had the legal right to amend, just prior to plan termination, the provision in the plan text dating from 1973 which stated that in the event of termination: "all the funds of the Plan shall be used solely for the benefit of Members and their beneficiaries...." Neither party disagreed that all residual assets would accrue to members had the plan been terminated with the above language intact. A&P's last-minute amendment on June 26, 1981, attests to this fact.

The plaintiff argued that A&P had freely, and without duress, placed this lucid statement into the official plan text for members to read and rely upon. He further argued that the company had no legal right to unilaterally withdraw or amend such commitment because, once freely entered into, it had become a part of the "work agreement" under which members served, and it had become a "liability" of the plan to its members. Further, both the rules of ERISA and the words of this plan text prohibit any amendment made to the plan for diverting funds for any use other than the exclusive benefit of members prior to the satisfaction of *all liabilities* to such members. Therefore, since the company had no right to amend the 1973 provision, it had no right to divert any surplus from the plan upon termination.

The District Court recognized that resolution of the amendability of the 1973 provision was the critical legal issue which might be resolved based upon the interpretation of the word "liabilities." While the court did not speculate whether this interpretation would be that of paid pension consultant affidavits or that of a jury of twelve, the court did note that "this multitude of complex legal and factual issues make inevitable lengthy and expensive litigation, indeed, given the many issues of first impression, the parties would face not only an appeal to the court of appeals but, as well, a likelihood of Supreme Court review."

The plaintiff was utterly amazed by the sworn affidavit which Bill Kane, former C.E.O., submitted to the court in 1982 in support of A&P's actions. In this affidavit, Kane for the first time publicly stated that the 1973 amendment (awarding residual assets to members) was inserted into the plan only as "shark repellant" to ward off unfriendly corporate raiders by making plan surplus appear inaccessible to them.

This plaintiff, who as a member of A&P's board of directors, voted approval of this amendment in 1973, had never earlier been apprised by Kane, or anyone else, that such ulterior motive (shark repellant) was the sole purpose of the amendment. I, and other board members with whom I have since discussed the matter, approved the amendment language on its face as codification of a similar promise made to members in the plan summary booklets since 1960. I believed, then and now, that the board approved this 1973 amendment to insure that all plan assets would remain safe for members at all times, which, of course, had the ancillary effect of keeping plan funds out of reach of friendly or unfriendly raiders from outside or inside A&P.

That A&P board also carried the fiduciary duty to administer the retirement plan solely in the best interest of members. Mr. Kane and the balance of the board approved the amended text language into the plan text without comment, explanation, or reservation. Had that board intentionally voted to mislead members while secretly planning to employ pension assets as shark repellant against unfriendly raiders, and as a lure to raiders friendly to management, such action would have constituted a grave breach of fiduciary responsibilities and a cruel and savage hoax upon plan members. Plaintiff argued that it would be a tragic irony if this friendly raider (Haub) should benefit now from A&P's shameful action in 1973.

At the September 21, 1982, final hearing, and for almost five months thereafter, plaintiff continued arguments against court approval of the proposed settlement, first, on the grounds that A&P had no right to amend the 1973 provision awarding all surplus termination assets to plan members, and, therefore, A&P had no right to divert any funds from the plan under any circumstance.

Second, plaintiff argued against approval on the grounds that the class in this action was not cohesively constituted, since unknown thousands of its members had never received adequate court "notice" of this action, and had been specifically excluded from sharing in the proposed settlement.

By court- and counsel-approved definition, this "class" included "all former Members of the Plan." Nevertheless, thousands of "former Members" were knowingly denied court-signed "Notice" of this action by first-class mail. Further, had any of these denied members (scattered across the entire United States) perchance stumbled across the court-signed "Notices" published only in *The New York Times* and the eastern edition of *The Wall Street Journal*, they would have been misinformed by the court.

This abused class comprised those thousands of members discharged as result of A&P's massive closing programs since 1975 whose individual terminations took place prior to their reaching age 32 and their completion of ten years of service. Upon being terminated, they were advised by A&P that they had no future rights under the plan, since they had not completed vesting requirement under the plan. They were not advised that under the rules of ERISA, plant or office closings, and closings of all operations throughout an entire marketing area, might be deemed to constitute "partial terminations" of the retirement plan. Further, ERISA stipulates that under either "complete" or "partial" termination of a plan, all members become "vested" by that act of termination and all are entitled to service benefits earned to that date of termination as well as any other termination benefits provided by the plan text.

Plaintiff argued that the rights of these individuals to due process were being flagrantly denied because they were being "bound" by the result of a class action which excluded them from benefits without adequate legal "Notice" of that action, and without being advised of their potential rights under the rules of "partial termination."

Plaintiff also argued that many of these massive closings of plants, and the termination of all operations throughout vast marketing areas such as Pittsburgh, Dallas, Houston, Cleveland, Kansas City, Buffalo and many others took place *before* A&P's amendment of the plan provision awarding termination assets to members. Therefore, covered "partial terminees" were entitled not only to their service benefit earned to the date of termination, but also their proportionate share of the entire surplus as proscribed by the text then governing the plan.

Counsel for both A&P and the class continued their arguments for approval of the proposed settlement on the grounds that it was fair, reasonable and equitable. They argued against upsetting the proposal because of plaintiff's "amendability" or "partial termination" arguments, and suggested plaintiff was merely employing tactics to delay the court's decision, and that this delay was against the best interest of many members.

These counsel prevailed, and on February 9, 1983, the court in a 46-page opinion approved the proposed settlement, concluding that litigation of the case would be long and costly, and even if the class prevailed and litigation determined A&P had no right to divert any assets from the plan, there was little likelihood that the class could force A&P to terminate the plan and distribute the surplus funds to members.

This court conclusion leads one to believe that the class case would have been stronger had class counsel not filed the action in October 1981 immediately following the announcement of the company's intention to terminate the plan on December 31, 1981, but had waited until after actual termination to file.

Obviously, the text bestowed had no power upon the membership to terminate the plan, and A&P had repeatedly warned the court and members that they would not terminate the plan if this settlement were rejected, or if later the class prevailed in litigation. Legally, there was little or any doubt that A&P had the right to continue the plan if they so chose.

To the plaintiff's dismay, the court took this A&P threat as gospel, dismissing his arguments that while A&P held this power legally, the threat itself was ludicrous for many reasons.

First: A&P held sole power to terminate all along. Here they had demonstrated an eagerness to forego over $50 million in cash because continuance of the plan was not a feasible option in their best interest.

Second: A&P's board was wily enough to understand the old "bird-in-the-hand" theory to which the court paid little heed. They knew a cash settlement for even half the surplus had far greater present value, and was far more desirable, than any possible recoupment of total surplus by attrition over the next thirty years, during which time any number of contingencies could arise to make recoupment impossible.

Third: The company realized any such recoupment of surplus was unrealistic because:

(a) Approximately 80 percent of plan members had been severed and were no longer accruing benefit costs.

(b) This huge surplus had been secured and locked in place through purchase of annuities at most favorable rates covering all members' service benefits earned through December 31, 1981.

(c) Despite no A&P cash contribution since 1980, the surplus had multiplied greatly by 1983, and it would continue to multiply because even under normal interest rate assumptions the annual income from the surplus would far exceed future annual funding costs for the relatively small number of members still actively accruing credits.

Fourth: The company realized that had the class prevailed in litigation, the company's ability to liquidate surplus through the sale, merger or consolidation of this plan with other plans would be blocked because ERISA prohibits any such transaction which would reduce benefits members would have been entitled to receive had their plan terminated immediately prior to any such merger, sale or consolidation.

In view of the above circumstances, the plaintiff and many members concluded that only a believer in the "tooth fairy" would put credence in A&P's threat to continue the plan in effect rather than increase the settlement offer.

Neither can the members understand how, because of this A&P threat, and despite the acknowledged uncertainty of resolution of the critical legal "amendability" issue, and the most serious questions regarding the denial of due process to thousands of former plan members, the court, in its wisdom, could possibly grant A&P the right to divert over $275 million from this trust and, at the same time, consider the distribution of $50 million to 30,000 members a fair and equitable resolution.

Members had initially filed action, not to secure a 15 percent share of the surplus but to prevent A&P's diversion of funds from the plan. Here we have a situation where justice hangs twisting in the wind, where the court held for the settlement approving A&P's diversion of over $275 million, not on the merits of proportionate equity in relation to the amount of surplus at issue, not on resolution of the critical legal issue, but obviously because the court considered its only choice to be between this settlement or no settlement. Under the influence of such reasoning, either a $5 million settlement or a $100 million settlement would have been considered fair, reasonable, and equitable had either been proposed by both counsel in place of the $50 million. In essence, the court held that the power to terminate is the license to seize pension assets. Such precedence jeopardizes the future of the defined benefit pension plan in the private sector.

Those many members who considered this a seriously flawed decision soon discovered they had no "class" right to appeal because class counsel had encouraged the settlement approval and refused to undertake any such appeal. In effect, the class had been dissolved by the court opinion, and any appeal would have to be undertaken singularly. The plaintiff, partially supported by contributions from approximately one thousand dissenting members, was successful in engaging an excellent New Jersey law firm to undertake the appeal to the Third Circuit. This firm, Williamson & Rehill of Newark, accepted the case on the basis of the modest contributions raised. They took the case on obvious short notice and considerable personal inconvenience and sacrifice of time and expense.

This appellant counsel advised from the onset how slim were the chances of overturning a court-approved class settlement sponsored by both counsel for the defendants and the class. However, plaintiff, holding to the belief, shared by many, that justice had not been well served, felt impelled to go this last mile in pursuit of more equitable resolution for the class.

The Appeals court on December 29, 1983, affirmed the opinion of the lower court, stating that its review did not re-appraise the merits or possible outcome of litigation but looked only for abuse of discretion on the part of the lower court. The Appeals court opinion added, moreover: "Great weight is accorded the views of the trial judge... he is exposed to the litigants... he is on the firing line and can evaluate the action accordingly."

To wrap things up, both counsels' agreement upon the settlement, and the District Court's approval of that settlement, were deemed to have been honest judgment calls by qualified legal authorities. In such circumstance the chances of reversal are as slim as reversing yesterdays' called strike by an umpire—even if it was a bad call. Tragically, the critical question of ownership remained untested, and we shall never truly know whether A&P is graciously sharing newfound wealth with old employees, or whether plan members were taken for over $275 million.

Considering the frequency with which our Supreme Court is badly split on decisions on which we would expect only one correct judgment, we must not expect perfection from the lesser courts, whose function, we find, is not dispensing pure justice, but attempting to interpret correctly our less than perfect existing code of law as it applies to an individual case.

Derek C. Bok, president of Harvard University, in a 1983 report to the Board of Overseers, criticized the American legal system as the "most expensive and least efficient in the world." Later he commented: "There is far too much law for those who can afford it and far too little for those who cannot." But despite all criticisms, including those of the author, our court system remains an essential asset to our social order. It is the system generations of Americans have struggled to build and which we now have the responsibility to preserve and improve. When our rights to court appeal have been exhausted, our right to remedy unjust law through legislation remains, and for that we must be grateful. If injustice has been served here, it is not the first nor will it be the last time. We must get on with life, supported by faith that final justice will inevitably prevail, perhaps not tomorrow, but sooner than many wish.

Now at last, in its 125th year, A&P had scored its greatest financial coup, not through retailing brilliance, but through its acuity in diverting some $275 million from an employee pension trust. The Tea Company not only pocketed a cash settlement more than five times greater than that awarded to all plan members, but as the cherry on this "bananza split" they sought and obtained a court judgment for, and then collected, $7,644.28 from this plaintiff as reimbursement of their legal costs in appeal. Finally, the District Court, in its wisdom, approved the rather princely sum of $2,126,229.00 as fair and reasonable payment to class counsel for their efforts in securing this settlement. Thus was justice serviced and equity resolved...?

But lo and behold, on March 7, 1985, just when everyone was convinced the pension struggle had ended, a new party was heard from. Jonathan L. Goldstein, former U.S. Attorney for New Jersey, filed civil action 85-1095 in the District Court in Newark, New Jersey, as a class action on behalf of all those former members of the retirement plan discharged as the result of A&P's closing programs before they, as individuals, had completed vesting requirements under the plan.

The new action names both A&P's plan trustees and the Internal Revenue Service as defendants. It charges that the plan's trustees breached fiduciary duties to this non-vested class through failure to proceed properly and provide IRS with the facts and circumstances which constitute partial terminations. It asks the court to order that A&P now present IRS with that information necessary for IRS to make the determination that "partial terminations" did, in fact, occur. And it asks the court to enjoin A&P from otherwise employing assets diverted from the retirement plan until this matter is resolved.

While this author was not party to this action and had no prior knowledge of its existence, much of the source material for this case springs from the class action just completed which is referred to often in the filings in the new case.

As plaintiff in the case now settled, I pleaded vigorously but vainly regarding the denial of rights to former plan members terminated as the result of A&P's many closings before they had completed vesting requirements.

In at least token recognition of those pleadings, the court in its February 9, 1983, opinion approving settlement included a final paragraph which said in part: "The court will order that, if the IRS determines that 'partial terminations' have occurred, A&P shall provide from that portion of the excess assets which it obtains as a result of this settlement sufficient funds to pay any newly vested benefits to these terminees, and increased benefits equal to those provided class members under the settlement."

Reminding the court that this vital addition to the settlement had never been included in any previously published "Notice," I begged, but in vain, for proper publication of such "Notice" without which affected members could not possibly learn of the existence of this order. We cannot predict the outcome, but we will follow the case with interest.

Fifteen

Renascence, or Rose Colored Glasses?

In the June 1983 annual report to stockholders, Mr. Wood described A&P's status: "We are today, a company on the threshold of a new era. Our reduced size, lower cost structure and substantially improved financial condition now provide the opportunity for significant growth."

Mr. Wood also explained: "Now that the turnaround has been accomplished," A&P is firmly committed "to our most important goal permanent profitability and a pattern of consistent growth, and progress toward these goals can be measured quantitatively by the basic yardsticks of earnings per share, and share of market." He then asserted these corporate goals would be achieved through close attention to the fundamentals of effective cost controls and dedication to development of retail operations that provide "maximum customer service."

This forceful statement provides still another new policy direction for an organization whose last twenty-five years have been characterized by consistent policy vacillation and change. Here A&P is placing primacy on the rather unlikely combination of "cost control" and "maximum service" as the means of achieving sustained profitability and growth; and, by silence on the subjects, this policy demotes "quality," "low price," and "selection" to positions of lesser importance.

Historically, in the supermarket derby, the consistent big winner has been "High Volume" out of "Low Price/High Quality." Over the years consumers have awarded their market share "Blue Ribbons" to the operators offering the lowest retails for good quality foods. Despite the multitude of other frills and niceties, price always has been, and will continue to be, the ingredient which separates the leader from the rest of the pack in the supermarket business. Long-term success for the other operators in the pack depends upon their ability to select and implement a policy strategy which can capitalize on some actual or perceived weakness in the leader's operation, and thereby enable them to generate both profit and growth. Among the most common elements which provide options for retail strategic planning are: "lower prices," "better service," "higher quality," "wider selection," and "more attractive stores."

With an abundance of competing supermarkets to choose from today, most consumers reject less attractive stores, or those offering sub-standard quality products. Therefore, the realistic policy options available to operators with lesser market shares are quickly reduced to (a) lower price, (b) superior quality, and (c) better service.

Before consideration of each of these options, we should briefly examine the advantages presently enjoyed by the market leaders. First, we recall supermarket results are commonly expressed in terms of percentage rates on sales. The industry has always taken public pride (but private remorse) in the fact that net profits average less than 1 percent of total sales. These industry leaders seldom make public mention that this 1 percent of sales should exceed 15 percent as a return on investment. Nonetheless, this 1 percent is achieved by insuring that gross margins exceed expense rates by 1 percent of total revenues.

The cost of goods is pretty much the same for most operators because they purchase similar products from similar suppliers, and while more astute buying practices, more effective shrinkage control and broader product-mix can have positive consequence on gross margins, the real supermarket competitive battle rages in the "cost of doing business," or the expense rate side of the equation. Long-term profitability and growth favor the operator who can scrape that 1 percent net profit out of a reduced expense rate, as opposed to the operator who must add 1 percent extra to an otherwise competitive price structure to achieve profitability.

Operators with dominant market share and/or the highest per-store volumes enjoy many expense rate advantages. In a typical trading area, (a) newspaper lineage rate contracts are available to all on equal terms, (b) utility rates are uniform, (c) equipment and fixture costs are similar, (d) rental costs per square foot of retail space tend to be comparable, and (e) union contracts usually provide comparable rates and fringe benefits. Thus, on a rate on sales basis, a full-page newspaper ad can cost the operator with 20 percent share only half what the same ad will cost the operator with 10 percent market share. Similarly, the operator enjoying the highest volume per square foot of rental space, or cubic foot of display case, will also achieve significant advantages in rent, utility and amortization expense rates. Finally, with comparable union contracts, the higher volume operator can more easily achieve higher productivity and lower wage expense rates on total sales.

Thus, we understand the complexity of the problem facing supermarket operators who enjoy only fragmentary market shares and lower per-store sales volumes than major competition in the trading area. This problem confronts A&P in many markets.

With the inherent cost advantages available to the market share leader, secondary competition has little chance to provide comparably attractive stores, similar service levels, and match across-the-board low prices, and still achieve satisfactory profit with some measure of growth. Further, the secondary competitor has even less chance of success through a frontal attack initiating a price war in the market. Very few dominant chains in a marketing area will permit themselves to be undersold on staple food items by any competitor offering comparable service, quality and store conditions. Usually, the competitor with the lesser market share will back off first when price wars occur. Unless a chain has major outside resources and a willingness to sacrifice profits for an interminable period, a frontal attack on the market leader's price structure offers small chance of success and is a poor business risk.

Dramatic undercutting of existing price structures only succeed when compensating cost reductions become available through changing the character of an operation from a "typical super-market" to perhaps a "warehouse store" concept offering markedly fewer services, smaller selection and a much less attractive store atmosphere. Also, such warehouse type store operations require high traffic locations with above-average selling space, and they are normally not suited to the typical size supermarket in the typical neighborhood shopping center.

Thus, we find the available strategic marketing policy options quickly narrow down to "higher quality" and "better service." In fact, in the real world, the option narrows down to offering both "higher quality and better service." Usually, a consumer perception of both "high quality/better service" linkage is needed to offset measurable price structure differences unless the market leader is running a rag-tag operation and abusing customers. In this context, "better service" is broadly defined to include many things including more accessible parking, an abundance of clean, operable customer carriages, a more attractive store atmosphere, faster more efficient checkout counters, a polite, efficient customer service desk, clean well-stocked shelves and courteous, knowledgeable service in the perishable departments.

A number of chains have achieved success operating under a policy which gives precedence to quality and service over low prices. However, such success has been earned by consistent high performance over many years during which consumers have become convinced that this "Quality/Service–Price" combination offers better total value than the "Price–Quality–Service" package offered by most supermarkets. A Quality/Service image cannot be achieved by mere management proclamation.

Operators will find the "superior quality" image more elusive and difficult to maintain than the "better service" perception which can be managed through more effective training and staffing. Since chains purchase the same national brand products from the same sources of supply, quality differences do not exist in the broadest segment of the product line. The notable exception in the grocery and dairy departments is the quality standard the store projects in private label products. No chain can hope to project a superior quality image if it permits less than top quality in the products which bear its name.

For over a century the Tea Company built a quality reputation by insisting upon national brand (or higher) quality specifications in every product which carried the "A&P" name. In its own plants,

A&P manufactured not simply to "a national brand standard" but to the quality and taste specifications of the "leading national brand item" in each particular category, and the company established and maintained elaborate inspection and testing procedures to assure this quality control.

Unfortunately, the Tea Company's policy of superior quality private label products went by the boards in the 1970's when "lowest cost" became the dominant factor in the private label strategy. This trade-off of quality for price not only resulted in a substantial lowering of private label sales but also contributed significantly to the diminished public reputation of the A&P name. Management, commenting upon A&P's present negative public image, suggests a name change may help upgrade customer perception. That will do about as much for the quality image as would hanging a "Naturally-Aged" sign over withered fruits and vegetables in the produce department.

Aside from private label products, quality differences can be found in the perishable departments of supermarkets. Some chains attempt to enhance their quality image through a wider selection of gourmet items, or the addition of a "health food" section on their grocery shelves. While customers do enjoy browsing and purchasing selected items in these specialty sections, they do little to enhance the quality image if the quality of the lettuce or ground beef is poor. Stocking Beluga caviar does not, of itself, create a quality store image.

A superior quality produce department image is achieved first by rigid high quality purchase and inspection standards at the source. It is enhanced, at store level, through attractive display of all currently available fruits and vegetables, and adherence to strictest policy standards which permit nothing but top quality product to remain on display. No one, in all history, has ever found a way to recondition an overripe banana, and any let down of quality standards at the purchasing, inspection, warehouse handling or trucking levels is impossible to reverse at store level. Additional damage to the quality image takes place when stores, in hopes of reducing shrinkage, permit marginal or sub-standard quality product to remain on display in the vain hope that some friendly, near-sighted customer will take the problem off their hands.

Fresh meat and fish items constitute the most sensitive and costly food purchases, and it is the quality comparison of these food items that separates superior quality markets from pretenders. There are damn few supermarkets (or private butcher shops) where every package sold would get high marks on a superior quality test, and qualify as a completely satisfactory purchase. Since most supermarket chains purchase to the same "choice grade" standards, meat quality assurance is dependent upon strict compliance to rigid corporate procedures by store meat department personnel. The quality reputation of the store is challenged with every package of meat sold. This reputation can only be protected and improved by meticulous adherence to established procedures with regard to sanitation, temperature control, handling, storage, cutting, trimming, packaging and freshness rotation. The superior quality meat department operates on the premise that every package prepared is good enough for meat department personnel to buy.

The better meat departments avoid deceptive packaging, with tails tucked under, and offer correctly cut product free of undesirable and unnecessary fat, gristle, bone or cartilage. Unfortunately some stores which have gone to the expense of installing service meat and fish departments to attract the most discriminating customers, fail because those departments do not live up to expected quality standards. Customers who have found a store where they can consistently purchase top quality meat and fish items at fair prices are seldom lured away by the siren songs of "special values" of other competitors where they liken buying meats to playing Russian roulette.

The old adage "there is no such thing as a free lunch" applies aptly to supermarkets. Every amenity has its special added cost for which some outlet, other than reduced profits, must be found. Invariably, that outlet is higher retail prices somewhere in the store. Better trim and quality controls add to labor and shrinkage costs of the store; quicker disposal of marginal fruit and vegetable items results in higher shrinkage in the produce department; better service normally results in higher labor costs; and, in the final analysis, consumer value assessments formulate buying decisions which, over time, determine the relative success of competing supermarkets.

Food shoppers are a great deal smarter than many retail executives realize. Being stupid enough to underestimate customer intelligence is perhaps the most common cause of retailing failures. Notice how those big-budget, full shopping cart customers always seem to congregate in the same store in any given neighborhood. After their own comparative testing, discerning shoppers usually give most of their trade to whom they consider the most honest operator who lives up to all claims in his ads, keeps his store fully stocked with a wide assortment of quality foods at competitively low prices, and shows respect for customers' time with efficient, fast checkout services.

The most successful operator is the one who best meets the quality/price/selection/service needs and standards of a particular trading area with minimum waste and unnecessary expense.

Coming back to our story, the July 1984 annual report included a personal message from Mr. Wood to the stockholders highlighting recent profit improvements. He touched first on the court approved settlement of the class action. In discussing the huge surplus to which A&P had, for the first time, gained legal access, he employs the expression "will be returned to the company." Realistically, nothing can be "returned to the company" that was not previously possessed by the company. However, perhaps such corporate literary license is excusable because, after all, it does sound so much more genteel and dignified than the more accurate expression, "seized by the company from the pension trust."

His message continues with mention of profit improvements stemming from elimination of manufacturing facilities, and the removal of significant disadvantages from labor contracts. Later, Mr. Wood reports completion of the first leg of a three-year plan for extensive store remodeling but neglects to disclose the number of stores remodeled. Finally, he predicts increased sales will result from internal marketing improvements and acquisitions.

You will recall the corporate game plan in 1983 asserted growth and profitability would be attained by emphasis both on effective cost control and maximum customer service. This unique dual emphasis, and the subsequent assertion that "even our largest, most complete and service oriented stores can maintain a low cost operating structure," combined to raise serious doubt. Experienced retailers know that "most service oriented" and "low cost" are paradoxical expressions possible of co-existence only in stores generating extraordinarily high sales volumes, and A&P has yet to demonstrate a consistent ability to attract such volumes in typical situations.

Fully consistent with past inconsistency, and perhaps in recognition of this apparent paradox, A&P's annual report in July 1984 simply dropped the reference to maximum customer service. Instead, the Haub/Wood ticket proclaimed: "Management was reshaping its operating policy to reflect a single-minded emphasis on cost effective retailing." Here we are now confronted with a carefully prepared written statement of corporate operating policy which excludes all mention of dependence upon either quality, variety, price, service or store ambiance in favor of a single minded emphasis on cost effectivness.

This abrupt single-minded emphasis on cost effectiveness is in stark contrast to more traditional retail philosophy which focuses upon awareness, concern and service to consumer interests as essential complementary adjuncts to efficiency in the pursuit of retailing success.

However, such pursuit of profit through emphasis only on efficiency does seem to be gaining popularity among a management cult which defines business purely as a "profit seeking activity" to the complete exclusion of any compensating need for "rendering some service of value to society."

Such hard-nosed managers lean to the notion that business is no more than a civilized dog fight where anything goes and only winners survive. To combatants so engaged, the employees, the public interest, one's word, loyalty, ethics and even the corporation itself are all just legitimate pawns to be played, or sacrificed, in the interest of winning.

The older concept of growth through re-investment in enlarged capacities is increasingly discarded in favor of the buy, sell, merge, borrow approach to effect instant improvement in the status quo, and thus attain at least a perception of upward momentum. All of which leads one to speculate whether humans will soon finally succeed in developing a computer with intellect, or whether the computer has already begun to robotize humanity?

No doubt it is far too early to suggest such hard-nosed solitary emphasis on efficiency will lead to an economic Armageddon for the nation or A&P. Clearly a far more imminent threat is posed by our apparently incurable national addiction to ever-increasing deficit spending in the face of the rapidly approaching inevitable consequence that debt service costs will strangle our productive vitality and diminish the economic freedom of future generations enslaved by inherited debt.

Certainly business history does not suggest such hard-nosed singular dedication to efficiency to the exclusion of consumer interests has ever met with noticeable success in retailing. Hopefully, it never will.

Surely, the retailing influences within A&P will attempt, at least outwardly, to modify this recently adopted operating policy to acknowledge and concern itself with consumer concerns and not just "reflect a single-minded emphasis on cost effective retailing." Still, one cannot forget that A&P is now a subsidiary of the Tengelmann Group and a part of the Haub business empire.

As tangible evidence of future direction, we find A&P operating stores under six separate flags, as 1984 comes to a close. These operations, "Super Fresh," "The Family Mart," "Super Plus," "Kohl's," "Pantry Pride," and "A&P" represent almost every known retail food format, and encompass the full spectrum from "help yourself" to "full service orientation." Under these circumstances it becomes increasingly difficult for A&P to espouse a uniform retail philosophy other than one of rigid cost and profit effectiveness.

A&P has affirmed its reliance on a profit-effective policy by eliminating unprofitable stores, divisions, and manufacturing facilities, and by securing labor cost reductions through negotiations under which employees had to choose between wage reductions or loss of jobs. Thus, management appears to have at least set aside a serious emphasis on the more difficult, more expensive, longer-term programs of restoring retail health to failing operations through improved merchandising techniques, job skills and store facilities. Rather, A&P appears to have clung to the hardline position that the weak must be abandoned to protect the strong. And results to date suggest management has made the right move.

Clearly, the enormous profit infusion from the employee retirement plan, together with the closure of almost every unprofitable facility, has provided a 180-degree turnaround in A&P's current profitability. Combined with the company's extraordinarily strong cash position, this bodes well for the future. To put things in better perspective, a comparison of A&P's and Safeway's results for the year 1983 proves interesting and informative. The Safeway annual report described 1983 as another year of excellent progress.

	Safeway	A&P
Number of retail stores	2,507	1,022
Annual Sales—in billions	$ 18.6	5.2
Annual Sales per store—in millions	$ 7.4	5.1
Annual Net Profit—in millions	$183.6	31.4*
Earnings per Share—in dollars	$ 3.26	.84*
Profit as a percentage of sales	.0099	.0060*

      * before extraordinary credits.

The theme of Safeway's annual report was TEAM SAFEWAY, and the cover message read: "Through individual contribution grows the corporate personality, something bigger, grander, more powerful than the mere sum of the parts." Of special note, the report acknowledges Safeway's continuing substantial investment in advanced technology including two ultramodern processing facilities, a charcoal briquet manufacturing plant, and a major addition to a modern dry pet food plant. Contrary to A&P's management, Safeway continues to believe that in-house product manufacture contributes favorably to both sales and profitability.

While A&P's 1983 results pale in comparison to Safeway's, they do reflect substantial improvement over the recent past, and did provide cause for celebration of the 125th anniversary of the company's founding. The occasion was marked in spectacular fashion by a lavish bash at the Washington, D.C., Hilton on July 10, 1984, the eve of the annual shareholders' meeting. The formal guest list of 600 included President Ronald Reagan along with many prominent politicians, government officials, media representatives, union leaders, suppliers and selected employees, but no ordinary shareholders, as such.

During 1984 A&P announced the acquisiton of twenty Pantry Pride supermarkets in Virginia. Commenting upon the purchase, an A&P spokesman said: "They're good stores" and "we want to operate them as Pantry Prides because they have a good name there." Later in 1984, the Justice Department, through a stipulation filed in Federal District court, consented to the termination of the 1954 Federal Court consent decree which for thirty years had forbidden A&P from operating stores at a loss for the purpose of eliminating competition, and also prevented A&P from engaging in wholesale or franchise distributions. In its stipulation, the Justice Department noted that over the past thirty years A&P had fallen, from being the nation's leading retailer with an 11.3 percent share of America's total food store sales, down to its present seventh place with an approximate 4 percent share of market. Apparently, this fact eased the concern of the Justice Department over A&P's future ability or incentive to attempt to monopolize retail markets. One might now expect A&P to experiment with the idea of wholesaling or franchising as a means of increasing volume and profits.

As further evidence of its game plan for allocation of the huge diversion of funds from the Retirement Plan of U.S. employees, A&P announced the signing of a definitive agreement to purchase 93 stores from Dominion Ltd. of Ontario, Canada. According to Chairman Wood, this acquisition will double A&P's present share of the Toronto market and bring A&P's annual Canadian sales volume into the $2 billion range.

Surely, these acquisitions and the termination of the consent decree justified Chairman Wood's earlier claim that: "momentum going into 1984 was strong." At year's end, A&P reported annual profits of $215.8 million or $5.74 per share on sales of 5.9 billion. However, as noted in *The Wall Street Journal* of March 21, 1985, these impressive totals included $135 million in additional extraordinary pension diversion credits, $30 million in tax loss carry forward credits, and $22.5 million gains from the sales of securities. Stripped of all this whipped cream not associated with normal retail operations, profits for 1984 were actually 10 percent less than the prior year, totalling only $28.3 million or .0048 rated on sales. Further, the old danger signs were reappearing as profits came from higher margins rather than from maintaining or lowering expense rates. Reflecting his lack of pride in 1984 profits, Chairman Wood pointed out that the prior year's results were helped by a four-week strike against competitors in New Jersey.

To date the Haub/Wood ticket has evidenced positive abilities in the diversion of enormous capital resources from the now defunct employee retirement plan by disposing of most unprofitable facilities and by timely renegotiation of unfavorable labor agreements. They have also demonstrated an eagerness to acquire stores which other owners appear anxious to sell. While this acquisiton policy has resulted in substantially increased sales, this management has yet to demonstrate an ability to achieve and sustain industry levels of profitability.

On the surface, the odds favor a continuing A&P recovery. However, putting matters in the parlance of the old music hall days, "The Show ain't over till the fat lady sings!"—and, She sure ain't sung yet! Pundits have previously hailed A&P turnarounds prematurely, and these two short years of recovery are but moments in time. No less a personage than Chairman Wood has testified that availability of pension surplus was the *sine qua non*, totally responsible for effectiveness of the revitalization program. Taking Mr. Wood at his word, the progress to date was financed by pension capital diversion. The burning unanswered question remains— "Can A&P management finally demonstrate a consistent ability to operate existing supermarkets at industry levels of growth and profitability?"

A partial insight into this managment's view of retailing's future is on display in Allendale, New Jersey. There on November 28, 1984, A&P announced with great fanfare the opening of its "Futurestore—with Warehouse prices."

Behind an enormous glass semi-umbrella facade this elaborate prototype, in reality, offers the customer nothing new. The interior appears to have been designed more for shock appeal than for effective high sales volume. The decor is an explosive repetition of blunt blacks against hospital whites. On the walls and interior signs, black blot images of fish, fowl, cattle, fruit, vegetables and mysterious sundries are apparently intended to whet appetites and lead customers to product displays. Pushing a carriage over the sterile white floor, one encounters a maze of angles, corners and turns leading to what appear to be under-sized departmental displays, on smaller than usual shelves, in rather narrow aisles, all of which mitigates against real high volume selling. To one observer, the total ambience generates all the charm of an operating room with little of the efficiency.

Despite the corporate fanfare, publicity and costly advertising proclaiming this "Futurestore" as a "giant step into tomorrow," one tends to hope this expensive prototype reflects no more than an experiment designed to project a corporate "forward look" and attract attention by capitalizing upon today's popular conception of a future space fashion. If, indeed, this store concept does reflect management's best appraisal of consumer trends and the future of food retailing, then a most serious question remains as to whether the future is bright or bleak, both for A&P and its customers.

Until more positive signs appear to evidence corporate commitment to proven sound retail policies, and until increased customer traffic and increased tonnage in existing stores provide proof of the implementation of needed improvements in merchandising, service levels and competitive pricing in those existing retail outlets, the longer term future success of A&P remains questionable. In his April 1985 message to shareholders, Jim Wood once more changed A&P's operating policy objective—this time for the better. A&P's dominant objective now is "the improvement of our stores to create the right environment for customers."

Now at last, the past has caught up with the present and the time has come to stand aside and watch as future A&P actions create the remainder of this history. How does one now briefly summarize 125 years or capsulize the lessons time has taught?

At the beginning there was a little company, born of a single handshake, without documentation to certify its parentage arrangement or exact date of birth. This, by itself, was not remarkable, for ten thousand such little companies are similarly born, flower briefly in the springtime of their youth, then tip-toe silently into eternity unmourned. The difference here was that two men whose basic goal was making money had decided on a plan whose implementation proved far more significant than their individual accumulations of wealth. This particular handshake united two men to the principle of "selling more for less" that was to revolutionize retailing in America and the world.

The company enjoyed fifty years of steady, prosperous growth selling tea, coffee and assorted sundries while holding relatively close to the lower price principle upon which it was founded. Then, early in this century, young John Hartford, son of A&P's owner, proved enormous additional sales and profit growth could be achieved through strengthening the "lower price" principle to a policy commitment to "sell the *most good food* for the *lowest* prices."

It was John Hartford's merchandising genius and lifelong dedication to this rigid policy that raised A&P to undreamed heights in retailing, and brought legitimacy to the word "Great" which had been brashly but prophetically prefixed to the name "Atlantic & Pacific Tea Company" back in 1869.

At John's death in 1951, A&P stood as the world's largest privately owned company, the world's largest retailer of any kind, and was second in total annual sales volume only to General Motors. And at his death John firmly believed that position, and A&P's 11.3 percent share of the total U.S. food sales, still represented only a modest beginning. It was not that his sales goals had been reached. It was just that his time ran out.

John with his brother George, who together ran A&P, left their entire combined shares of A&P stock to the Hartford Foundation. John had established this foundation in his later years with the understanding that a succession of A&P executives would manage it, and as trustees would nourish its assets and faithfully execute its charitable purposes.

The Hartford brothers also expected the A&P executives who controlled the foundation and voted its 40 percent of A&P's stock would see to it that the company, its policies and organization would continue, in perpetuity, to grow and prosper as a lasting, living memorial to their father who had founded the business. Unfortunately, those expectations were never fulfilled.

Under the terms of the family trust to become effective upon the death of the founder, all equity and profits of the company were to be shared equally with each of his five children, or their heirs. However, the trust provided that John and George together, or either as survivor, were to exercise complete and absolute control over the operation of A&P with no voting rights granted to the other three children, or their heirs, until the dissolution of the trust which would occur with the death of the last surviving child of the founder.

Accordingly, the trust was dissolved in 1957 following the death of George L. Hartford, the last surviving child. Thereupon 60 percent of A&P's stock and voting control of the company was suddenly turned over to a small group comprising the ten heirs of the two sisters and one brother of John and George Hartford. None of this group had any significant experience in, or knowledge of, the food business. They were not aware how precarious the operating position had already become, and as individuals the group shared little interest in common other than the inheritance, and a joint desire for continuing dividends and increased stock valuation.

The Hartford Foundation, with its 40 percent control of company stock and its dual obligation to charitable purposes and the perpetuation of A&P, found itself a minority party facing a totally unpredictable 60 percent majority. There was reason to fear that large controlling blocks of stock might soon be assembled by some corporate raider unless management could secure sufficient voting loyalty of the heir group, and continuance of generous dividends seemed the most likely means to that end. Suddenly, management found itself swinging in the breeze hoisted on a Hartford family petard, a position which John and George never experienced and never dreamed possible. While the heirs as a group never did rebel, that threat of rebellion was always in the air and a succession of A&P chief executives found their survival increasingly contingent upon dividend payments considered excessive by normal standards.

After a century of remarkable growth under family control of a father and sons during which consideration for future growth always took precedence over immediate profitability, those longer-term interests now became captive to un-realistic demands for short-term profits and the long steep slide from the summit accelerated.

Hindsight might suggest that no self-respecting chief executive worthy of the name should have yielded or remained under such pressures. However, everyone could not desert the sinking ship and, even if only out of loyalty to the company and the organization, some with knowledge of the business had to remain and try to make the best of the situation.

Those who succeeded Mr. John were dedicated, honest employees who had carried out John's policies out of a deep sense of obedience and respect, but probably never truly appreciated the intensity of his commitment to the policy of "selling the most good food at the lowest prices." They were more inclined to attribute A&P's success to his dynamic leadership and the organization, stores and factories he had built. They envisioned A&P as a goliath that should enjoy steady growth based merely upon the strength of past achievements.

Whereas John devoted his life protecting A&P's empire by expanding its territorial boundaries, his successors now set out to protect that empire by building moats around its borders. Apparently unmindful that in nature death begins the moment growth ceases, their defensive strategies managed only to imprison the company and melt its muscle into flab. All seemed to have forgotten John's very own words which had warned: "I don't see how any businessman can limit his growth and stay healthy." How very apt here would have been the phrase, "John, we hardly knew ye."

Over the passing years all sorts of diagnoses, explanations and solutions were offered to resolve A&P's problems. None hit the mark. All kinds of management changes, reorganizations and new programs were tried. None hit the mark. None of the experts had uncovered the simple truth, that with John's death, the soul had left the body and the company had then become just a huge paper tiger without spirit, energy, principle or purpose.

Surely, all of the above reminds us that our power over others ends at the grave, and that the greatest of corporations like the greatest of men must all fall victims of mortality.

With the passage of time the erosion deepened until it eventually threatened the company's existence. Thereupon a systematic liquidation process began by orderly disposal of the most economically diseased corporate organs until some 3000 stores and most manufacturing facilities were discarded along with many thousands of long-term employees.

In 1979 the foundation, having suffered losses of over $400 million in A&P stock devaluation, abandoned the struggle and offered to sell all of their A&P holdings as a block. A number of heirs simultaneously joined in offering blocks of their remaining shares. Shortly thereafter, Erivan Haub of West Germany announced his purchase of 42 percent of A&P's stock. By 1981, Mr. Haub had gained control of more than 50 percent of A&P's shares.

Once more A&P's control is centered in a principal owner and management is free of the need to serve divergent interests. Buoyed by a massive inflow of cash from the employees' retirement plan, the company is now in a strong position from which to launch new growth. Little else is known about Mr. Haub other than the obvious fact of his great wealth which springs from retailing success in Germany. His approval of the pension cash diversion was by far the most significant A&P management decision since 1979 and there is little other evidence to reveal his retail business philosophy.

It is known that huge fortunes have been amassed through many diverse business philosophies, ranging from "Never give a sucker an even break" to A&P's old "Sell the most quality product for the lowest price." Long term, the best deal is the deal that benefits both parties to the transaction. Therefore, A&P's long-term success might well depend upon its choice of policy, and ability to bring that policy to life in every store. Thus, success can result from a return to real values, from playing down frills and hype, from reducing emphasis on the trite "P's and Q's" and "Futurestores," from reestablishing competitive pricing, from improved meat merchandising, and a return to retailing with the consumers' real interest in mind.

And now this story which had to be told has been. It seeks a new perspective, a fair and accurate inside view without embellishment nor omission of fact. At times critical of given corporate decisions, it is not intended to demean named individuals, each of whom has contributed much to A&P. Finally, on behalf of all those many to whom A&P meant so much—and, who meant so much to A&P—and with lasting personal respect and gratitude, we now offer this final salutation. Hail and farewell—Grandma!

Index

251